Oliver Wendell Holmes, Jr., Legal Theory, and Judicial Restraint

Oliver Wendell Holmes, Jr., is considered by many to be the most influential American jurist. The voluminous literature devoted to his writings and legal thought, however, is diverse and inconsistent. In this study, Frederic R. Kellogg follows Holmes's intellectual path from his early writings through his judicial career. He offers a fresh perspective that addresses the views of Holmes's leading critics and explains his relevance to the contemporary controversy over judicial activism and restraint. Holmes is shown to be an original legal theorist who reconceived common law as a theory of social inquiry and who applied his insights to constitutional law. From his empirical and naturalist perspective on law, with its roots in American pragmatism, emerged Holmes's distinctive judicial and constitutional restraint. Kellogg distinguishes Holmes from analytical legal positivism and contrasts him with a range of thinkers, including John Austin, Thomas Hobbes, H. L. A. Hart, Ronald Dworkin, Antonin Scalia, and other leading legal theorists.

Frederic R. Kellogg has been Visiting Scholar in the Department of Philosophy at the George Washington University, Senior Fulbright Fellow at the University of Warsaw, and Visiting Professor at Moscow State University. He is the author of *The Formative Essays of Justice Holmes: The Making of an American Legal Philosophy*, as well as numerous articles on legal philosophy and jurisprudence.

Oliver Wendell Holmes, Jr., Legal Theory, and Judicial Restraint

FREDERIC R. KELLOGG

CAMBRIDGE
UNIVERSITY PRESS

CAMBRIDGE UNIVERSITY PRESS
Cambridge, New York, Melbourne, Madrid, Cape Town,
Singapore, São Paulo, Delhi, Tokyo, Mexico City

Cambridge University Press
32 Avenue of the Americas, New York, NY 10013-2473, USA

www.cambridge.org
Information on this title: www.cambridge.org/9780521321921

frederickellogg@cs.com

First published 2007
First paperback edition 2011

A catalog record for this publication is available from the British Library

Library of Congress Cataloging in Publication data

Kellogg, Frederic Rogers.
Oliver Wendell Holmes, Jr., legal theory, and judicial restraint /
Frederic R. Kellogg.
p. cm.
Includes bibliographical references and index.
ISBN-13: 978-0-521-86650-7 (hardback)
ISBN-10: 0-521-86650-2 (hardback)
1. Holmes, Oliver Wendell, 1841–1935. 2. Judges – United States – Biography.
3. United States. Supreme Court – History. 4. Law and politics.
5. Law – Philosophy. I. Title.
KF8745.H6K45 2007
340′.1–dc22 2006011715

ISBN 978-0-521-86650-7 Hardback
ISBN 978-0-521-32192-1 Paperback

In memory of Paul A. Freund and Elliot L. Richardson

Contents

Preface

I have a learned friend, whose name would be well recognized if I were to disclose it, who though active in supporting conservative judicial nominees confides deep misgivings about the philosophical basis of contemporary judicial conservatism. For my part I have long had misgivings about contemporary legal philosophy, which I find to be illuminating, if not parallel, in regard to my friend's central concern, the basis for judicial restraint. In part, this book is an attempt to place this issue in a broader historical and theoretical context, I hope neither innately liberal nor conservative, as those terms are popularly understood.

More important, this is a book about Oliver Wendell Holmes, Jr., and his contribution to legal theory. These subjects converge because, even while Holmes was engaged in refining a concept of law grounded in the philosophy of the common law, the intellectual landscape in England and America was changing. Holmes's classic treatise, *The Common Law*, has never been adequately understood as a reconceptualization of common law opposing the legal positivism of John Austin and Thomas Hobbes. Legal positivism became influential in England and America with John Austin's *Lectures on Jurisprudence* (1861) and was reinforced by H. L. A. Hart in the following century. It has come to dominate theories of law, both liberal and conservative. Now, with legal positivism at an impasse, a reconsideration of Holmes may be welcome.

This study is dedicated to the late Professor Paul A. Freund of Harvard Law School, who ignited my original interest in Justice Oliver Wendell Holmes and the insights to be gained through careful mining of his complex and controversial work. It is also dedicated to the late

Elliot L. Richardson, whose combination of scholarly intelligence and public service set a motivating, while equally impossible, example.

I would like to recognize an early and broad-ranging influence of members of the Harvard University faculty, especially Bernard Bailyn, my senior tutor Gordon S. Wood, Talcott Parsons, Erwin Griswold, Clark Byse, Mark deWolfe Howe, and Harold Berman. My interest in Holmes is partly traceable to an early fascination with the question of whether law and morals are separate, which was treated in a compilation entitled "Introduction to Law" distributed to students at Harvard Law School in the 1960s. Prompted by the insights of Professor Howe, I sensed then that Holmes's position in the famous 1897 essay "The Path of the Law" was subtle and unlike that of either Lon L. Fuller or H. L. A. Hart,[1] but I could find little elucidation in *The Common Law.*

Between law school and practice I studied social theory under Talcott Parsons, and I read much of Emile Durkheim's work. Rereading *The Common Law,* I was struck by the comparison between Durkheim's evolution from mechanical to organic social solidarity and Holmes's evolution from moral toward external standards. Having had the opportunity to observe something close to Holmes's notion of specification[2] in my exposure to legal practice, I was prompted to look for the origins of his thought in the early writings.

This led to research at George Washington University, where I went through the masters and doctoral programs in jurisprudence at the National Law Center, concentrating on Holmes. A comment by Grant Gilmore on a work submitted for publication encouraged me to improve my understanding of pragmatic philosophy and Holmes's relation to it. I eventually published *The Formative Essays of Justice Holmes: The Making of an American Legal Philosophy* in 1984 treating this connection, but I was not alone in being unsatisfied that it adequately addressed the more difficult questions.

I later read Gerald J. Postema's *Bentham and the Common Law Tradition,* published in 1986, and I saw how strongly Holmes's theory opposed legal positivism while fitting the common law tradition; it struck me

[1] Mark DeWolfe Howe, "The Positivism of Mr. Justice Holmes"; Henry M. Hart, Jr., "Holmes' Positivism – An Addendum"; Howe, "Holmes' Positivism – A Brief Rejoinder"; H. L. A. Hart, "Positivism and the Separation of Law and Morals"; Lon L. Fuller, "Positivism and Fidelity to Law – A Reply to Professor Hart"; in *Introduction to Law, Selected Essays Reprinted from the Harvard Law Review* (Cambridge, Mass.: Harvard Law Review Association, 1968).

[2] See discussion of "successive approximation," chapter 3.

then that Holmes had updated common law theory with a concept of community inquiry parallel to that of the classical American pragmatists, with whom he associated in mid-nineteenth-century Cambridge. I tested various aspects of this hypothesis in several papers,[3] culminating in one delivered at the 2001 meeting of the American Philosophical Association, Eastern Division, entitled "The Construction of Positivism and the Myth of Legal Indeterminacy." My commentator, Brian Bix, gave me helpful guidance.

Since 1984, Holmes has received much attention. There have been four biographies, four symposia, two new collections of his writing, two volumes of essays and one evaluating his contemporary influence, and numerous articles and monographs.[4] The evaluation is Albert W. Alschuler's *Law without Values: The Life, Work, and Legacy of Justice Holmes.* My own study might be considered as an alternative evaluation from the perspective of contemporary theory. I take a more sympathetic view of Holmes's contribution. As Professor Matthias Reimann, who wrote more favorably of Holmes before Alschuler's book, notes in his review of it,

[3] Frederic R. Kellogg, "Pragmatism and Liberalism: Two Distinct Theories of Law and Justice," paper delivered at the Eastern Division of the American Philosophical Association, December 1991; "Common Law and Constitutional Theory: The Common Law Origins of Holmes' Constitutional Restraint," 7 *George Mason L. Rev.* 177–234 (1984); "Learned Hand and the Great Train Ride," 56 *American Scholar* 471 (1987); "Legal Philosophy in the Temple of Doom: Pragmatism's Response to Critical Legal Studies," 65 *Tulane L. Rev.* 15–56 (1990); "Who Owns Pragmatism?" 6 *Journal of Speculative Philosophy* 67 (1992); "Justice Holmes, Common Law Theory, and Judicial Restraint," 36 *John Marshall L. Rev.* 457 (2003); "Morton White on Oliver Wendell Holmes," 40 *Transactions of the Charles S. Peirce Society* 559 (2004).

[4] Gary J. Aichele, *Oliver Wendell Holmes Jr.: Soldier, Scholar, Judge* (Boston: Twayne Publishers, 1989); Liva Baker, *The Justice from Beacon Hill: The Life and Times of Oliver Wendell Holmes* (New York: Harper Collins, 1991); Sheldon M. Novick, *Honorable Justice: The Life of Oliver Wendell Holmes* (Boston, Toronto, and London: Little, Brown, 1989); G. Edward White, *Justice Oliver Wendell Holmes: Law and the Inner Self* (Oxford: Oxford University Press, 1993); Robert W. Gordon, "Holmes' Common Law as Legal and Social Science," 10 *Hofstra L. Rev.* 719 (1982); "Symposium: The Path of the Law after One Hundred Years," 110 *Harv. L. Rev.* 989 (1997); "Symposium: The Path of the Law 100 Years Later: Holmes' Influence on Modern Jurisprudence," 63 *Brook L. Rev.* 1 (1997); "Symposium: The Path of the Law Today," 78 *B. U. L. Rev.* 691 (1998); *The Collected Works of Justice Holmes: Complete Public Writings and Selected Opinions of Oliver Wendell Holmes*, ed. Sheldon Novick, 3 vols. (hereafter "*Collected Works*") (Chicago and London: Chicago University Press, 1995); Richard A. Posner, ed., *The Essential Holmes: Selections from the Letters, Speeches, Judicial Opinions, and Other Formative Writings of Oliver Wendell Holmes, Jr.* (Chicago and London: Chicago University Press, 1992); Albert W. Alschuler, *Law without Values: The Life, Work, and Legacy of Justice Holmes* (Chicago and London: University of Chicago Press, 2000). Many of the articles are listed in the Bibliography.

"its main importance lies in a simple but valuable reminder: if American legal culture continues to revere a Nietzschean nihilist, a power-addicted war enthusiast, and an emotional cripple without sympathy for the underdog, it is flirting with moral bankruptcy."[5] While aware of the basis for such criticism, I will try to present a balanced picture, grounded in an admittedly condensed consideration of Holmes's huge output.

The arrangement of the book is as follows. In the first two chapters I describe the general contours of Holmes's judicial restraint and intellectual background. In the third I compare his conception of law and its origins to the reigning theory, legal positivism. In the fourth I address its relation to the tradition of common law. In chapters 5 and 6, I trace the original emergence of Holmes's conception in the years of scholarship following the Civil War, to document my controversial dissociation of it from the analytical positivism within which Holmes is commonly included. Chapter 7 elaborates on Holmes's famous skepticism and his view of the relation of law and morals. In chapter 8, I address the continuing misunderstanding of Holmes's approach to principles and "policy." In chapter 9, I present a common law–based elucidation of his constitutional restraint, and in chapter 10, I evaluate his thought from the perspective of contemporary legal and political theory.

I am grateful to various journal editors and other commentators, on a number of papers, including Andrew Altman, Patricia Beard, Brian Bix, Philip Bobbitt, R. Paul Churchill, Larry Goffney, Peter Hare, Catherine Kemp, David Lyons, Edward H. Madden, Mark Medish, Kevin Mellyn, James Oldham, Lucius Outlaw, Robert Park, Ferdinand Schoettle, Thomas L. Short, Beth Singer, Mark Tushnet, and Kenneth Winston, for their helpful comments and criticism; to William A. Truslow and Dale Brunsvold for their timely help; and to many members of the Society for the Advancement of American Philosophy for their enlightenment and encouragement. While I hope the cautious faith of these people in my purposes was not misplaced, I admit to a dimness of vision of things poorly understood, and a natural blindness to my errors, with confidence that many more are yet to be uncovered, for which all of the above should remain blameless.

Special thanks are owed to Erika S. Chadbourn and David Warrington and the staff of the Special Collections department of the Harvard

[5] Matthias Reimann, "Lives in the Law: Horrible Holmes," 100 *Mich. L. Rev.* 1676 (2002); Reimann, "Why Holmes?" 88 *Mich. L. Rev.* 1908 (1990).

University Law School Library; to the George Washington University and R. Paul Churchill, then Chair of the Department of Philosophy; and to the staffs of the Burns and Gelman Libraries at the George Washington University, Professor Charles Karelis for his intensive commentaries on my manuscript, and most of all to my wife Molly Shulman Kellogg, for the immeasurable support that made this project possible.

1

A Time for Law

> It cannot be helped, it is as it should be, that the law is behind the times. As law embodies beliefs that have translated themselves into action, while there still is doubt, while opposite convictions still keep a battle front against each other, the time for law has not come; the notion destined to prevail is not yet entitled to the field. It is a misfortune if a judge reads his conscious or unconscious sympathy with one side or the other prematurely into the law, and forgets that what seem to him to be first principles are believed by half his fellow men to be wrong.
>
> Justice Oliver Wendell Holmes, 1913[1]

I begin this exploration with a comment by Justice Holmes at seventy-one, speaking to the Bar Association of the City of New York. He is discussing the role of timing in judicial decisions, timing indeed in constitutional law. Holmes is alone as a legal theorist in focusing so heavily on it – on the notion of readiness or unreadiness, of a social context within which legal and constitutional rulings are made. But consider: what of court intervention in public school segregation, in prosecutorial fairness and police coercion of confessions, disparate state laws against abortion, affirmative action in employment discrimination, the constitutionality of laws barring same-sex marriage, the juvenile death penalty? Has not the context and timing of judicial rulings in these matters, for good or ill, been a large measure of their apparent justification – or lack thereof?

[1] Holmes, "Law and the Court," speech at a dinner of the Harvard Law School Association of New York on February 15, 1913, in Mark deWolfe Howe, ed., *The Occasional Speeches of Justice Oliver Wendell Holmes* (Cambridge, Mass.: Belknap Press, 1962), 168.

Separation of the races could hardly seem unconstitutional to a mostly white America in 1896, when it was upheld in *Plessy v. Ferguson.*[2] Integrating the public schools would have been unthinkable then, but in 1954? After passage of the Civil Rights Act of 1964, judicial orders decreeing affirmative action in employment were common, after findings of race discrimination. Leading universities soon took affirmative steps to increase the enrollment of minority students. Such programs came under attack for reverse discrimination. In 2002, after wrestling with this question (and with itself) for two generations, the Supreme Court upheld a carefully tailored University of Michigan affirmative action plan in *Grutter v. Bollinger*,[3] but set a time limit for constitutionality of twenty-five years, after which, presumably, affirmative action is due to become unconstitutional.

What is involved here? As the constitutional scholar Paul A. Freund repeatedly asked, should the Court serve as the "conscience of the country"?[4] The very idea of a *moving* national conscience is murky and uncertain. In his 1969 Oliver Wendell Holmes Lectures, Alexander Bickel thoroughly deflated the notion that the court could associate its rulings with an inexorable "progress."[5] Conservatives irk any liberal crowd with their caricatures of a "living constitution." As history reveals, the Court can get carried too far. In abortion, there was no uniform drift of national consensus to support a wholesale removal of traditional state jurisdiction in *Roe v. Wade.*[6] The Court's actions under the Constitution are final, save a curative amendment, and they short-circuit more natural movements of national conscience, they close off further civil debate, leaving room only for vitriol. When the Massachusetts Supreme Court found a constitutional right to same-sex marriage, it affected the politics of the 2004 national elections.

The recent case of *Roper v. Simmons* illustrates the problem. There the Court held by a slim 5–4 majority that capital punishment was unconstitutionally "cruel and unusual" when applied to juveniles (having upheld it only sixteen years before). The *Roper* decision was guided in part by

[2] *Plessy v. Ferguson*, 163 U.S. 537 (1896).

[3] *Grutter v. Bollinger*, 539 U.S. 306, 342 (2003): "It has been 25 years since Justice Powell first approved the use of race to further the interest in student body diversity in the context of public higher education. Since that time, the number of minority applicants with high grades and test scores has indeed increased. We expect that 25 years from now, the use of racial preferences will no longer be necessary to further the interest approved today."

[4] E.g., Paul A. Freund, *On Law and Justice* (Cambridge, Mass.: Belknap Press, 1968), 35.

[5] Alexander Bickel, *The Supreme Court and the Idea of Progress* (New York, Evanston, and London: Harper & Row, 1970).

[6] *Roe v. Wade*, 410 U.S. 113 (1973).

the fact that a growing number of states that authorize capital punishment (although not yet a majority) now outlaw it for juveniles. It was guided also by the observation that juvenile executions are banned in an overwhelming majority of foreign countries. This reasoning inflamed the conservative dissenters. Wrote Justice Antonin Scalia, "The court thus proclaims itself the sole arbiter of our nation's moral standards – and in the course of discharging that awesome responsibility purports to take guidance from the views of foreign courts and legislatures."[7]

There are searching questions raised by Holmes's observation. Is the division on the current Court to be explained by the line he draws in warning that the Court should stay "behind the times"? What is the role of popular consensus in legal interpretation? A student curious about such questions would seek with difficulty any satisfactory explanation in the university library under "theories of law."[8] Perhaps more elucidation might be found under the catalogue of "politics," not reassuring to anyone who imagines that unchanging "principles" govern the Bill of Rights. Still, as Holmes said in 1913, battles before the Court generally rage among and between *opposing* principles (is there any such thing as a "neutral" principle?). The cases that work their way up through the courts are the most difficult, not the most obvious. Stubborn controversies can prove relentless in finding a way, through experienced counsel, to entail the jurisdiction of the U.S. Constitution.[9]

How then did Holmes, at seventy-one, come to explain the plight of his court, besieged by criticism for having overturned much (though by no

7 *Roper v. Simmons*, No. 03–633 (U.S. Supreme Court, March 1, 2005), 125 S. Ct. 1183, 1222. "[N]o national consensus exists here." 125 S. Ct. 1183, 1222 n. 8 (Scalia, joined by Thomas, dissenting).

8 This is not to suggest that theories of law and constitutionalism in which popular consent plays an important part are by any means novel. The English scholar Thomas Smith (1514?–77) saw a strength of English legal practice as resting on the participating co-determination of the people. Carl J. Friedrich, *The Philosophy of Law in Historical Perspective* (Chicago: University of Chicago Press, 1967), 67. Richard Hooker (1553–1600) wrote that "laws they are not therefore which public probation hath not made so" and "laws therefore human of what kind so ever are available by consent." From the *Laws of Ecclesiastical Polity* (New York: Legal Classics Library, 1998), I, x, 8; Friedrich, *Philosophy of Law*, at 75. Bruce Ackerman notes the role of consensus in *We the People* (Cambridge Mass.: Belknap Press, 1991). It is rather the place of prevailing standards in immediate decisions that distinguishes Holmes's view.

9 "Given a sufficient hardihood of purpose at the rack of exegesis, and any document, no matter what its fortitude, will eventually give forth the meaning required of it." Edward S. Corwin, "The Supreme Court and the Fourteenth Amendment," in *American Constitutional History: Essays by Edward S. Corwin*, ed. Gerald Garvey and Alpheus T. Mason (New York, Evanston, and London: Harper & Row, 1964), 68.

means all) state regulatory legislation for over a decade, as a misreading not of principle but of timing? Holmes had the reputation then, as now, of a deep but dimly visible foundation beneath his fluent utterances. The invisibility of the ostensible ground beneath his frequently skeptical remarks has left his skepticism open to characterization as cynicism.[10] This impression is buttressed by a lifelong tendency to glorify struggle, in a way that often seemed "childish" to his friend William James.[11] The role of conflict is easily oversimplified in interpretations of Holmes; though he had a personal side, and experiences as a soldier, to reinforce the impression, a cynical deference to power has on careful examination almost nothing to do with his judicial philosophy.

My purpose is to explore the background to Holmes's 1913 comment, to focus on its derivation in Holmes's development as a scholar and theorist, and to consider its intellectual contours, how it fits into a theory of law and compares with other leading theories – both historically and in a contemporary context, especially as regards the leading theories of this past century, those expounded by H. L. A. Hart, Joseph Raz, Ronald Dworkin, and their contemporary critics and followers.

First I note a connection between Holmes's 1913 comment and three writers and jurists whose thoughts and lives overlapped with his: James Bradley Thayer, lawyer, scholar, and Harvard law professor through whom the younger Holmes gained editorship of *Kent's Commentaries on American Law*, a move that would profoundly affect his thinking; Felix Frankfurter, the Harvard law professor who supplied Justice Holmes with his personal secretaries and later became a Supreme Court Justice himself; and Learned Hand, by all accounts "the greatest judge never appointed to the Supreme Court," who venerated Holmes and seems to have influenced his attitude toward free speech in time of war.[12]

Characterizing the spirit of judicial restraint, Thayer would write in 1893: "The safe and permanent road towards reform is that of impressing upon our people a far stronger sense than they have of the great range of possible harm and evil that our system leaves open, and must leave open, to the legislatures, and the clear limits of judicial power; so that responsibility may be brought sharply home where it belongs." This runs counter to the common acceptance of final judicial interpretations

[10] E.g., Alschuler, *Law without Values*.

[11] William James to Frances R. Morse, April 12, 1900, in Ignas K. Skrupskelis and Elizabeth M. Berkeley, eds., *The Correspondence of William James*, vol. 9 (Charlottesville and London: University Press of Virginia, 2001), 184.

[12] See Kellogg, "Learned Hand and the Great Train Ride," 56 *American Scholar* 471 (1987).

of the Constitution. There is a renewed concern among legal scholars that the public, in our litigious society, is being left out of the shaping of constitutional law and hence of our most fundamental rights. Mark Tushnet, in his book *Taking the Constitution Away from the Courts* (1999), and Larry D. Kramer, in *The People Themselves: Popular Constitutionalism and Judicial Review* (2004), have lately brought this concern back to the forefront.[13]

The sentiment, or one very like it, goes back to Thayer (1901):

> [T]here has developed a vast and growing increase of judicial interference with legislation. This is a very different state of things from what our fathers contemplated, a century or more ago, in framing the new system. . . . Great, and indeed, inestimable as are the advantages in a popular government of this conservative influence, – the power of the judiciary to disregard unconstitutional legislation, it should be remembered that the exercise of it, even when unavoidable, is always attended with a serious evil, namely, that the correction of legislative mistakes comes from the outside, and the people thus lose the political experience, and the moral education and stimulus that come from fighting the question out in the ordinary way, and correcting their own errors.[14]

Citing this passage in a dissenting opinion, the famous 1943 flag salute case, Felix Frankfurter at the height of World War II opposed the court majority in its decision to reinstate a young Jehovah's Witness expelled from school for refusing on religious grounds to participate in the Pledge of Allegiance. "The reason why from the beginning even the narrow judicial authority to nullify legislation has been viewed with a jealous eye is that it serves to prevent the full play of the democratic process." We can imagine the outcry if the current Court were to stay its hand in such a case.[15]

Even more extreme, consider Learned Hand, who in the Oliver Wendell Holmes Lectures at Harvard in 1958 (funded by the Holmes Devise, created after the childless Holmes willed the balance of his estate to the federal government), caused an academic uproar by denouncing the Bill of Rights as grounds for overturning legislation, likening such Supreme Court jurisdiction to the ordination of a council of moral censors: "For myself it would be most irksome to be ruled by a bevy of

[13] Mark Tushnet, *Taking the Constitution away from the Courts* (Princeton: Princeton University Press, 1999), and Larry D. Kramer, *The People Themselves: Popular Constitutionalism and Judicial Review* (Oxford: Oxford University Press, 2004).

[14] James B. Thayer, *John Marshall* (Boston: Houghton Mifflin, 1901), 106.

[15] *West Virginia State Board of Education v. Barnett*, 319 U.S. 624, 667–71 (1943) (Frankfurter, dissenting).

Platonic Guardians, even if I knew how to choose them, which I most assuredly do not. If they were in charge, I should miss the stimulus of living in a society where I have, at least theoretically, some part in the direction of public affairs."[16]

Insofar as there is a connection with Holmes, the notion of timing in judicial self-restraint is connected with the preservation of democratic debate, of the popular grounding of democratic institutions. What do we know about this reason, and what are its contours? How may it be understood as a consistent, coherent theory of law – if a theory of law at all? The popular constraint on judges is the claim of a dominant text, illuminated only by its putative "original understanding." But we are in a skeptical moment just now; textualism as a judicial guide to final constitutional meaning cuts both ways, and can result no less in the exercise of a constitutional litmus test.

The two competing notions, that of an authoritative law that always contains the right answer, and that of a law of timing, of consensus, are radically opposed. The notion of a judicial system that somewhere holds a right or better answer for every legal question is found in Ronald Dworkin's *Taking Rights Seriously*, where if necessary the judge must turn to principles and rights. Here we encounter Holmes's second point above: "It is a misfortune if a judge reads his conscious or unconscious sympathy with one side or the other prematurely into the law, and forgets that what seem to him to be first principles are believed by half his fellow men to be wrong."[17]

What guidance can Holmes give us? Perhaps his notion here, though sounding conservative, may hide a licentious set of assumptions – that there is *no* legal answer, that the justices simply hoist their fingers to the wind. They sit down to assess the state of the national conscience, whatever that means, and decide whether the time is right to implement the enduring principles of the United States Constitution as they see them.

This book addresses a threefold subject: the intricate intellectual path of Justice Holmes, his relation to contemporary legal theory, and the controversial subject of judicial restraint. Oliver Wendell Holmes, Jr., was the rare son who could eclipse a famous and dominant father, an acutely

[16] Learned Hand, *The Bill of Rights* (Cambridge, Mass.: Harvard University Press, 1958), 73.

[17] Ronald Dworkin, *Taking Rights Seriously* (Cambridge, Mass.: Harvard University Press, 1977); Holmes, supra n. 1.

ambitious workaholic without children, a prodigious scholar who mastered in his time the history, theory, and practice of American law (a feat perhaps never again to be matched), judge for fifty years on the highest courts of Massachusetts and the United States. He has cast a long shadow upon the judges and scholars of our time – over a century now since he took a seat at sixty-one on the highest court of the land. Yet Holmes scholarship has been disorderly, even schizophrenic. His influence is undoubted, but its source ill-understood, giving rise to cycles of severe criticism. We are in one now.

Much of this criticism is responsible and illuminating. Once an icon, Holmes has been humanized. Where it falls short is in understanding the sources and development of his thinking. Confusion is understandable, given his unusual path and the subtlety of the original position, established early in his career. Before trying to characterize it, and where it might enlighten us, I give an example that demonstrates both the problem of understanding Holmes and its potential.

Two eminent scholars, Louis Kaplow and Steven Shavell, have recently published a controversial book about law entitled *Fairness versus Welfare* (2002), addressing a fundamental question about law. To what degree should we consider the impact on general welfare, as opposed to notions of fairness, in deciding legal matters? The authors take an extreme position against the advocates of fairness; they claim, and attempt to demonstrate, that any policy pursued on grounds other than social welfare – including fairness among the parties in the case – may end up making everyone worse off.[18]

Holmes, as many scholars have noted, often sounded a similar view in such comments as "I think that the judges themselves have failed adequately to recognize their duty of weighing considerations of social advantage" and "Moral predilections must not be allowed to influence our minds in settling legal distinctions."[19] Such comments sounded radical in their day and have maintained a ring of contemporary relevance. Did Holmes adopt a position similar to Kaplow and Shavell, as has often been suggested? That would be inconsistent with the distinctive position that is captured in his 1913 speech. The law is behind the times; while

[18] Louis Kaplow and Steven Shavell, *Fairness versus Welfare* (Cambridge, Mass.: Harvard University Press, 2002).

[19] Holmes, "The Path of the Law," in *Collected Legal Papers* (New York: Harcourt Brace, 1920), 184; *The Common Law* (Boston: Little, Brown, 1881), 118.

convictions still clash, they are not to be preferred; judges should avoid reading their own convictions into the law. There is such a thing as "a time for law."

While these three comments, from widely separated decades, may at first seem incongruous, there are hints of consistency. It is not morals or fairness per se that Holmes eschews in 1881, writing his major treatise *The Common Law*. It is moral *predilections*. The notion of deep uncertainty, of a process akin to a search, is embedded in his thinking about law. A search for what? Where does this idea come from, and what is it like? Nor indeed is it social advantage, or perhaps I should say the matrices of economic advantage or disadvantage presumed discoverable by Kaplow and Shavell, that he advocates in 1897 (in "The Path of the Law," his best-known essay). Rather, it is a *recognition* that he urges, a form of honesty: the judges "have failed adequately to recognize" their involvement in this aspect of the search, however murky the waters. There are inklings here of a complex venture, with hidden perils lurking to shipwreck the unready, rather than a socio-economic calculus.

Judicial restraint – a phrase hardly common in Holmes's time – is in his case associated with a theory of the law as a process of critical inquiry, a dynamic rather than static enterprise, but one involving a high degree of caution, of perspective, of learning. Holmes as a judge was not always a paragon of such restraint. He had a powerful mind and a sophisticated set of views – indeed a theory of history – that he sought constantly to bully past his colleagues on the Supreme Judicial Court of Massachusetts and write into the law. In 1902 he would arrive on a Supreme Court of the United States that was embroiled in controversy not unlike our own, over judicial invocation of the due process clause of the Constitution[20] to invalidate state social welfare legislation. Here his fame would be made in several ringing dissents, although his actual record is not as pure as the dissents might suggest; he did not resist all, or even most, substantive interventions under the due process clause.

The search for what lies beneath this unique vision of judicial restraint, unlike anything that can be found among the writings of judges or scholars today, takes us back to the earlier days of intensive study and conversation following Holmes's return to Cambridge and Boston from the Union Army in 1863. I will connect him more clearly with the influences

[20] "No state shall . . . deprive any citizen of life, liberty, or property, without due process of law. . . ." United States Constitution, Amendment XIV, sec. 1 (1868). A similar provision in Amendment V (1789) constrains the federal government.

of this period, from both New England and abroad, establishing how his legal conception developed and how it might fit into a larger picture that is usefully comprehensible today.

The slogan "popular constitutionalism" has emerged in the recent writings of certain legal scholars. I already mentioned Tushnet and Kramer, reacting to the fact that virtually all contemporary debate over judicial review of legislation, liberal or conservative, accepts the assumption of judicial supremacy, or more precisely judicial "determinism." That is, the context of *all* contemporary argument over judicial activism versus restraint is one in which no real alternative exists to the *courts* finally deciding, one way or the other, under one sweeping constitutional principle or another, the outcome of controversies affecting fundamental values. Hence the battle comes down to membership on the courts themselves. This has led some liberals to advocate what used to be conservative political tools for controlling federal court nominations, lest they become vested with politically approved nominees, such as congressional filibusters of controversial nominations or stripping the federal courts of controversial areas of jurisdiction.

There is revelation here – the notion that judicial determinism is embedded and will not yield easily to argument – but it is not enough revelation to work a revolution. Whether such political measures would be effective is not within my purview – but rather the question of whether there is any alternative comprehensive context within which judicial determinism is *not* accepted unquestioningly, indeed one in which it is convincingly overthrown. A revolution might then begin with new understanding and belief, leading to a new standard for both public and professional conduct.

2

Playing King

Connections and Misconceptions

> What intellectual fun all of this is! It explains why first-year law school is so exhilarating, because it consists of playing common-law judge, which in turn consists of playing king – devising, out of the brilliance of one's own mind, those laws that ought to govern mankind. How exciting! And no wonder so many law students, having drunk at this intoxicating well, aspire for the rest of their lives to be judges.
>
> Supreme Court Justice Antonin Scalia, *A Matter of Interpretation* (1997)

On a December day in 1882, Oliver Wendell Holmes, Jr., at forty-one, was at lunch in Cambridge, Massachusetts, with a colleague on the faculty of Harvard Law School. He had recently published a book, *The Common Law*. It was the culmination of fifteen years of effort, including numerous scholarly essays and a grueling revision of the leading American legal encyclopedia, *Kent's Commentaries on American Law*. His scholarship had been mixed with work as a private lawyer, half of them bachelor years of evening and weekend conversation with friends such as the James brothers, William and Henry, and a long visit to England in 1866. His wedding to Fanny Dixwell in June 1872 was curtly noted along with new editorial responsibilities in a diary devoted mainly to his reading and writing. ("June 17. *Married[.] sole editor of Law Rev.* July no. *et seq.*").

The book had gained the serious attention Holmes longed for. It had received highly respectful reviews by American journals, albeit traced with caution. A favorable review by the British legal historian Frederick Pollock, whom he had met on a visit to England with Fanny in 1874, as well as a strong but conditional endorsement by the prominent English legal scholar Albert Venn Dicey, would soon appear. Unhappy with private practice in Boston, already unsuccessful in obtaining a judicial appointment, he had accepted a professorship endowed on his behalf by the Weld family at the behest of James B. Thayer. To Thayer's considerable distress, Holmes would teach for only two months.[1]

His lunch on Friday, December 8, 1882, and his academic career, was abruptly cut short by George Shattuck, a recent law partner, who had Fanny Holmes in a carriage waiting to rush him to the governor's office in Boston. The retiring Republican John Long had been persuaded by Shattuck and others to appoint Holmes to an unexpected opening on the Supreme Judicial Court of Massachusetts. Formal acceptance of the nomination would have to reach the Governor's Council by three that afternoon. An anxious ride through what is now East Cambridge and across the Charles River was all that stood between the forty-one-year-old lawyer-scholar and his forty-nine-year judicial career.[2]

Several components frame my account of Holmes. One is the vainglorious self-regard he carried from his days of scholarship to the Massachusetts high court, where, according to Patrick J. Kelley, he forced an unorthodox legal theory into the law like the king in Justice Scalia's comment above.[3] This characteristic would repeatedly haunt him, in the regard of his oldest friends, in the way he framed and argued his book and in its effect on his language, the pithy, rhetorical facility with words and ideas, shared with his famous doctor-poet father but formally dense and informally often inclined to the shocking one-line closer. Along with his celebration of struggle and conflict, it overshadows his reputation today.

Another less-noted problem is the derivation and design of the theory itself, influenced by diverse sources, the English scholars John Austin and Henry Maine, as well as American literary and philosophical friends, such as the Jameses, Chauncey Wright, Nicholas St. John Green, and Charles S. Peirce, and the unique and changing literary, theological, and philosophical attitudes of nineteenth-century Cambridge and the continuing influence of leading figures of the Scottish Enlightenment. Evidence of influence is circumstantial; Holmes dispensed little credit.[4]

1 Novick, *Honorable Justice,* 164–5; White, *Justice Oliver Wendell Holmes,* 182–191.

2 Id.

3 Antonin Scalia, *A Matter of Interpretation: Federal Courts and the Law* (Princeton: Princeton University Press, 1997), 7.

4 There are several excellent references for the early and formative intellectual influences on Holmes. He grew up in a family prominent among the Cambridge and Boston intelligensia, with family friends including Ralph Waldo Emerson and the William James

Still another is the unsettled place of his theory in the also unsettled context of legal theory today, suggested in the passage above wherein Scalia rejects the common law tradition as devoid of intellectual legitimacy. All this is linked to the dubious place of Holmes's *The Common Law*, for reasons that go back to the comments of Dicey, who called it "the most original work of legal speculation which has appeared in English since the publication of Sir Henry Maine's *Ancient Law*," even while finding his "attempt to unite the historical with the analytical method" at the root of a "doubt whether Mr. Holmes is contending that a given principle is in conformity with the decisions to be found in the year-books, or that it is in conformity with the dictates of right reason, or expediency."[5]

Misunderstanding of the main thrust of his research and writing, combined with his frequent celebration of soldiering and social struggle, has given rise to Holmes's reputation as a power-oriented amoral relativist, recently elaborated at book length by Albert W. Alschuler. It must be addressed if Holmes's contribution is to be recognized as more than a clever but quirky nineteenth-century comment on Thomas Hobbes, the still-influential seventeenth-century philosopher of law and the modern state.

In a commentary in the *New York Times*, "The Competing Visions of the Role of the Court," the *Times*'s Supreme Court editor Linda Greenhouse observed that the main dividing line on the late Rhenquist Court has been between textualists, led by Justice Antonin Scalia, and *con*textualists, typified by Justice Stephen G. Breyer:

family. His Harvard education and associations make Bruce Kuklick's *The Rise of American Philosophy: Cambridge, Massachusetts 1860–1930* (New Haven and London: Yale University Press, 1977), detailing the role of both Harvard and the intelligensia in shaping contemporary attitudes, an important reference. Kuklick pays particular attention to the influence of non-university intellectuals, such as Chauncey Wright, and teachers, such as Alford Professor of Philosophy Francis Bowen (who influenced Holmes's generation even while finding Holmes an occasionally obstreperous student – see White, *Justice Oliver Wendell Holmes*, 44, – and who may have participated in the revived Metaphysical Club in 1876), and emphasizes the profound and lasting Scottish influence, as do Elizabeth Flower and Murray G. Murphey in *A History of Philosophy in America* (New York: G. P. Putnam's Sons, 1977).

Also helpful are H. S. Thayer, *Meaning and Action: A Critical History of Pragmatism* (Indianapolis and New York: Bobbs-Merrill, 1977); Herbert W. Schneider, *A History of American Philosophy* (New York: Liberal Arts Press, 1946); and Philip P. Wiener, *Evolution and the Founders of Pragmatism* (Cambridge, Mass.: Harvard University Press, 1949).

5 Albert V. Dicey, "Holmes's Common Law," 55 *The Spectator* (Literary Supplement, June 3, 1882), reprinted in Saul Touster, "Holmes a Hundred Years Ago: *The Common Law* and Legal Theory," 10 *Hofstra L. Rev.* 673 (1982).

For Justice Scalia, who focuses on text, language is supreme, and the court's job is to derive and apply rules from the words chosen by the Constitution's framers or a statute's drafters. For Justice Breyer, who looks to context, language is only a starting point to an inquiry in which a law's purpose and a decision's likely consequences are the more important elements.[6]

Textualism has had many precursors, including the political slogan "strict construction," popular among conservatives in the Nixon era. It has come into renewed prominence, reflected in the publication of Justice Scalia's *A Matter of Interpretation*, in 1997. This consisted of his 1996 Tanner Lectures at the Center for Human Values at Princeton University, with four critical commentaries by distinguished scholars: historian Gordon S. Wood, law professors Laurence Tribe and Mary Ann Glendon, and the renowned American legal philosopher Ronald Dworkin.

In that remarkable essay, Scalia derides the common law, notwithstanding its prominence within the American law school, as a license for judges to do as they please. He anoints a strict textualism as the only sure restraint on freewheeling judges. Not one of the commentators has much in particular to say in defense of common law as a legal theory.[7] Strangely, there appears no recognized authoritative text or treatise on common law, contemporary or otherwise, with which these or other critics of textualism are comfortable. But if indeed there is any theory against pure text and in favor of context in legal interpretation, it must in some fashion derive from or reflect the common law.

Holmes, although commended in Scalia's lecture for his strict adherence to the objective interpretation of a legislative text, developed a distinctive conception of the common law during the years 1865–80, after he had returned from the Civil War and had entered the study of law, first as a student at Harvard Law School, then as a reader and private practitioner, and eventually as an independent scholar (including a lectureship on constitutional law at Harvard College in 1870–71 and on jurisprudence at Harvard Law School from 1871 to 1873). It was influenced by editing *Kent's Commentaries on American Law*, framed in a series of published articles from 1870 to 1880[8] and reflected (though not, I argue,

[6] Linda Greenhouse, "The Competing Visions of the Role of the Court," *New York Times*, sec. 4, July 7, 2002.

[7] Gordon Wood does bring up the subject in a historical context in his comment on Justice Scalia's essay. Scalia, *A Matter of Interpretation*, 59.

[8] These were reprinted in Frederic R. Kellogg, *The Formative Essays of Justice Holmes: The Making of an American Legal Philosophy* (Westport: Greenwood Press, 1984) (hereafter *Formative Essays*). They are now also available in vols. 1 and 3 of *Collected Works*. While

adequately explained) in his book *The Common Law*, delivered as the Lowell Lectures in 1880 and published in 1881.[9]

As his own title suggests, it is a view based on the common law that characterizes Holmes's depiction, or perhaps reconstruction, of the general conception "law." The conception draws heavily from the historical debate between English legal theorists over the nature and source of legal rationality.[10] It also finds remarkable parallels to certain ideas of Holmes's nonlawyer friends, Chauncey Wright, Charles S. Peirce, William James, and others, among whom were founders of the American school of philosophical thought known as pragmatism, growing out of the multi–faceted influence of the Scottish Enlightenment on American thought and the response of Cambridge intellectuals to Darwin's *Origin of Species*.[11]

Holmes may have formulated some of his theory before 1870, as Sheldon M. Novick suggests, there is little clear evidence of it in the published writings. 1 *Collected Works*, 7 n. 2, 183–212.

9 Holmes received his bachelor's degree from Harvard College in 1861, and began a two-year course of study at Harvard Law School in the fall of 1864. He had been discharged from the Twentieth Massachusetts Regiment on July 17, 1864. He left law school in the middle of his second year to finish his studies as a reader in the office of attorney Robert M. Morse of Boston. The Harvard law faculty consisted of three men, Theophilus Parsons, Joel Parker, and Emory Washburn, all former practitioners and none original scholars, although Parsons's treatise on contracts made him for many generations the leading authority on the subject in America. They gave no examinations, and the only requirement for a degree was occasional attendance at lectures. Holmes received his degree in the summer of 1866. He later (1870) published anonymously the comment that "for a long time the condition of the Harvard Law School has been almost a disgrace to the Commonwealth of Massachusetts." Mark DeWolfe Howe, *Justice Oliver Wendell Holmes: The Shaping Years, 1841–1870* (Cambridge, Mass.: Belknap Press, 1957), 205.

Seeking roots of his later theory in Holmes's diaries of his early reading, several items stand out. Foremost among them is the originating work of legal positivism, John Austin's *Lectures on Jurisprudence*, begun in April 1861, his final term of Harvard College, while he was awaiting a commission in the Twentieth Massachusetts Regiment. Holmes records reading Austin again in 1865–66, again in 1868, and still again in 1870 and 1871; he notes that on December 5, 1871, he finished reading it twice. Henry Maine's *Ancient Law*, a major originating work in historical theory of law, appears on the list for 1865–66, and had been finished twice by October 1868. Sir William Blackstone's *Commentaries on the Laws of England*, the highly influential eighteenth-century exposition of the common law and its underlying theory, appears at the very beginning of the diaries in 1865, later in the 65–66 term, and again in 1867 and 1868. Jeremy Bentham, founder of utilitarianism and leader of the challenge to common law theory, appears once in 1865–66 (*Defence of Usury*), twice in 1871 (*Theory of Legislation* and *General View of a Complete Code of Laws*), and 1872 (*Fragment on Government*). See Eleanor Little, "The Early Reading of Justice Oliver Wendell Holmes," 8 *Harvard Library Bulletin* 163, 169–85 (1954).

10 See, e.g., Friedrich, *Philosophy of Law in Historical Perspective* 67–100.

11 See n. 4 supra.

Because he did not regard a legal text as hieratic, even while applying a strict standard of interpretation,[12] Holmes was not a textualist in Scalia's sense. Nor was he in any strong sense an "originalist." The appeal to original understanding, while in many instances useful and some cases essential, sheds little light on novel questions. It is like the rhetorical one put a century ago by Holmes's friend and colleague John Chipman Gray: "What was the Law in the time of Richard Coeur de Lion on the liability of a telegraph company to the persons to whom a message was sent?"[13] What was the original understanding of the Fourteenth Amendment, adopted on the heels of the Civil War in 1868, regarding remedial or affirmative steps to end race or gender discrimination? Or, for that matter, regarding state-sponsored suppression of free speech, the indigent right to counsel in a criminal case, or privacy? All of these issues are now part of Fourteenth Amendment law.[14]

It is a sign of misunderstanding Holmes that we have failed fully to investigate the roots of his cautionary language in the Supreme Court dissents and the connection, if any, with his early scholarship and his major work, *The Common Law.* The explanation may be the obscure language and shifting focus of the early scholarly work, especially the condensed style and heavily historical bent of *The Common Law,* with its widely discredited thesis of an evolution from moral to external standards, worked so insistently into his treatise and later his Massachusetts opinions.

The Common Law is considered supplanted and no longer relevant. But defects aside, an account must be provided for the idea, sounding radical but also conservative, that premature judicial intervention and resolution may in some serious and coherent sense be illegitimate, that a final judicial prerogative to interpret and pronounce constitutional rights may be associated with a flawed conception of law itself.

If Holmes is to be reread in search of this connection, the deficiencies of *The Common Law* and the excesses of his Massachusetts opinions need to be not overlooked, but rather illuminated as part of a larger context.

[12] See Holmes, "Legal Interpretation," *Collected Legal Papers,* 203.

[13] John Chipman Gray, *The Nature and Sources of the Law* (Gloucester, Mass.: Peter Smith, 1972), 99.

[14] The Fourteenth Amendment was passed by the Reconstruction Congress in 1866. Included in it is the phrase "[n]o state . . . shall deprive any person of life, liberty, or property, without due process of law." While there is no evidence of an original intent in 1866 to include the rights of free expression, fair trials in criminal cases, and privacy, such rights have been "incorporated" from other rights applying against the federal government so as to apply against the states. This issue, and Holmes's attitude regarding it, is further discussed in chapters 9 and 10.

This might best be described by showing how Holmes painstakingly recovered and redescribed the tradition of the common law, eventually to address a new problem of now massive dimensions: the interpretation of a written constitution as it applies to the most vexing legal controversies of modern society.

It is, moreover, a context that should be connected to the path of Anglo-American legal philosophy since Thomas Hobbes. In the seventeenth century, amidst the conflict engendered by the English Civil War, Hobbes solidified a concept and philosophy of law rooted in the power of the central state that might be said, like the British royal family, to be a paradigm that reigns even while surrounded with evidence of its own obsolescence. I mean by this the notion of law as a certain and definable analytical entity, which the English scholar John Austin affirmed for Holmes's generation and which Professor H. L. A. Hart of Oxford University carried forward in the twentieth century. It is a context in which we may understand and actually resolve the problem that Dicey noted immediately in 1881, the confusing "attempt to unite the historical with the analytical method," which, I suggest, underlies the main controversies about Holmes today.

The tradition that Holmes brought forward is the fundamental relation of law to the voluntary, embedded patterns of social life. We live in an age of legislation and administrative regulation, accompanying the fact of enormous growth in the size and scope of government. This development, traceable back to origins in the sixteenth century and before, has brought with it a set of assumptions about law. Those assumptions have evolved, but on balance they reflect a vision of law as autonomous, determinative, largely coherent, and textual. Against that, the old idea has emphasized the larger context of law embedded in social practices and emerging from the resolution of disputes. It appeared distinctly as a theory of the common law.[15]

[15] The idea that law is embedded in society and its order is in some fundamental sense independent of state enforcement is developed in the writings of F. A. Hayek, most recently in *The Constitution of Liberty* (Chicago: University of Chicago Press, 1960), 148–61. Hayek (id. at 452) notes that the idea goes back at least to David Hume (1711–76). Hume's likely influences were Anthony Ashley Cooper, Lord Shaftsbury (1671–1713), Francis Hutcheson (1694–1746), and Henry Home, Lord Kames (1696–1782), as well as Charles de Secondat, Baron de Montesquieu's (1689–1755) *L'esprit des lois* (1748). See chapter 3, n. 24.

This broad insight does not on its own meet the question of how such ordering operates and what it entails for the problems of legal interpretation, a need that Holmes would address by his original analysis of the common law.

When Holmes wrote his famous dissent in *Lochner v. New York*,[16] resisting the judicial overruling of reform legislation at the beginning of the twentieth century, the old idea had been transformed by him to apply, as never before, to the adjudication of disputes arising from the language of the United States Constitution. This was an approach to constitutional adjudication derived from the tradition of the common law. His approach can be traced from his early research to the dissenting opinions in the Fourteenth Amendment cases of his late career.

It is a path in which the fortune of ideas is remarkably linked to that of a man and his legacy. Holmes's reputation has traced a roller-coaster path in the seventy years since his death. After reaching an apotheosis during the 1930s around Holmes's death, it was challenged in the 1940s during years of world conflict in which his outspoken skepticism of moral certainties ill suited the nation's mobilized mood.[17] It rose in mid-century with a sincere, but incomplete, recognition of his contributions to a flourishing of constitutional doctrine and legal philosophy in America. After a somewhat bumpy period of interest, it plummeted again in the 1980s, driven down once more by the more skeptical – many say cynical – aspects of his thought and writing. H. L. Pohlman has noted the tendency toward polemical abuse of Holmes's influential writings, leading to "cycles of intellectual anachronism, panegyrics, and condemnations."[18]

In 1997, Professor Albert W. Alschuler of the University of Chicago Law School wrote his disapproving and highly readable book about Holmes's life and legacy, with the title *Law without Values*, echoing attacks from patriotic and natural law theorists during the Second World War. The idea that Holmes's conception of law was value-*less* rather than value-neutral (or, as I suggest, value-*transparent*) betrays a misunderstanding of his overall career and a marked tendency to miss the intellectual context of his skepticism itself. Alschuler is hardly alone. The principal missing piece of the puzzle, whose incompletion may explain the widely shared attitude, is the period after Captain Holmes returned to Cambridge in 1864 from the Civil War, having been thrice wounded

16 *Lochner v. New York*, 198 U.S. 45, 74–76 (1905) (Holmes, dissenting).

17 See Touster, "Holmes a Hundred Years Ago," 675.

18 H. L. Pohlman, *Justice Oliver Wendell Holmes and Utilitarian Jurisprudence* (Cambridge, Mass., and London: Harvard University Press, 1984), 1. Pohlman has been a leader in reading Holmes strictly in historical context. He argues forcefully for a closer identification with Bentham and Austin than would appear consistent with the early critique of Austin and the turn Holmes's thinking took in the mid-1870s. See chapter 6 and 10 infra.

with the Twentieth Massachusetts Regiment at Ball's Bluff, Antietam, and Second Fredericksburg.

In 1864, after Grant took over the Army of the Potomac and began his relentless drive toward Richmond, Holmes was detailed as a staff officer to General Horatio Wright and witnessed the extraordinary carnage of the battle of the Wilderness and the Bloody Corner, reinforcing a reluctance to extend his enlistment and return to the line with the Twentieth Massachusetts, a regiment that suffered singular casualties throughout the war. Holmes went to Cambridge and began the formative period of his scholarship, including a decade of still obscure essays that reveal his commitment to a common law tradition and eventually his transformation of it.

To explore the transformation I address the progression of Holmes's thought in an updated context, comparing it along the way with more recent ideas concerning law, as well as earlier ones stemming from the seminal Hobbes. Now may be a propitious moment to separate Holmes from an important aspect of the analytical positivist tradition, with which Alschuler and many others have identified him, and to show how his overall perspective compares with other contemporary approaches to legal philosophy, especially the forms of legal positivism still maintained today, and the influential anti-positivist position painstakingly elaborated by Ronald Dworkin.

Holmes's association with the common law tradition is a key to the overall puzzle. Common law has perhaps had no other explicit constructive theorist, effectively since Sir Edward Coke (1552–1634), Sir Matthew Hale (1609–1676), and Sir William Blackstone (1723–1780) – also scholar-judges – in the seventeenth and eighteenth centuries.[19] Common law theory has been considered by most scholars to have been eclipsed for two centuries by the legal positivism of Hobbes (1588–1679) and a succession of positivist theorists from John Austin (1790–1859) to Hans Kelsen (1881–1973), H. L. A. Hart (1907–1994), and their contemporary successors.[20] Even so, the term and practice of "common law"

[19] Other common law theorists may be found among the legal realists of the early twentieth century, but none advance as comprehensive a theory as Holmes. See, e.g., Karl Llewellyn, *The Common Law Tradition: Deciding Appeals* (Boston: Little, Brown, 1960).

[20] The roster of contemporary legal positivists is too long to enumerate; useful recent references are Brian Bix, "Positivism," in *The Blackwell Guide to the Philosophy of Law and Legal Theory*, ed. William A. Edmundson and Martin P. Golding (Oxford and Malden, Mass.: Blackwell, 2004), 29; Jules L. Coleman and Brian Leiter, "Legal Positivism," in

endures in England, America, and elsewhere (there is now said to be an emerging "common law of Europe"[21]), embedded in legal education and research, and reasoning from precedents. It is the quintessential decentralized or "bottom-up" theory of law, as opposed to one stemming from Hobbes that might be characterized as fundamentally centralized and "top-down."

Understanding the connection between Holmes's eventual judicial restraint and his theory of the common law requires taking the good with the bad. There are aspects of his theory, as originally formulated in the period of scholarly research, that have not withstood scrutiny. This includes the notion of an external standard of liability sweeping inexorably throughout the entire body of the law, removing all traces of subjectivity, and his effort to apply and later to amend the notion as an appellate judge. It also includes his own occasionally idiosyncratic use of reasons and precedents, in judicial rulings that have troubled contemporary scholars.[22]

Yet there are broad aspects of the theory that remain relevant, in particular the ideas of common law method as case-specific inquiry, of the tentative and experimental nature of legal thinking and common law rule making, of the skepticism of abstraction, and of the importance of and respect for community practice and participation in the courtroom law-making process. These ideas may sound unrealistic in light of current legal culture, but Holmes affirmed them as part of the Anglo-American legal tradition. They contribute to a particular image or ideal of a judge that may yet be valuable and worth preserving, especially given the extreme politicization of judicial selection that prevails at the federal level.

My first task is to reexamine Holmes from the perspective of the early writings leading to his Lowell Lectures of 1880, published as *The Common Law*. From the period of exploration, 1866–80, emerges a picture of his

Dennis Patterson, ed., *A Companion to Philosophy of Law and Legal Theory* (Oxford and Malden, Mass.: Blackwell, 1996), 241; and Stephen R. Perry, "The Varieties of Legal Positivism," 9 *Canadian Journal of Law and Jurisprudence* 361–81 (July 1996).

21 See, e.g., Bruno de Witte and Caroline Forder, *The Common Law of Europe and the Future of Legal Education* (Deventer, The Netherlands, and Cambridge, Mass.: Kluwer 1992).

22 See Patrick J. Kelley, "Holmes on the Supreme Court; The Theorist as Judge," in Russell K. Osgood, ed., *The History of the Law in Massachusetts: The Supreme Judicial Court 1692–1992* (Boston: Supreme Judicial Court Historical Society, 1992), 275–352; Alschuler, *Law without Values*.

conception of common law with a distinctiveness that cannot be fully retrieved from the 1880 lectures, or the later essays, opinions, and letters. My approach follows intellectual rather than psychological or sociocultural sources in the development of his thinking. Primacy is given to the period in which the main lines of his philosophy were formed, followed by connecting later developments to the original patterns of thought.

A useful device in understanding Holmes may lie in considering his overall method and theory in comparison to the founder of legal positivism, Thomas Hobbes. For both men, the fundamental nature of law was associated with conflict. Born in 1588, as the Spanish fleet prepared its ill-fated invasion of England, Hobbes commented, "My mother brought forth twins, both me and fear." Also a speculative scholar (though not as empirical as Holmes), his approach reflects the powerful influence of mathematical and mechanistic logic.[23] Greatly impressed by his exposure to Euclid in 1630, he was inclined toward argument from principles to necessary conclusions.[24] Holmes, on the other hand, refrained from abstraction until surrounded by facts, in great detail, largely acquired while editing a contemporary encyclopedia of American law.

For Hobbes, who viewed the civil strife of his era as reflecting an ugly and brutish state of nature,[25] law emerged from the considered decision by the citizenry to yield certain of their natural rights to the sovereign state. Law thereby became, by a deductive if not Euclidean necessity, an entity with the overall form of a system of sovereign commands. From this assumption, it followed for Hobbes that law's internal reasoning should reflect a unitary form of authority and coherence, or be subject to constant doubt and dispute by a quibbling citizenry. Hobbes found himself obliged to reject the common law, in continuous flux from particularized cases and influences, in favor of absolute sovereign power and, where applicable, the legislative text. It followed that all legal reasoning should be derived from its sovereign source.[26]

[23] Leo Strauss, "On the Spirit of Hobbes's Political Philosophy," in K. C. Brown, *Hobbes Studies* (Cambridge, Mass.: Harvard University Press, 1965), 1–29.

[24] Id. at 17: "The attempt to deduce the natural law or the moral law from the natural right of self-preservation or from the inescapable power of the fear of violent death led to far-reaching modifications of the content of the moral law. The modification amounted, in the first place, to a considerable simplification."

[25] Michael Oakshott, "Introduction to *Leviathan*," in *Rationalism in Politics and Other Essays* (Indianapolis: Liberty Fund, 1991), 279.

[26] "Hobbes, as his opponents understood him, identified the moral with the positive law. That is wrong, he said, which the sovereign forbids; that is right which he allows."

Two centuries later, John Austin, influenced less by Hobbes than Jeremy Bentham and lecturing in London during Holmes's youth, filled out (for different reasons) what such a unitary system might look like in considerable and impressive detail. A generation after this, Holmes, who would first read Austin while preparing to become a Union soldier and would continue to reread him, immersed himself in a revision of *Kent's Commentaries on American Law*, the encyclopedic reference work of its day, perhaps the ideal reality test for any analytical scheme of law. Recruited as an assistant editor by Thayer, he had brashly taken the project over.[27] Updating this legal catalogue with Austin's framework in mind, he grew increasingly doubtful not just of Austin's classifications but of the project of classification itself. In a decade of essays we find a unique commentary by Holmes on analytical legal reasoning – itself at times analytical, empirical, and historical.

This development of his thought – a growing skepticism concerning pure analytical method leading to a historical conception of the law's (including analytical method's) own formation and usage – is largely missing from *The Common Law*. There, the historical conception is transformed into a new evolutionary thesis, a direct challenge to Sir Henry Maine, as Dicey noted. Yet influence of the analytical framework remains, since Holmes had concluded (in a somewhat Hegelian move) that aspects of Austin's positivism could be the result, *mutatis mutandis*, of the historical process. This replacement of Hobbesian foundations explains Dicey's confusion about the relation of the two in the final overall scheme. Against the weight of scholarly opinion, Holmes had found not internal coherence throughout law, but rather the scattered evidence of a process of growth and adjustment, leading nevertheless to an increasingly systematic order. Obscured from view amidst the subsequent confusion has been the residue of his early critical insights, his conception of rule formation and the resolution of conflicts among competing precedents and legal authorities.

Though personally bloodied by a far more intense, fiery, and deadly fratricidal conflict than Hobbes could have witnessed or perhaps even imagined, Holmes nevertheless conceptualized law with a theory not to

Sir Leslie Stephen, *History of English Thought in the Eighteenth Century*, vol. 2 (London: Smith, Elder, 1902), 5. Friedrich identifies Jean Bodin (1530–96) as the originator of the view of law as properly deriving from the sovereign. Friedrich, *Philosophy of Law in Historical Perspective*, 57.

27 Mark DeWolfe Howe, *Oliver Wendell Holmes: The Proving Years, 1870–1882* (Cambridge: Belknap Press, 1963), 11–15.

control conflict but to assimilate it. His conception was embedded within the perennial turbulence of society, not superimposed upon it. It embodied not deductive reasoning from a set of unquestioned assumptions but a messier, collective form of thinking, growing out of the turbulence itself. It would grow despite the lack of an innate unitary rational coherence, though Holmes attempted to attribute an overall historical direction. Meanwhile, the process of collective reasoning amidst conflict remained keenly local and specific in origin and left ample room for social competition and change.

This account of a perennial misunderstanding renders Holmes's thought both more coherent and consistent than the prevailing interpretation of him as a late Hobbesian positivist. Times had changed from the common law of Hobbes's day, and part of the change was the widespread growth and acceptance of centralized republican government. Holmes was obliged to make room for the positivist ethos of legislation, but in a way that could be incorporated into a larger understanding, consistent with common law tradition. Here lies a nuance in Holmes's thought that seems crucial for us to recognize in escaping the Diceyan confusion. It is easier to miss if the reader is embedded in the set of assumptions that accompany analytical positivism.

For a vision that is fundamentally open to transformation, as Holmes's vision was, room had to be left for collective attitudes that could turn with relative freedom, such that a public choice might exist whether and how to turn away from turbulence, toward order. Holmes conceded reform legislation as a legitimate turn, defending it against constitutional attack, and in so deferring to the state, and demanding strict adherence to the text of legislation insofar as it was indisputable, he has seemed to have put himself on a parallel course with Hobbes, Bentham, and Austin. This is a good part of the reason why the majority of scholars now see Holmes as a "positivist."

If we were to define positivism broadly, as (in the formulation of Brian Bix) "a study of law in the scientific spirit," rather than an attempt to separate it definitively from morals or "law as it should be," Holmes is indeed a positivist. But legal positivism in the twentieth century has been characterized by a strict separation of law and morals, and this does not suit the common law-based conception developed by Holmes. We should take care to distinguish Holmes from this aspect of the Hobbesian tradition.[28]

[28] James Herget notes that the use of the term "legal positivism" to characterize the radical separation of law and morals flourished after Lon L. Fuller, in *The Law in Quest of*

For Holmes a pervasive skepticism forever remained the prominent feature of his thought. The manifestations, indeed the very nature, of legal argument and rationalization required cautious evaluation. The assumptions of lawyers or philosophers, no matter how widespread, are not necessarily evidence of conclusive and permanent aspects of law, though they may be evidence of the process through which it is changing. Arguments and rationalizations themselves are not evidence of analytical truth – even those that may have acquired a seemingly permanent consensus.[29] Nevertheless, conclusive weight is placed by contemporary legal philosophers on precisely this sort of evidence.[30]

Holmes's famous skepticism, for all its negative overtones, may be defended as an antidote to this form of thinking. For Holmes the judge, a high premium lay with what we would today call "transparency," the unblemished reality behind the varnished product. It was to be found in a realistic assessment of the history of legal development, and thus of the judges' appropriate institutional place in the legal process. He sought a perspective that would genuinely reflect historical reality, from which he could define what he saw as judicial error or abuse. He saw these as frequently arising from reliance on sweeping and "empty" generalizations,

Itself (Chicago: Foundation Press, 1940), challenged the extreme empiricist strain of legal realism together with John Austin for failing to account for values and purposes in jurisprudence. Herget, *American Jurisprudence 1870–1970* (Houston: Rice University Press, 1990), 253–56. Herget usefully distinguishes Anglo-American jurisprudence into three camps, the "moral," "expository," and "evolutionary" models or paradigms, and notes Holmes's dramatic shift from an expository to an evolutionary model in the 1870s, id. at 43, which I attempt to explain as essential to understanding his conception of law.

29 See Basil Willey, *The Eighteenth Century Background* (New York: Doubleday, 1953), 99–100: "What we have to look out for, in reading the philosophers of Western Europe, is the emotional or social determinant which makes their work what it is, and this is usually implicit rather than explicit. As I have attempted to suggest above, what will seem 'true' or 'explanatory' to any age or individual is what satisfies current demands and interests. What has this writer most urgently demanded from life? is the question we must constantly ask ourselves. The original impulse, towards, say, 'materialism,' or 'idealism,' is usually something sublogical; not, that is, a 'conviction' resulting from an intellectual process, but a quite simple set of the whole being towards a particular way of life. The direction once given, the subconscious affirmation once made, the character of the metaphysical superstructure is determined accordingly. It would be well if it were more generally realized that metaphysical utterances which appear to be statements of 'fact' are disguised imperatives, or at least disguised optatives; and our studies of the philosophers would be more remunerative if we went to them, not for 'truth,' but in order to discover what particular *fiat* or *utinam* their teaching implies.

"Few of our modern classical philosophers illustrate these considerations more than Thomas Hobbes."

30 I discuss this throughout chapters 6 through 9, in the context of Holmes's opposition to the use of moral arguments from general propositions in deciding particular cases.

whether time-honored legal maxims or abstract constitutionally based "principles." In his ongoing opposition to this tendency, Holmes sought to force difficulty and complexity to the surface – although once in the open, he could, to the discredit of his later reputation, be doctrinaire in his treatment of it and surprisingly quick to lay down his own rule.

After what I have called the formative period, after Holmes was appointed in December of 1882 to the Supreme Judicial Court of Massachusetts, he served there for twenty years. He was appointed by Theodore Roosevelt to the Supreme Court of the United States in 1902, retiring in January 1932 at the age of ninety. He applied and adapted his early conception of law to issues that faced him as a judge; and Holmes throughout his career was a prodigious worker. In his forty-nine years of service as a judge, Holmes compiled a huge inventory of over two thousand signed opinions (and many unsigned memorandum opinions), which Sheldon Novick has suggested may be more than any other judge writing for a supreme appellate court.[31] Several excellent studies of the Massachusetts opinions have been published;[32] the Supreme Court years are less well charted.[33]

The span of Holmes's scholarly and judicial career is so great, and the social, economic, and military events that touched it so significant, that no writer can approach the subject without humility. While I have focused mainly on the years of scholarship, Holmes's views on law (as Morton Horwitz also maintains) were influenced by his judicial experience.[34] I have suggested somewhat less of a transformation than Horwitz, along a far more consistent path, leading to and elucidating the pronounced judicial restraint and skepticism that Horwitz views as having changed from the early years.[35]

David Rosenberg has recently explored the difficulty of accurately tracking Holmes's thought in *The Hidden Holmes* (1995). Focusing mainly on his theory of tort and personal injury, he has shown how inaccurate

[31] Sheldon M. Novick, *Honorable Justice: The Life of Oliver Wendell Holmes* (Boston, London, and Toronto: Little, Brown, 1989), 406.

[32] White, *Justice Oliver Wendell Holmes*; Mark Tushnet, "The Logic of Experience: Oliver Wendell Holmes on the Supreme Judicial Court," 63 *Virginia L. Rev.* 975–1052 (1977); Patrick J. Kelley, "Holmes on the Supreme Court: The Theorist as Judge," 275–352.

[33] A careful and illuminating exploration of Holmes's due process decisions is found in Michael J. Phillips, "The Substantive Due Process Decisions of Mr. Justice Holmes," 36 *American Business Law Journal* 437–77 (Spring 1999).

[34] Morton J. Horwitz, *The Transformation of American Law 1870–1960* (New York and Oxford: Oxford University Press, 1992), 109–43.

[35] Id. See chapter 8, n. 36.

misconceptions have become mainstream opinion, and how a strict attention to the entire chronology of Holmes's writing is essential in getting him right.[36] While we may disagree in the overall characterization of Holmes's theory, I agree with Rosenberg's observation that Holmes did not adopt the strict separation of law and morals.[37]

Following the discussion of the early scholarship, I have focused my attention largely on Massachusetts decisions that reflect and elucidate his scholarly concept of law, and those from early in his Supreme Court tenure that form a part of the history of the Court's interpretation of the due process clause of the Fourteenth Amendment. This is a choice dictated by space and narrative coherence; there is much more to be explored of Holmes's judicial career, and there is much of considerable value and insight in the existing literature, that I unfortunately cannot address here.

[36] Rosenberg, *The Hidden Holmes: His Theory of Torts in History* (Cambridge, Mass.: Harvard University Press, 1995), 163–69 (noting the tendency of mainstream scholarship to overlook the place of Holmes's tort theory in the context of his overall thought and to associate Holmes with opposition to strict liability, limiting the corporate exposure to damages, which Rosenberg refers to as the "industrial-subsidy" thesis).

[37] Id., 49–50. Rosenberg's central thesis, with which I agree, is that scholars have misinterpreted Holmes as a opponent of strict liability. Our principle disagreement lies in Rosenberg's account of what he refers to as Holmes's "new jurisprudence," in particular supporting judicial law making in "proceed[ing] opportunistically, with courts fashioning and enforcing their views of expedient policy for the particular situation at hand." Id. at 44. I address this topic at length in chapters 7 and 8.

3

Holmes's Conception of Law

> It is the merit of the common law that it decides the case first and determines the principle afterwards.
>
> O. W. Holmes, 1870

Before tracing Holmes's intellectual path, which I do in the following chapters, I should highlight a broad distinction between common law conceptions and their more recent alternative, analytical legal positivism. John Dewey, the American philosopher much admired by Holmes, held that law is "through and through a social phenomenon" and that all legal theories should be judged as programs for action. Hence Dewey warned against use of the word "law" as a "single general term." Law, he explained, must be viewed as intervening in the complex of other activities, and as itself a social process. Hence (in Dewey's words) "'law' cannot be set up as a separate entity, but can be discussed only in terms of the social conditions in which it arises and of what it concretely does there."[1]

This is a classic statement of law as boundaryless, endogenous, and embedded, as a social theorist might say, an "open system." It emerges in part from, and is applicable to, common law. It is distinct in several crucial respects from the dominant vision of legal positivism, which sees law as fundamentally separate, *ex*ogenous, autonomous, acting on society rather than acting within.[2] Both models are in some degree reflected in the current methodology of American law; yet the two are at odds. They

[1] John Dewey, "My Philosophy of Law," in *Credos of Sixteen American Scholars* (Boston: Boston Law Book, 1941), 77.

[2] See Gerald J. Postema, *Bentham and the Common Law Tradition* (Oxford: Clarendon Press, 1986), 314.

imply a deep inconsistency in our corporate belief in what law *is*. What difference does it make which assumption is taken?

For the present purposes, we may find an operational contrast between the two views, in their different approaches to legal interpretation. According to the positivist model of law as a separate, autonomous, and bounded entity, law (when deciding a case) either succeeds or fails on its own. That is, all positivists would agree that it is *law only* that must determine the outcome, but when law is defined as a static textual or analytical entity, as "positive" law, the outcome of a case must be recognizably attributable to it without regard to human intervention and foible. When it comes to deciding difficult cases, this means the positivist legal theorist must accept the real and problematic possibility of "legal indeterminacy." What is stated as a metaphor becomes real; the issue of the boundary location of law itself becomes intimately involved with the question of legitimacy of judicial decisions.[3]

For the endogenous or embedded model, that of the common law, legal indeterminacy carries a very different meaning, denoting degrees of uncertainty and difficulty. The term "legal indeterminacy" can, of course, be understood conversationally to mean a high degree of difficulty, but this is not its meaning under positivism. The core issue of positivist jurisprudence, lending itself to the technique and style of analytical philosophy, is the definition and boundary of the concept of law. When the entire authoritative text of the law does not appear to have any clear answer to a pertinent question, the positivist paradigm forces the conclusion that it is "indeterminate" and the answer must lie, in some crucial respect, outside the boundary. This bears an obvious implication for the conduct of judges: if the decision of an unclear case is not covered by what is inside the accepted boundary, it must have been guided by something outside, not belonging within the proper definition of "the law." The decision must be tantamount to judicial "activism" or "legislation."

In a now famous remark about law that appears altogether unlike the positivist model, Holmes in 1870, at the age of twenty-nine, wrote:

> It is the merit of the common law that it decides the case first and determines the principle afterwards.... In cases of first impression Lord Mansfield's often-quoted advice to the business man who was suddenly appointed judge, that he should

[3] Brian Leiter incisively sets forth the grounds for concluding that "the real debate about indeterminacy is, in fact, coextensive with the debates already central to analytic jurisprudence, for example, about the legitimate sources of law and legitimate ways of interpreting statutes and precedents." Leiter, "Legal Indeterminacy," 1 *Legal Theory* 481–492 (1995).

state his conclusions and not give his reasons, as his judgment would probably be right and the reasons certainly wrong, is not without its application to more educated courts.[4]

Here the legal decision is described as coming before the reasoning; the boundary of the law, and the appropriate rule of decision, would appear surprisingly irrelevant. This somewhat hyperbolic comment implies – perhaps too much so – that there is no clear rational itinerary from the written law to the specific decision. More important, it implies a sort of common law judicial minimalism, deciding "one case at a time." This phrase has most recently been deployed by Cass Sunstein, referring to decisions of the Supreme Court that avoid formulae and withhold sweeping generalization.[5] Holmes had in 1870 proposed a quite sophisticated model through which common law rules are ideally formulated:

It is only after a series of determinations on the same subject-matter, that it becomes necessary to "reconcile the cases," as it is called, that is, by a true induction to state the principle which has until then been obscurely felt. And this statement is often modified more than once by new decisions before the abstracted general rule takes its final shape. A well settled legal doctrine embodies the work of many minds, and has been tested in form as well as substance by trained critics whose practical interest it is to resist it at every step.[6]

Holmes called this process "successive approximation." Legal rules are viewed historically, and Holmes here proposes that they be understood as emerging from classes of activity, or more precisely from classes of disputes within discrete activities. As new cases arise within a given class, for example, vehicular accidents or communications among people forming contractual arrangements, they are initially decided on their facts, a case at a time. Eventually, a body of decided cases can be "reconciled," with the laying down of a general rule, after time has permitted sufficient case-specific analysis, probing the relevant varieties and conditions of accidents or contractual communications.

[4] Holmes, "Codes, and the Arrangement of the Law," in *Formative Essays*, 77, and in 1 *Collected Works*, 212.

[5] Cass Sunstein, *One Case at a Time: Judicial Minimalism on the Supreme Court* (Cambridge, Mass., and London: Harvard University Press, 1999); *Legal Reasoning and Political Conflict* (New York and Oxford: Oxford University Press, 1996), 68 (crediting Holmes for saying that ideas are developed with close reference to the details, rather than imposed on them from above).

[6] Holmes, "Codes, and the Arrangement of the Law."

Whereas legal positivism emphasizes language and text, which gives the appearance of fixity, the common law model emphasizes patterns of conduct, which may be in the process of gradual development. While the positivist model sees legal development as possible mainly through legislation, Holmes saw it as ongoing in areas even already covered by statute; and finality of generalization is elusive. The introduction of new forms of travel or communication may require new amendments to the rules of travel or contract, as did the airplane and the telegraph in the previous century. And even new legislation will need to be interpreted and applied on a case-by-case basis.[7]

Opposing this version is the textualist idea that a judicial decision should derive directly from the written law. We may take an example made famous by the leading British positivist legal philosopher of the last century, H. L. A. Hart of Oxford University, who conceived the law as embodied in language and viewed indeterminacy as deriving from legal language's "open texture." A local ordinance bans vehicles from a public park. Competent users of English are uncertain or disagree about whether bicycles are vehicles. Hart infers that the rule banning vehicles from the park has a core of determinate meaning and a penumbra of indeterminate meaning, into which the bicycle would fall.[8]

For Hart, deciding the bicycle case requires a court to assign to the rule an increment of determinate meaning that it did not previously have.[9] The American legal philosopher David Lyons has pursued the implications of this to a troublesome conclusion.[10] Lyons demonstrates that positivist open texture theory, adopting the conception of metaphorical space in an open-textured entity "law," either renders the project of legal interpretation impossible or the language of judges and lawyers fraudulent. For the metaphorical space to be truly empty, any gap in a rule must

[7] As developed below, Holmes applied this to legislation. Statutes too are the work of many minds, in elected bodies. Diverse circumstances are explored all at once, in legislative committees, instead of seriatim through litigation. Again, unclear circumstances remain, to be addressed in a case-specific manner by the judiciary, if not through legislative amendment. See, e.g., Roscoe Pound, *The Spirit of the Common Law* (Boston: Beacon Press, 1921), 174; Edward H. Levi, *An Introduction to Legal Reasoning* (Chicago: Chicago University Press, 1949), 27–33.

[8] H. L. A. Hart, *The Concept of Law* (Oxford: Oxford University Press, 1994), 123–127.

[9] Hart, supra n. 10, 127. This reading is reinforced by Hart's own remarks in the Postscript responding to Ronald Dworkin added to the second edition of *The Concept of Law*, 252–53, 272–73.

[10] David Lyons, "Open Texture and the Possibility of Legal Interpretation," 18 *Law and Philosophy* 297–309 (1999).

be a gap in the law as a whole, as there would otherwise be someplace else within the law to find an answer. Hence for such gaps there is no possibility of deciding a case by interpreting "the law." Lyons observes that this is inconsistent with what happens in actual legal disputes.[11]

Lyons notes that filling such gaps assumes a logical step that is not necessary in actual practice. Assume that a judge decides for the defendant; this would not require incremental meaning for the term "vehicle." The case could simply be decided under the principle that "conduct that is not legally prohibited is legally permitted." Although there might be an appearance of open texture in the language of authoritative legal materials, this does not in practice give rise to gaps in the law, as there is no gap-filling required to decide the matter. A court deciding a paradigmatic "open texture" case need not become a surrogate legislature by contributing new meaning to the indeterminate term. This is reinforced by the working assumption of lawyers and judges who speak and act in such cases as if they are applying the law. To hold otherwise would imply that judges and lawyers are massively confused or deceitful in purporting to resolve difficult cases according to "the law."[12]

We may wonder whether law can be conceived as a separate entity without bringing on some form of the problem that Lyons identifies. To be separate philosophically implies having a distinctive and coherent form, such that a comparative judgment can be made between what is within and what is without. Whether or not the internal form is seen as a "texture," it must be distinctive enough to be described – and, implicitly, inert at the moment of analysis and insulated from revision by the deciding judge. But as courtroom experience reflects, "uncertain" and indeed "original" cases do indeed arrive and must be decided. Little philosophical analysis precedes the decision of lawyers and litigants to file a lawsuit. From a practical perspective – the one taken by Lyons – the term "law" should be broad enough to encompass any claim that can be stated within the rules of pleading. Even a denial of relief reflects the operation of "law." Anglo-American law began as a process of controlling disputes, and it has been largely dispute-driven throughout its history.

It seems that this is the sort of issue that Dewey sought to avoid through his warning. He would not have been sympathetic to the debate of whether law and morals are separate, which has gone on in some form for centuries. Hart, at mid-twentieth century, famously upheld the strict

[11] Id., 300–303.
[12] Id., 303.

separation of law against Professor Lon L. Fuller of Harvard, who maintained that there were several enumerable aspects of "inner morality" to the law.[13] But for Dewey it would seem that the question was not a proper question at all, as it required "setting law up as a separate entity." The choice, it would appear, is a radical one: is law an entity identifiable from moment to moment, even as it develops, or is it something rather more amorphous, a term of convenience or method – as Dewey said, "a process"? Does it contain all of the elements necessary to decide a case in advance, or do its very decisions "make" the law, as suggested by Holmes's dissent in *Northern Securities v. United States*: "great cases, like hard cases, make bad law"?[14]

Indeterminate cases more often involve the conflicting effects of multiple applicable rules than the extension of just one. In the positivist texture model, the aggregate of all legal rules (common law as well as statutes, constitutions, and accompanying principles) is presumably already interconnected in its recognizable form, despite having arisen from diverse unrelated human pursuits. But this is not so for the alternative model; any such consistency as might exist must be worked in as part of the ongoing project. In Holmes's model, as it further developed in 1873, the resolution of interaction among conflicting cases is handled in roughly the same case-specific experimental manner as was the original formulation of the rules themselves:

> The growth of the law is very apt to take place in this way: Two widely different cases suggest a general distinction, which is a clear one when stated broadly. But as new cases cluster around the opposite poles, and begin to approach each other, the distinction becomes more difficult to trace; the determinations are made one way or the other on a very slight preponderance of feeling, rather than articulate reason; and at last a mathematical line is arrived at by the contact of contrary decisions, which is so far arbitrary that it might equally well have been drawn a little further to the one side or to the other.[15]

Such interactions are not resolved all at once, through interpretation and application of an antecedent underlying pattern by a Herculean intelligence. Instead, they are addressed in appropriately timed retrospective

[13] Lon L. Fuller, *The Morality of Law* (New Haven: Yale University Press, 1969), 33–41.

[14] 193 U.S. 197, 400 (1903).

[15] Holmes, "The Theory of Torts," in *Formative Essays*, 119, and in 1 *Collected Works*, 327. A possible source for this model may indeed be Austin's discussion of the "competition of competing analogies," found by his wife Sarah in "loose papers" and published along with the *Lectures in Jurisprudence* in 1863. John Austin, *Lectures on Jurisprudence or the Philosophy of Positive Law*, vol. 2 (London: John Murray, 1869), 660–62.

examinations of an array of specific prior decisions. Decisions based on different case-specific considerations are depicted as gradually filling a metaphorical space between the two rules ("cluster[ing] around the opposite poles"). Judges eventually resolve the conflict by recognizing and describing a "line" between the opposing poles.

From this image it can be better understood what Holmes might have in mind as an indeterminate case. It would be described as the case that does not nicely fit the otherwise emergent "line" between opposing poles, that cannot readily be "reconciled" with the patterned trend of other cases in the same metaphorical space. This image can be seen projected into such later comments as the familiar *Northern Securities* dissent (1903):

> Great cases like hard cases make bad law. For great cases are called great not by reason of their real importance in shaping the law of the future but because of some accident of immediate overwhelming interest which appeals to the feelings and distorts the judgment. These immediate interests exercise a kind of hydraulic pressure which makes what previously was clear seem doubtful, and before which even well-settled principles of law will bend.[16]

It should be noted parenthetically that this case involved the interpretation of a federal statute: the vague and sweeping Sherman Act, forbidding "unreasonable restrictions of trade." Although thirty years later and still applying common law imagery, Holmes is not quite consistent (he has moved from electromagnetics to fluid dynamics), and his terminology can be confusing. He suggested earlier that in ideal circumstances "a mathematical line is arrived at by the contact of contrary decisions." *Beadel v. Perry*, an English case, was cited to elucidate this: the standard of "substantial damage" to neighboring property from construction near a boundary, gradually abstracted into a judicial rule that the height of the new building must not exceed "the distance of its base from the base of the ancient windows."[17]

16 Holmes, dissenting, in *Northern Securities Co. v. United States*, 193 U.S. 197, 400 (1903). It should be noted that "hard cases" referred not to indeterminacy but to matters that had a legally clear but inequitable or "hard" result under applicable precedents, e.g., *County of Morgan v. Allen*, 103 U.S. 498, 515 (1880). The term is now often understood to refer to the case that has no clear result under the applicable law, as opposed to the "easy" case. E.g., Frederick Schauer, "Easy Cases," 58 *So. Cal. L. Rev.* 399–440 (1985).

17 Holmes, "The Theory of Torts," in *Formative Essays*, 120, and in *Collected Works*, 328, citing *Beadel v. Perry*, L. R. 3 Eq. 465, 467 (1866). Frederick Pollock would later complain that the case does not adequately elucidate the principle. Pollock to Holmes, July 3, 1874, Howe, ed., 1 *Holmes-Pollock Letters* (Cambridge, Mass.: Harvard University Press, 1946), 4.

Holmes's choice of terms is unfortunate; it is rare that conflicts among cases are resolved "mathematically." The next sentence suggests that the line has nothing to do with mathematical logic: it is drawn "so far arbitrary that it might equally well have been drawn a little further to the one side or to the other." His point is rather that case-specific decisions based on a general standard, such as "substantial damage," are bound to vary somewhat from one case to the next, like sentences for similar crimes. "[B]etween these clearly opposed cases there lie a great number of others which may as well be decided one way as the other, and so the exact limit of the defendant's duty is measured by the opinion of the jury. But all the elements of these cases are permanent, and there is no reason why a case should be decided one way to-day, and another tomorrow. To leave the question to the jury forever, is simply to leave the law uncertain."[18]

Despite some problems in Holmes's exposition, it can now be seen where he finds the critical point for the judge's active contribution: after the practical contours of an issue have been surveyed and assessed by case-specific decisions, it becomes necessary to remove the issue from the gray area of case-specific decision and to abstract a rule and rationale. In this notion lay the germ of his 1913 comment about a "time for law" – his eventual sense of the boundary between activism and restraint. It emerged as a question of consensual judgment and timing. It implies an image of disputes plotted on a rough intellectual graph, working their way into the courts in related clumps, to be sorted out individually until patterns of decision emerge. The patterns consist of relatively clear cases at opposite "poles," separated by a more dimly visible "line" where the distinctions are less clear, such that close cases may be decided "one way [or] the other." Without judicial intervention, the law will remain "uncertain." It is better – at some appropriate point – for the judge to exercise what Holmes called "the sovereign prerogative of choice"[19] than to leave future actors to guess where the limits of legal liability lie.

There are a number of assumptions behind this model. The judicial role, while important, is not envisioned as the primary creative force in the development of legal rules. It is limited in an important respect: the courts take notice of the relation of disputes to the practices that give rise to them, and let the practices, insofar as possible, dictate the solutions. Second, the process involves, as Holmes explicitly says, "many minds." It suggests an ongoing community exploring common problems. In this it

[18] In *Formative Essays*, 119–20, and in 1 *Collected Works*, 328.
[19] Holmes, "Law in Science and Science in Law," in *Collected Legal Papers*, 210.

bears remarkable similarities to the model of scientific inquiry emerging at roughly the same historical period in the writings of Holmes's controversial friend Charles S. Peirce, a model later adopted by John Dewey. All thought and its conceptual products were for Peirce a response to human problems, driven by doubt and seeking commonly accepted belief. Such belief would be expressed in language as principles of knowledge, but the language was itself fallible. New circumstances were bound to arise that could not possibly have been foreseen, and hence expressed.[20] Dewey applied the model to logic in general, in his 1939 *Logic: The Theory of Inquiry*.[21]

Thus Holmes in the early 1870s was advancing a theory of law as itself a process of critical inquiry. Like the scientific philosophy of Peirce, it was driven by something akin to problematic doubt, more specifically by the problem of disputes flowing into the courts, and resolved by the formulation of general rules and principles. And as with Peirce the language was subject to modification while new circumstances were still forthcoming. Holmes's 1870 article notes hypothetically that even if a code were adopted by a committee of lawyers (thus bringing the law closer to a legislative model), "New cases will arise which will elude the most carefully constructed formula. The common law, proceeding, as we have pointed out, by a series of successive approximations – by a continual reconciliation of cases – is prepared for this, and simply modifies the form of its rule."[22]

Holmes's vision is unique among theories of the common law. As a comprehensive conception, it could hardly avoid affecting his approach to constitutional law. For the traditional areas of the common law, yet unregulated by legislation, it emerged from his scholarship as a new hypothesis and remained (as it still does) surprisingly untested by broad scholarly criticism. Undaunted, Holmes proceeded to document it himself, by fiat, simply writing it into his opinions on the Supreme Judicial Court at every

[20] Charles Sanders Peirce, *Collected Papers*, vol. 5, ed. Charles Hartshorne and Paul Weiss (Cambridge, Mass.: Belknap Press, 1978), 231.

[21] John Dewey, *Logic: The Theory of Inquiry* (New York: Henry Holt, 1938).

[22] Holmes, "Codes, and the Arrangement of the Law." Others have made a similar observation, including Edward Levi in *An Introduction to Legal Reasoning*, 27–33. One issue that perhaps deserves more specific discussion than I have given it here is the different conceptions of rules and principles and their operation found in Holmes, and those of Hart and Dworkin, especially in the latter's *Taking Rights Seriously*, 24–58, and in Hart's Postscript to *The Concept of Law*, 259–65. While I have not addressed this specifically, I hope the distinction becomes clear in chapters 7–10 treating Holmes's approach to precedents, principles, and legal texts.

available opportunity. It rested on the notion of a cumulative community consensus, involving judicial rule making only after a clear standard of conduct was evident. But if it were to apply to constitutional cases, could Holmes fairly find a comparable process? And would a common law approach simply unfetter constitutional decision making, rendering it free to be applied without restraint to a broad range of issues? Or might it instead have an opposite effect when lacking an evident consensual grounding?

At stake is the question of judicial supremacy – the notion that judges are final interpreters of all law including the Constitution. Holmes offers a perspective that escapes what I have portrayed as the positivist trap. A perspective that accepts and conditions the traditional involvement of judges in the growth of legal rules may provide a keener awareness of the historical conditions of the judicial role. It may, indeed, be all the more effective in preserving realistic constraints. Positivism, in restricting the judge to the confines of an identifiable entity, denies with excessive strictness any creative role to the judge and the entire courtroom context. This may have an unintended effect where, in a close, novel, or highly controversial case, the sweeping generalities of a constitution are relied on as deriving from an authoritative text to support a conclusion that is permitted to ignore, and thus disregard, competing laws and precedents.

Common law has always conceded a prominent role for judges. The traditional explanation, that they were "finding" the preexisting law of a difficult case, was no longer acceptable when Holmes wrote in the nineteenth century; it was unacceptable to Hobbes in the seventeenth. To Holmes it raised the specter of something "out there," a "brooding omnipresence in the sky," as he derisively called it.[23] But no cognizable alternative theory existed to account for the common law process, in which judges were directed not just to the authoritative materials of law but to the context of a dispute and of prior similar disputes, embodied in previous decisions or precedents. On what authority did they depart from the authoritative written materials of the law? Was this authority a blank check, to depart whenever they saw fit? What principles of legitimacy governed the common law method?

In laying down a positivist theory of law in the seventeenth century, Thomas Hobbes had addressed the problem of legitimacy with a clarity

[23] *Southern Pacific Co. v. Jensen*, 244 U.S. 205, 222 (1917): "The common law is not a brooding omnipresence in the sky but the articulate voice of some sovereign or quasi-sovereign that can be identified."

largely absent in the common law tradition. A Hobbesean view, detailing the law as a comprehensive set of sovereign commands, had been reaffirmed and elaborated by John Austin in the generation preceding Holmes. Over the centuries since Hobbes, positivists have kept issues of legitimacy in the forefront of their thinking. For the theory of common law, it has, surprisingly, been largely ignored since the eighteenth century.[24]

The writings of Hobbes and Austin laid down a strict definition of law that had the merit of separating it clearly from "morals": law was the command of the sovereign, as Austin noted, command enforced and habitually obeyed. This antiseptic, test-tube–like separation was seen as a path toward clear and objective, if not indeed scientific, understanding of law. It was a bulwark against subjectivism and libertinism: the removal of all doubt and dispute. To make matters confusing, emphasis on a certain kind of separation of law and morals is found prominently in the writings of Holmes. This has led to the conception of Holmes as a positivist; but there is a critical difference, in that the positivist separation is analytical, going to the essential nature of law, while that of Holmes is historical and found in the transformation of liability. Austin's separation was expressed in 1832 as follows:

> In consequence of the frequent coincidence of positive law and morality, and of positive law and the law of God, the true nature and fountain of positive law is often absurdly mistaken by writers upon jurisprudence.[25]

Holmes's attitude, as expressed in 1881, ran thus:

> [W]hile the terminology of morals is still retained, and while the law does still and always, in a certain sense, measure legal liability by moral standards, it

[24] The natural affinity between common law practice and a decentralized, naturalistic ethics was observed by writers of the Scottish Enlightenment in the seventeenth and eighteenth centuries, especially Lord Kames (1696–1792) and Adam Smith (1723–90); if moral conduct was rooted in the natural moral sense of individuals and communities, courts and their judgments could be seen as its embodiment. Smith, *Lectures on Jurisprudence* (Oxford: Clarendon Press, 1978); Cairns, "Legal Theory," in A. Broadie, ed., *Cambridge Companion to the Scottish Enlightenment* (Cambridge: Cambridge University Press, 2003), 234 ("[C]ourts ... managed to inscribe into rules of law the needs of justice as identified by the moral sense or moral sentiments by responding appropriately to individual cases"). Such a foundation for common law has never been persuasively and comprehensively established, and while Holmes was not an ethicist, I suggest that his approach might form a critical part of such a foundation.

[25] John Austin, *The Province of Jurisprudence Determined and the Uses of the Study of Jurisprudence* (London: Weidenfeld and Nicolson, 1955), 162–163.

nevertheless, by the very necessity of its nature, is continuously transmuting those moral standards into external or objective ones, from which the actual guilt of the party concerned is wholly eliminated.[26]

The different perspectives expressed here embody substantially different approaches to, and assumptions about, both law and knowledge.

Both scholars were products of the intellectual climate of their time and place. A full understanding of Holmes's judicial philosophy has been obstructed largely by an unexamined association of him with the positivist analytical separation of law from morals. While supported in part by his deference to sovereign power, this is often based on a speech given at mid-career at Boston University Law School, "The Path of the Law," where he advanced and elaborated on the view that he "often doubt[s] whether it would not be a gain if every word of moral significance could be banished from the law altogether." But Holmes had in mind a quite specific notion of "words of moral significance" and their abuse by lawyers and judges; this speech was not a departure from the view developed earlier, wherein the law does "in a certain sense" measure liability by moral standards. He significantly noted in the speech that, standing back with the view of the historian, "[t]he law is the witness and external deposit of our moral life."[27]

I have argued, against the grain of mainstream scholarship, that Holmes's assessment of the relation of law and morals was and remained fundamentally distinct from the tradition of legal positivism. I do not claim that there are no problems with his overall theory nor that he was always a paradigm of restraint himself. But lest Holmes appear incoherent, it is imperative to show conclusively that Holmes came down on Dewey's side of the larger issue, and this accounts for his distinctive approach to legal interpretation, as well as to judicial restraint.

The relation between law and morals has been an important topic throughout the past century, in part due to the revival of legal positivism by H. L. A. Hart at Oxford University, and also because of its obvious bearing on public attitudes toward global conflict and ideological polarization. During this period we have seen a continuing transformation of legal positivism from the concept introduced by Hobbes. The most influential version in the past century was Hart's. The issue came to new life when, in the 1950s, the Harvard philosopher Morton G. White arranged

[26] Holmes, *The Common Law*, 33.

[27] Holmes, "The Path of the Law," in *Collected Legal Papers*, 170. This lecture, and its consistency with Holmes's overall theory, is discussed at greater length in chapter 8, n. 36.

to have Hart visit Harvard University. Thus began Hart's debate with Lon Fuller.[28]

Professor Fuller at Harvard Law School had gained considerable eminence through his Rosenthal Lectures given at Northwestern University Law School, later published as *The Law in Quest of Itself.* He had launched a severe attack on the "positivist" separation of law and morals and called upon a new generation of lawyers to return to the healthier conviction, traditionally associated with natural law, that law and morals can and must be associated. Holmes came in for especially heavy criticism as chiefly responsible for "why American legal scholarship has remained so unseasonably positivistic."[29] A scholarly exchange of views between Fuller and Hart whether law and morals are separate hardly resolved the question, but led to the full exposition of their views in Hart's *Concept of Law* and Fuller's *The Morality of Law.* White, in *Social Thought in America: The Revolt against Formalism,* had already taken Holmes's skepticism as an aspect of America's unique philosophical innovation, pragmatism, while identifying an apparent inconsistency in his approach to the relationship of law and morals that now appears to be at the root of a deep division in Holmes scholarship. In his famous lecture "The Path of the Law," where he defined law as the prediction of the courts' use of official coercion, Holmes seemed to deny "that the rules of law can be deduced from the principles of ethics," while asserting in the same lecture that "the law is made by judges who do draw upon considerations of social and moral advantage."[30] Clearing away the apparent incoherence requires that we consider the roots of his conception itself.

An extreme workaholic, Holmes was in the 1870s juggling several intellectual agendas: the philosophical commitments influenced by Chauncey Wright and (according to Charles S. Peirce) the Metaphysical Club; a comprehensive analysis of the influential lectures of the Benthamite legal philosopher John Austin; a painstaking revision of the leading comprehensive American legal treatise, *Kent's Commentaries on American Law*; and his own ambitious (but ultimately flawed) evolutionary theory of the common law. From the first two emerged what White has called Holmes's holistic pragmatism, such as it is: implicit and poorly articulated, but

[28] Morton G. White, *A Philosopher's Story* (University Park: Pennsylvania State University Press, 1999), 217.

[29] Lon L. Fuller, *The Law in Quest of Itself* (Boston: Beacon Press, 1966), 117.

[30] Morton G. White, *Social Thought in America: The Revolt against Formalism* (Boston: Beacon Press, 1947), 69–70, discussing Holmes, "The Path of the Law," in *Collected Legal Papers,* 172.

revolutionary. Within the latter is found a dense and aphoristic style, marked by extravagance, allusion, and difficulty of interpretation. Within the mixture there came a sophisticated insight regarding the nature of law.

In his early essays, Holmes compared the positivist catalogue of legal concepts detailed by John Austin against the actual encyclopedia of the law of his time in *Kent's Commentaries.* He came, through analytical and historical criticism, to reject the former – Austin's system of duties and rights – as an Aristotelian attempt to assign potency and actuality to fixed natures or essences, and instead to view the actual law as revealing the historical emergence and transformation of legal concepts born of repeated inquiry into classes of repetitive disputes. He thus replaced the internal taxonomic permanence and authority of legal positivism with a fallibilist skepticism combined with a community-based deference to ongoing, transgenerational consensus. Law received authority and legitimacy less by logic or fiat than by inheritance, and an officially sanctioned process of inquiry and revision. Consistency was gradually, if imperfectly, worked in:

> The truth is, that law hitherto has been, and it would seem by the necessity of its being is always approaching and never reaching consistency. It is for ever adopting new principles from life at one end, and it always retains old ones from history at the other which have not yet been absorbed or sloughed off. It will become entirely consistent only when it ceases to grow.[31]

Worked in along with consistency was something he called "policy" or considerations of "social advantage." The law gradually adapted itself to its time. But it is clear that this process is retrospective. As Justice Holmes explained it to the Harvard Law School Association of New York in 1913: "It cannot be helped, it is as it should be, that the law is behind the times." The context of this insight, the root of Holmes's restraint, has been obscured by misinterpretation of his position on law and morals. The definition of law as prediction emerged during the period of intense critical analysis of the legal taxonomy of John Austin and his revised form of the command theory of Thomas Hobbes. Beneath it lay Holmes's observation that the courtroom operates through "successive approximation," guided by precedent but adapting prior rules to conform to unanticipated circumstances. In so noting, Holmes rejected a rigid separation

[31] Holmes, "Common Carriers and the Common Law," in *Formative Essays,* 201, 223, and in 3 *Collected Works,* 60, 75–6.

of law from morals, or more precisely from the moral force of indigenous custom and practice, advancing instead a conception of law that denies any ontological segregation or separation. White perceived this in 1947 as one side of Holmes's inconsistency. In retrospect, it now appears that Holmes was breaking with the positivist tradition in a manner more profound than White or anyone else gave him credit.

In fact, Holmes was rethinking the common law. It had never entirely recovered (nor has it still) as an intellectual account, Edmund Burke notwithstanding, from the positivist attack begun by Hobbes and continued by Bentham. In place of the earlier appeal to tradition, Holmes introduced a theory of socially rooted inquiry with remarkable parallels to the scientific philosophy of Peirce. This was a conservative application of the pragmatic attitude, not the more progressive one associated with John Dewey. Nor is it comparable to the neopragmatic "ironism" of Richard Rorty.[32] Both attitudes noted by White toward Holmes's skepticism are misguided: he was siding with neither Fuller nor Hart.

Seeking a foundation for universal deference to sovereign power, Hobbes conveyed supreme legal authority (and control of its rationale) to the state. With this centralizing turn, traditional common law theory was rejected, and law became (under all subsequent versions of positivism) separate and exogenous, acting *on* society, rather than *within*. A strict separation of law and morals reflected Hobbes's rejection of individual subjective judgments as potential grounds for disobedience. Thus, influencing legal theory for the next three hundred years, was priority given to theories of state sovereignty over the quibbling common lawyer.[33]

[32] See Kellogg, "Who Owns Pragmatism," 6 *Journal of Speculative Philosophy* 67 (1992), and ch. 7, n. 26.

[33] Hobbes, *Elements of Law* (Cambridge: Cambridge University Press, 1928), 87. It should be noted that an influential line of criticism of Hobbes originating with Lord Shaftsbury (1671–1713) and Frances Hutcheson (1694–1746) supports an alternative to Hobbes that is parallel in important respects to the common law approach of Holmes. Shaftesbury argued, against Hobbes's emphasis on fear as the principal motivating factor in human social ordering, that human affections support the tendency to live in community and that social ordering through the ideal of ethical conduct is founded on a natural "moral sense." Hutcheson developed moral sense theory into an articulate moral naturalism, influencing a great many Scottish theorists from Adam Ferguson and Thomas Reid to Adam Smith and David Hume. He was well known in America and his influence was acknowledged by John Adams and Thomas Jefferson and later generations of Americans. Flower and Murphey, *A History of Philosophy in America*, 224ff.; see also L. Turco, "Moral Sense and the Foundations of Morals," in Broadie, *Cambridge Companion to the Scottish Enlightenment*.

Another Scot, Lord Kames, in *Historical Law-Tracts* (1758), extended moral sense as a theory of law and legal development, drawing on the comparative law insights of Montesquieu's *L'esprit des lois* (1748). Commenting on the movement for law reform in

Twentieth-century positivists gave up the command theory as untenable, but they have held fast to the ontological separation. In his renewal of positivism as a system of primary and secondary rules, governed by a Rule of Recognition, Hart, not a Holmes scholar, and misled (as many are) by "The Path of the Law," simply packaged Holmes up with John Austin as a proto-command-theorist, ignoring the early writings that reveal Holmes's rejection of a strict separation of law and morals for a holistic version of pragmatic inquiry and fallibilism: the notion that general conceptions must be open to revision to accommodate new experience. The pathbreaking Peirce scholar Max Fisch even suggested, in 1942, that Holmes introduced his evidence of common law fallibilism into discussions of the Metaphysical Club and that it influenced Peirce's philosophy.[34]

Whether that happened is hardly crucial; the point is that Holmes's association with Wright, James, and Peirce, and the readings that influenced them all, elucidates the origin and nature of his intellectual attitude. One of a very few explicitly given credit by Holmes was Wright,

eighteenth-century Scotland, Kames stressed the importance of courts over legislatures in developing the law (as Holmes would do a century later in "Codes, and the Arrangement of the Law"), exercising their natural "moral sense." He argued (as Holmes would do in *The Common Law*) that "[l]aw in particular, becomes then only a rational study, when it is traced historically, from its first rudiments among savages, through successive changes, to its highest improvements in a civilized society." *Historical Law Tracts* iii (Edinburgh: T. Cadell, Bell and Bradfute, and W. Creech, 1792). Montesquieu's *L'esprit des lois* appears in Holmes's reading diaries in December 1871 and July 1873.

In keeping with the widespread regard for Kames, and deeply influenced by David Hume, Adam Smith proposed that moral judgment derived from the ability to evaluate the behavior of others in particular situations through natural sympathy, and putting oneself in the position of an "impartial spectator," a trope strikingly parallel to Holmes's emphasis on juries applying the standard of the "prudent man." Smith developed a view of justice that arose from the confrontation with particular episodes of wrong demanding redress, and influenced by custom – comparable to the idea of common law rules arising from repeated applications of the prudent man standard to determine accepted standards of conduct. Adam Smith, *The Theory of Moral Sentiments*, ed. Knud Haakonssen (Cambridge: Cambridge University Press, 2002), 182–83, 234–47; see J. W. Cairns, "Legal Theory," in Broadie, *Cambridge Companion to the Scottish Enlightenment*, 222–42.

There is scant evidence that Holmes drew directly from these writers (though he did study Hume), and his theory is distinct enough to suggest that he did not. However, there is ample evidence that the empirical and moral naturalism of the Scottish Enlightenment had a profound influence on the intellectual climate of the Boston and Cambridge in which he grew up and was educated, and that later Scots, including Alexander Bain, directly influenced the discussions of the Metaphysical Club. Kuklick, *Rise of American Philosophy*, 10–62; Flower and Murphey, *A History of American Philosophy*, 203–69, 567ff.

34 Max Fisch, "Justice Holmes, the Prediction Theory of Law, and Pragmatism," 39 *Journal of Philosophy* 85, 94 (1942).

and his diaries reflect both meeting with and reading Wright, specifically the latter's important 1865 essay "The Philosophy of Herbert Spencer." Holmes's diary for 1867 reveals several trips to see the reclusive bachelor (October 20, 1867: "Went out and had a long palaver with Chauncey Wright also with Wm James on philosophy") and a "reread[ing]" of Wright's article on Spencer (September 12, 1867). In a letter to Frederick Pollock written many years later, Holmes would recall, "Chauncey Wright, a nearly-forgotten philosopher of real merit, taught me when young that I must not say *necessary* about the universe, that we don't know whether anything is necessary or not. I believe that we can *bet* on the behavior of the universe in its contact with us. So describe myself as a *bet-abilitarian*" (emphasis in original).[35]

The connection would appear to be with Wright's insistent criticism of Spencer for misconstruing Darwin and interpreting nature in terms of a teleological principle. Although Spencer had sought to avoid grand overgeneralizing in his "law of evolution," Wright commented that "teleology is a subtle poison and lurks where least suspected." Wright suspected all cosmological "systems" to be essentially teleological, "a fine composition of poetry under the forms of science." In place of the lure of evolutionary cosmology, Wright suggested an alternative he called "cosmic weather," the notion that there is only movement and countermovement, that "there is no production in nature from which in infinite ages there can result an infinite product." There remain mere probabilities; hence, we might surmise, Holmes's language of *bet*ability and prediction.[36]

The roots of this are important. At Harvard, Emerson had been Wright's main influence, but he was soon immersed in Francis Bacon and William Whewell, who together established and reinforced a strong empiricism and mistrust of teleological anticipations of nature. Next to engage him was William Hamilton, from whom Wright took "the salutary lesson that the capacity of thought is not to be constituted into the measure of existence." Wright's attention was then captured by John Stuart Mill, especially the critical *Examination of Sir William Hamilton's Philosophy*, generating a wholesale rejection of a priori thinking that would lead his Darwinian empiricism toward the radically anti-Cartesian idea that

[35] Chauncey Wright, "The Philosophy of Herbert Spencer," 100 *North American Review* 427 (1865); Holmes to Pollock, August 30, 1929, 2 *Holmes-Pollock Letters*, 252.

[36] Gail Kennedy, "The Pragmatic Naturalism of Chauncey Wright," in *Studies in the History of Ideas* (New York: Columbia University Press, 1935), vol. 3, pp. 482–83. See also Kuklick, *Rise of American Philosophy*, 63–79.

natural selection had formed the very process of thought as a means of human adaptation to the environment.[37]

In deriving from this a holistic account of the socially rooted development of perception, cognition, and language, Wright anticipated by nearly a century the radical anti-Cartesianism – resisting the separation of mind and world – of John Dewey.[38] It is striking to find in Holmes's diaries of his readings, for the years immediately following his return to Cambridge from the Civil War, reference not only to Wright's essay on Spencer but to the very authors that had influenced him in that direction: Whewell, Hamilton, Spencer, and Mill, interspersed among Bentham, Austin, and various legal treatises. Like Wright, Holmes had read Emerson before the war. Wright and Holmes, though a decade apart, were graduates with James and Peirce of Harvard College, lived in Cambridge, and shared and nurtured a distinct intellectual climate.[39] If indeed Holmes attended the informal Metaphysical Club (something like it is suggested by the diary entry for October 20, 1867), Peirce's tribute to Wright's role as "boxing master" on those discussions is telling.[40]

This suggests deep roots to Holmes's holistic pragmatism, though of course his position must be fixed by extrapolation, acknowledging his own rejection of the pragmatist label as it was popularized in later years by James ("*I* think pragmatism an amusing humbug – like most of William James's speculations, as distinguished from his admirable and well written Irish perceptions of life"[41]). Wright and his readings seem to have pulled the already Emersonian and anti-Platonist Holmes sharply away from the foundationalist and teleogical strain that has characterized legal positivism since Hobbes, as well as the associated tendency to, in Joseph Margolis's apt description, "assign fixed potency and actuality to fixed 'natures' (or essences) or essences to fixed potencies." Although

37 Id.

38 See Wright, "The Evolution of Self-consciousness," *North American Review* 245 (April 1873), in Wright, *Philosophical Discussions* (New York: Henry Holt, 1877), 205–29.

39 Kuklick, *Rise of American Philosophy*, 10–62; Flower and Murphey, *A History of Philosophy in America*, 507, 535–53, 567–68; see chapter 2, n. 4, supra.

40 Id., 537; Max H. Fisch, "Was There a Metaphysical Club in Cambridge?" in *Studies in the Philosophy of Charles Sanders Peirce*, ed. Edward C. Moore and Richard S. Robin (Amherst: University of Massachusetts Press, 1964), 15; see also chapter 5.

41 Holmes to Pollock, June 17, 1908, in Howe, *Holmes-Pollock Letters*, vol. 1, pp. 138–39. A year earlier Holmes wrote more sympathetically about James's views to James himself: "We start from surprisingly similar premises and our conclusions fit as opposites sometimes do." Holmes to James, April 1, 1907, in Skrupskelis and Berkeley, *The Correspondence of William James*, vol. 11, p. 338 (acknowledging receipt of an essay on pragmatism).

one might argue that the subtle poison of teleology crept into *The Common Law* and certain of Holmes's judicial decisions, he seems to have believed, with Wright before him and Dewey later, in what Margolis calls "the flux."[42]

Assuming this condensed account is satisfactory to place Holmes and his relation to both holism and the positivist tradition, we may proceed to its relevance for legal interpretation. What difference can such philosophy make to legal theory, and ultimately to practice itself?

First, where did Hart lead legal positivism? He saw his task as maintaining the foundation for law's autonomous authority and reason (though without the original Hobbesean explanation) such that law kept its authority *as law*, not open to influence from moral opinion, however principled. Defending against the challenge from Lon Fuller, who insisted on certain basic moral principles inherent in contemporary law, Hart deftly incorporated them as part of the hierarchy of legal rules. Thus the ontological separation of law and morals was maintained, with the reassuring myth that law operates determinately insofar as it extends.

Applied to the judicial process, this conceptual picture leads to a persistent dilemma. The project of conceptual separation of "law" goes hand in hand with the project of definition and delineation of it and concedes the possibility of legal *indeterminacy*, the real existence of cases that are not covered by the law as defined and delineated. There is a vast literature on this in contemporary analytical positivism. Hart addressed it as an indeterminacy of text, such that matters outside the "penumbra" of legal terms require interstitial judicial "legislation." Constitutional textualists such as Justice Antonin Scalia, in dealing with the problem, look to the original understanding of the founding generation.

The defect of this model lies in creating an ontic gap or cavity wherein either legitimate judicial decision is foreclosed or judicial resort is conceded "outside" legal texts to something the judge finds subjectively compelling, whether "moral principle" or a putative historical necessity. Holmes saw cases not as "determined" vel non by an existing "law" or its inexorable logic, but as bearing varying levels of difficulty or novelty. He sought to identify the undeniably original aspects of difficult cases as leaning more or less toward distinct lines of prior decision or precedent. This focused the judicial role on the refined and fact-specific question

[42] Joseph Margolis, *Reinventing Pragmatism: American Philosophy at the End of the Twentieth Century* (Ithaca, N.Y.: Cornell University Press, 2002), 117, 126.

of which precedent should prevail and where the immediate controversy could be situated in the progression from old to new consensus.

Holmes accordingly rejected judicial appeal to "principle" as a dereliction of the judicial role. This was to step entirely away from the delicate process of building or rebuilding transgenerational consensus. Such was the import of his constant critique of moral language, notable in "The Path of the Law." Herein lies the resolution of the inconsistency White noted in 1947. What Holmes meant in eschewing moral language was not an ontological separation but a fallibilist insight, that competing principles can generally be found on both sides of a controversial case, and moral argument from them amounts to "hollow deduction from empty general propositions."[43]

Moreover, by 1902 when Holmes joined the Supreme Court, the expansion of constitutional jurisdiction had brought conflicts into the courts among competing interests where no consensus had yet emerged. Judicial restraint thus became something quite distinct from judicial circumspection, or even a policy of cautious governance; it was seen as a limiting condition of collective inquiry into the conditions of consensual social ordering, of which law and governance are contributing, but hardly the only, factors. If judges blithely assumed that sweeping constitutional "principles" were part of the legal fabric, trumping precedent and legislation, the legal process could be used to short-circuit democratic deliberation and the more cautious legislative process. Judicial teleology could be a subtle poison. As the famous dissent in *Lochner v. New York* notes, "The Fourteenth Amendment does not enact Mr. Herbert Spencer's Social Statics."[44]

Although Holmes's frequent discussion of the effect of "policy" on the growth of the law would appear to elevate expediency in judicial decisions, what White calls his "holism," emerging from Wright's critique of teleology, and from his application of it to the positivist paradigm, ultimately supports a cautionary approach to judicial policy where no clear path has yet been publicly sanctioned. In constitutional law, privileging the text, with its sweeping terms such as equal protection and due process, short-circuits the mechanics of social and political intercourse.

[43] Holmes, "Privilege, Malice and Intent," *Collected Legal Papers*, 117, 120.

[44] *Lochner v. New York*, 198 U.S. 45, 75 (1905).

4

Common Law Theory Revisited

> The common law is the absolute perfection of reason.
>
> Sir Edward Coke, *Institutes of the Laws of England*

> Would you have every man to every other man allege for law his own particular reason? There is not amongst men a universal reason agreed upon in any nation, besides the reason of him that hath the sovereign power. Yet though his reason be but the reason of one man, yet it is set up to supply the place of that universal reason, which is expounded to us by our Saviour in the Gospel; and consequently our King is to us the legislator both of statute-law, and of common-law.
>
> Thomas Hobbes, *A Dialogue between a Philosopher and a Student of the Common Laws*

I have claimed that Holmes's overall conception of law is rooted in the common law tradition in the novel theory he proposes. There are strands that recognizably link the two together. We may trace the origins of Holmes's common law vision back to Sir Edward Coke's comment above, associating common law with "the perfection of reason," and just below it the rhetorical question inspired by it, put to an imaginary seventeenth-century common law theorist by Thomas Hobbes, in a manuscript written late in his life in the 1670s. The manuscript, with its questioning by the "Philosopher" of the "Law Student," introduces the resolution that Hobbes gave to the problem of the relation between reason and authority in the law, one based on sovereign command and inhering in coherence and determinacy. This writing is generally consistent with Hobbes's better known works, though specifically designed as a challenge to Coke and his defense of the common law.[1]

In a mocking tone similar to Scalia's recent attack on common law three centuries later, Hobbes derides Coke's notion of an innate rationality to the common law. He ridicules the possibility of a universal or natural reason that can supply coherence and consistency in the search for answers to troublesome legal questions. For Hobbes, Coke's assumption would let "every man to every other man allege for law his own particular reason." Law can have coherence and determinacy only if its reason comes from a single source, a fully empowered sovereign – or, as Scalia claims, from an authoritative text and its original understanding.

The conditions surrounding Holmes's early life and research differ markedly from those of Coke and his contemporaries. The sovereign power of nineteenth-century America lay in a republic of divided powers, not a monarch asserting royal prerogatives in the face of challenges from rising and shifting economic and social forces. Nevertheless, both Hobbes and Holmes wrote in defense of central authority in a century of political disorder, radical revolution, and eventual restoration. Coke, and anyone else asserting common law reason in his time, would have had in mind professional and political interests different from those of post–Civil War America. Groups favoring legislation or executive authority would be as different in their interests and temperaments from each other as they would be from Thomas Hobbes. The targets of persuasion and the stakes of belief differ greatly over this long span. But there is remarkable common ground.

Where did the peculiar "model" of common law interpretation and decision derive in Holmes's early research? It would seem that nothing quite like the intellectual background of Darwinian evolution and Wright-influenced fallibilism could be found in previous theoretical writings about the common law, and it is evident that Holmes himself believed his theory to be original.[2] In certain basic respects it clearly is not; the comment that Holmes in 1870 attributes to Lord Mansfield, for instance, evokes claims and observations about the nature of common law that were

[1] See Postema, *Bentham and the Common Law Tradition*, 46 n. 13; see J. Cropsey, Introduction to Thomas Hobbes, *A Dialogue between a Philosopher and a Student of the Common Laws of England* (Chicago and London: University of Chicago Press, 1971).

[2] See Howe, *Justice Oliver Wendell Holmes: The Proving Years*, 137. For some of the possible sources that might have contributed to the intellectual climate surrounding his eventual outlook, even if Holmes believed that he came to it largely on his own; see chapter 3, n. 33.

made by its defenders during the period of its defense in the sixteenth and seventeenth centuries. Its principal expositors were engaged in various phases of the political conflict over increasing centralization of authority in England: Sir Edward Coke (1552–1634), Sir Matthew Hale (1609–76), and Sir William Blackstone (1723–80).

The common law, according to Blackstone, was "That antient collection of unwritten maxims and customs, which is called the common law, however compounded or from whatever foundations derived, [that] had subsisted immemorially in this kingdom; and though somewhat altered and impaired by the violence of the times, had in great measure weathered the shock of the Norman Conquest."[3] The common law is seen here as *universal*, shared by the people of England notwithstanding the history of divisions and conflicts. It is "a law *common* to all the realm, the *jus commune* or *folcright* mentioned by King Edward the elder, after the abolition of the several provincial customs and particular laws beforementioned"[4] (emphasis in original). As can be seen from Blackstone's comment on the Norman Conquest, it is also *continuous*. Its validity lies in the fact that it is of long standing:

> [T]he maxims and customs, so collected, are of higher antiquity than memory or history can reach: nothing being more difficult than to ascertain the precise beginning and first spring of an antient and long-established custom. Whence it is that in our law the goodness of a custom depends upon it's[*sic*] having been used time out of mind; or, in the solemnity of our legal phrase, time whereof the memory of man runneth not to the contrary. This it is that gives it it's [*sic*] weight and authority; and of this nature are the maxims and customs which compose the common law, or *lex non scripta*, of this kingdom.[5]

Legislation, the *lex scripta*, was written or in some form *enacted* law; "the written laws of the kingdom, which are statutes, acts, or edicts, made by the king's majesty by and with the advice and consent of the lords spiritual and temporal and commons in parliament assembled."[6] When Blackstone wrote, the *lex scripta* and *non scripta* were considered to be of the same substance: "Statutes also are either *declaratory* of the common law, or *remedial* of some defects therein." The same was true of "constitutional law," as it emerged in England.[7] Coke and Blackstone were skeptical

[3] W. Blackstone, *Commentaries on the Law of England*, vol.1 (New York and London: Garland Publishing, 1978), 17.

[4] Id. at 67.

[5] Id.

[6] Id. at 85.

[7] John Hudson, *The Formation of the English Common Law* (London and New York: Longman, 1996), 220–37.

and often severely critical of legislation as the product of a temporary consensus among arbitrary wills:[8]

> The mischiefs that have arisen to the public from inconsiderate alterations in our laws, are too obvious to be called in question; and how far they have been owing to the defective education of our senators, is a point well worthy the public attention. The common law of England has fared like other venerable edifices of antiquity, which rash and inexperienced workmen have ventured to new-dress and refine, with all the rage of modern improvement. Hence, frequently it's [*sic*] symmetry has been destroyed, it's [*sic*] proportions distorted, and it's [*sic*] majestic simplicity exchanged for specious embellishments and fantastic novelties. For, to say the truth, almost all the perplexed questions, almost all the niceties, intricacies, and delays (which have sometimes disgraced the English, as well as other, courts of justice) owe their original not to the common law itself, but to innovations that have been made in it by acts of parliament.[9]

Blackstone's emphasis on custom suggests a different view common lawyers had of *reason*; for Coke, Blackstone, and Hale all insisted that (in Coke's terms) "the common law is the absolute perfection of reason."[10] This special common law reason has been described as "artificial" and "*within* the law,"[11] but like the Holmesian model it had much to do with conduct and practice. As Gerald Postema has noted, it was "inseparable from the particular situations brought to the law and resolved by it. It is the reason not of rules and principles, but of cases."[12] It may be misleading to describe this reason as internal to the *law*, as it reflects the fact that cases are the by-product of problematic interaction among humans engaged in social and economic activities, which fall naturally into patterns that might qualify as "custom," from which reason cannot be detached. It is distinct, then, from the meaning given to the term by Hobbes.

[8] As Postema has noted, after the sixteenth century, common law theory struggled to find a satisfactory explanation of legislation, as the latter took on an ever greater importance in English life and society. The medieval notion of legislation as merely another form, with adjudication, of discovering preexisting law gave way to the realization that law could be created anew; "[l]aw could be seen not merely as the formal and public expression of an existing social (or even natural) order, but as an instrument with which that order could be altered or even recreated." Postema, *Bentham and the Common Law Tradition*, 15.

[9] Blackstone, 1 *Commentaries* 10.

[10] Sir Edward Coke, *The Second Part of the Institutes of the Laws of England* (Buffalo, N.Y.: William S. Hein,1986), 179.

[11] Postema, *Bentham and the Common Law Tradition*, 30.

[12] Id., 31. See also Postema, "Philosophy of the Common Law," in *The Oxford Handbook of Jurisprudence and Philosophy of Law*, ed. Jules Coleman and Scott Shapiro (Oxford: Oxford University Press, 2002), 593–95.

When Hobbes asks, "Would you have every man to every other man allege for law his own particular reason?" he has accepted that individuals will disagree about legal questions according to their differing interests. Although it might be applied to particular situations, this reasoning is essentially, like Hobbes's own reasoning, abstract and analytical. Hobbes had no confidence in Coke's claim that common law reason will resolve close cases, but in an important way Hobbes misconstrued Coke's perspective. Coke accepted the fact of complexity and diversity of opinion; his observations in the *Institutes* reflect a sense of great difficulty "to reconcile doubts . . . arising either upon diversity of opinions or questions moved and left undecided."[13] He recognized that judges often disagreed.[14] "The learned" had to "perplex their heads, to make atonement and peace by construction of law between insensible and disagreeing words, sentences and provisoes."[15] How best to do this? "It is the best manner of expounding, so to interpret the laws that they may agree with one another," and "The best interpreter of the law is custom."[16] Through such arguments Coke implied removal of the analytical thinker as the source of logic, and the replacement of it, as eventually also by Holmes, with patterns of communal action.[17]

Hobbes's attack on Coke was not published until well after his death in 1681; it was apparently circulated widely enough in manuscript form to come to the attention of Matthew Hale. Hale's reply, *Reflections by the Lord Chiefe Justice Hale on Mr. Hobbes his Dialogue of the Lawe*, was unpublished until 1921 when its importance was recognized by the British legal historian Frederick Pollock, by then a forty-seven-year friend and correspondent of Holmes. It engages Hobbes on the subject of legal reason as well as on sovereignty, and although in 1870 it remained as yet undiscovered by Pollock and unread by the young Holmes, it stands as an important precursor to Holmes's nineteenth-century views.[18]

[13] Coke, *Reports of Sir Edward Coke* sig. D 3b (Dublin: J. Moore, 1793), vol. 3.

[14] Id.; *Reports*, vol. 1, Preface to the Reader.

[15] Coke, *Reports*, vol. 2, To the Learned Reader, 7.

[16] Coke, *Reports*, vol 2, p. 81; *Reports*, vol. 10, p. 70. ("Optimus legum interpretes consuetudo.")

[17] See D. E. C. Yale, "Hobbes and Hale on Law, Legislation and the Sovereign," 31 *Cambridge Law Journal* 25–26 (1972): "[I]n Coke's theory the common custom of the realm was totally reasonable, in the sense that it represented the product of a professional skill working a refinement and co-ordination of social habits into a system of rules."

[18] Sir Matthew Hale, *Reflections*, printed in William Holdsworth, *A History of English Law*, 7th ed. (London: Methuen, 1956), 499–513. There is no evidence that Holmes made any focused study of Hale until 1876, and then only by way of Andrew Amos, *Ruins of Time Exemplified in Sir Matthew Hale's History of the Pleas of the Crown* (London: V. and R. Stevens and G. S. Norton, 1856) (see Holmes, *The Black Book*, Harvard Law School

Hale begins his *Reflections* with an elaborate demonstration that reason is by no means univocal as applied to different subjects of inquiry, such as mathematics, physics, and politics, and that it must be permitted to assume a special meaning in the difficult field of law. This is because "ye texture of Humane affaires is not unlike the Texture of a diseased bodey labouring under Maladies, it may be of so various natures that such Phisique as may be proper for the Cure of one of the maladies may be destructive in relation to ye other, and ye cure of one disease may be the death of the patient."[19]

Hale's comparison of law to a curative introduced into the "texture of human affairs" separates both his notion of reason and his conceptualization of law from those of Hobbes. His "texture" terminology anticipates Hart's "open texture" of legal language; but unlike Hart, the texture of interest to Hale is *outside* the law, a texture of "affaires" or *activity*, and the element of difficulty would necessarily be located there instead of within the isolated text. His analysis resists separating law, whether as language or reasoning, from the disputes that engage the courts and the generality of human activity giving rise to them. The reasoning of the common lawyer is not only different from that of the moral philosopher, it is directed at a different subject matter, a distinct type of problem. It is not, for Hale, akin to a mathematical or scientific dissection of a preexisting system of rules. Based on experience, it looks beneath rules and decisions to an organic reality, from which the consideration of rules by themselves cannot be separated. "There is no sharp conceptual boundary between law and other social phenomena because, on this view, there is no sharp difference between them in the community governed by law."[20]

The contrast between Hobbes's *Dialogue* and Hale's *Reflections* is obscured by the use of similar terms. Both disputants in the *Dialogue*, the Law Student and the Philosopher, are in agreement that law has a rational basis – that law must be informed by reason and cannot be law if it conflicts with reason. Hobbes's point is simply that the claim of a "universal" or "natural" reason accessible to common lawyers opens the way to disobedience by any who set up their own individual reason against that of the law: it is the nature of law to command, and commands require obedience. It is the nature of "universal" reason to be open to question. Thus

Library (1876–1935), 17). Frederick Pollock never mentions discovering the *Reflections* in his surviving letters to Holmes. However, there is no way of assessing the content and influence of conversations between Holmes and English common law scholars such as Pollock and James Fitzjames Stephen on his trips to England beginning in 1866.

[19] Hale, *Reflections*, 503.

[20] Postema, *Bentham and the Common Law Tradition*, 38.

the reason of law must emanate from a single commanding sovereign source.

Hobbes's Philosopher asks the imaginary Law Student to explain how Coke can avoid the charge that in tying the law to reason he is discouraging obedience. The Law Student's defense of Coke, demonstrating Hobbes's personal view of common law theory, falls back on the claim of special legal training ridiculed lately by Justice Scalia: he cites Coke's dictum that the law is based on what is reasonable not to any individual man but to the reason of men specially trained and possessing the legal art: "because by so many successions of ages it hath been fined and refined by an infinite number of Grave and Learned Men." This removes from its context the common law argument from experience, the identification of reason with a deference to the established practices of the relevant community. Hobbes's Law Student, in identifying reasoning as mere subjective individual judgment, albeit coming from a profession claiming special expertise, would not have received a passing grade from Sir Matthew.[21]

Hale's *Reflections*, in contrast, binds the definition of reason closely to the nature of the inquiry:

> It is taken complexedly when the reasonable facultie is in Conjunction w[i]th the reasonable Subject, and habituated to it by Use and Exercise, and it is this kind of reason or reason thus taken that Denominates a Man a Mathematician, a Philosopher, a Politician, a Phisician, a Lawyer; yea that renders men excellent in their p[a]rticular Acts[22] as a good Engineer, a good Watchmaker, a good Smith, a good Surgeon – all w[hi]ch consists in the application of the Facultie of reason to the particular Subject. . . . [23]

Hereupon Hale anticipates the later comment of Lord Mansfield, quoted by Holmes in 1870, to the effect that the business man suddenly appointed judge should avoid abstract reasoning and rely on common sense:

> And upon this acco[un]t it is that when men of observation and Experience in Humane affaires and Conversation between man and man make many times good Judges, yett for the most part those men that have greate reason and Learneing w[hi]ch they gather up of Casuists, Schoolmen, Morall Philosophers, and Treatises touching Moralls in the Theory, that So are in high Speculations and abstract Notions touching Justice and Right, and as they differ Extreamely among

[21] Hobbes, *Dialogue*, 109.

[22] A note appears here in Pollock's text: "This should probably be 'Arts.' – F.P."

[23] Hale, *Reflections*, 501–2.

themselves when they come to particular applications, So are most comonly the worst Judges that can be, because they are transported from the Ordinary Measures of right and wrong by their over fine Speculacons[,] Theoryes and distinctions above the Comon Staple of humane conversations.[24]

Hobbes could not appreciate the common law argument from custom and practice, because he could not see how custom or precedent could have any special authority apart from their explicit adoption into the law by an empowered sovereign on strictly legal or equitable grounds:

I deny that any Custome of its own nature, can amount to the authority of a law: For if the Custome be unreasonable, you must with all other lawyers confess that it is no law, but ought to be abolished; and if the Custome be reasonable, it is not the custom, but the equity that makes it law.[25]

He failed to accept that common lawyers conceived the notion of custom not in isolation but as the continuing effect of public practices on the substantive framework of law. We see here the danger of which Dewey warned: using "law" in such a way as to set it up as a separate entity. In Hobbes's usage, custom is objectified as a discrete entity, set off from a similarly objectified entity "law," while insofar as the common lawyers had conceptualized law, custom was already at work within it. For Hobbes a presumptive boundary preexisted the analysis; any given custom must be separately evaluated as part of the law or not.

What Hale, especially, seems to be driving at by "custom" are the settled and orderly habits of economic and social activity that provide the basis for a coordinate legal order; both law and custom are organically connected and integrated.[26] This order is constantly interrupted and threatened by dispute and conflict, which would cause considerable disruption to the social fabric were the law not available to restore it, first by explicitly identifying and recognizing the integrated fabric, notwithstanding its complexity, then by gradually and experimentally crafting a coherent and consistent response.

First, The Common Law does determine what of those Customs are good and reasonable, and what are unreasonable and void. *Secondly,* the Common Law gives to those Customs, that it adjudges reasonable, the Force and Efficacy of their Obligation. *Thirdly,* the Common Law determines what is that Continuance of Time that is sufficient to make such a Custom. *Fourthly,* the Common Law

24 Ibid., 503.
25 Hobbes, *Dialogue,* 96.
26 See Postema, "Philosophy of the Common Law," 592.

> does interpose and authoritatively decide the Exposition, Limits and Extension of such Customs.[27]

The above is from Hale's posthumous *A History of the Common Law of England*; in *Reflections* Hale makes clear that his concept of custom, seen through the eyes of the judge, is akin to experience, and law should be based on as wide a variety of experience as possible:[28]

> Againe I have reason to assure myselfe that Long Experience makes more discoveries touching conveniences or Inconveniences of Laws then [*sic*] is possible for the wisest Councill of Men att first to foresee. And that those amendm[en]ts and Supplem[en]ts that through the various Experiences of wise and knowing men have been applyed to any Law must needs be better suited to the Convenience of Laws, then the best Invention of the most pregnant witts not ayded by Such a Series and tract of Experience.
>
> All these thinges are reasonable, the particular reason of the Laws & Supplem[en]ts themselves perchance are not obvious to the most Subtill Witts or Reason.
>
> And this adds to ye difficultie of a present fathomeing of the reason of Laws, because they are the Production of long and Iterated Experience....[29]

This point, made after the lengthy argument concerning the nature of reasoning itself, provides a striking historical precedent for Holmes's famous passage, written two centuries later, at the beginning of *The Common Law*: "the life of the law has not been logic, it has been experience."[30]

Legal positivism emerged – we may portray it here as an outgrowth of political developments in seventeenth-century England – as a defense of central government entirely compatible with democratic theory: what the sovereign commands, whether by fiat or majoritarian legislation, *is* the law. Holmes wrote much that seems consistent with this simple dictum, and most scholars understandably characterize him as a positivist.[31] But legal positivism has evolved in a manner that renders it quite incompatible

[27] Hale, *A History of the Common Law of England*, ed. C. M. Gray (Chicago: University of Chicago Press, 1971), 18.

[28] Yale, "Hobbes and Hale," 126–27.

[29] Hale, *Reflections*, 504–5.

[30] Holmes, *The Common Law*, 1.

[31] E.g., White, *Justice Oliver Wendell Holmes*, 161, 221, 388. Patrick J. Kelley, "Was Holmes a Pragmatist? Reflections on a New Twist to an Old Argument," 14 S. *Ill. L. J.* 427 (1990); Sheldon M. Novick, "Holmes's Constitutional Jurisprudence," 18 *S. Ill. L. J.* 347, 348 (1994): "The assumption of all [Holmes's] thinking was that government rested on violent force"; Posner, Introduction to *The Essential Holmes*, xxiii; Posner, *The Problems of Jurisprudence* (Cambridge, Mass., and London: Harvard University Press, 1990), 20.

with Holmes's most basic insights, and its recent development highlights the very criticisms of it that are embedded in his early writing.

Many now view the early common law theorists as engaged in a holding action, defending judicial prerogative against a transformative tide toward both majoritarian legislation and central government. Common law itself is seen as radically diminished in size as well as importance. Scalia quotes the legal historian Lawrence Friedman in saying that even private law has become statutory and that "[t]his is particularly true in the federal courts, where, with a qualification so small that it does not bear mentioning, there is no such thing as common law. Every issue of law resolved by a federal judge involves interpretation of text – the text of a regulation, or statute, or of the Constitution." But while marginalizing common law, Scalia undercuts his own textualism with the observation, "We American judges have no intelligible theory of what we do most."[32]

Until quite recently, "common law" perspectives on law have persisted apathetically. Allusions to common law have been found at the margins of theoretical debate, such as that over interpretative approaches in Supreme Court jurisprudence. Common law has suffered from the fact that it is perceived as ungrounded in any current or comprehensive legal philosophy. It can be neither explained nor ignored. Bentham considered the common law "sham," "mock," or "impostrous," equivalent to the exercise of arbitrary power; he called it "fictitious" and a "mere nonentity."[33] A. W. B. Simpson has more recently written that it is "more like a muddle than a system," "essentially shadowy," and operates "as if [it] placed particular value upon dissention, obscurity, and the tentative character of judicial utterances."[34]

In the course of his early scholarship, Holmes did indeed give common law a theory, as had the English scholar-judges of the seventeenth and eighteenth centuries. Theirs is now seen as a defense of embedded, and not entirely well reasoned or intentioned, practices. They were pitted

[32] Scalia, *A Matter of Interpretation*, 14, quoting Henry M. Hart, Jr., and Albert M. Sacks, *The Legal Process: Basic Problems in the Making and Application of Law* (Westbury, N.Y.: Foundation Press, 1994), 1169: "The hard truth of the matter is that American courts have no intelligible, generally accepted, and consistently applied theory of statutory interpretation."

[33] Stephen R. Perry, "Judicial Obligation, Precedent, and the Common Law," 7 *Oxford Journal of Legal Studies* 215 (1987), 234.

[34] Id., 250; A. W. B. Simpson, "The Common Law and Legal Theory," in Simpson, ed., *Oxford Essays in Jurisprudence: Second Series* (Oxford: Clarendon Press, 1973), 90.

against a nicely simple theory – perhaps too simple – of both state and democratic power. The early articulation of both theories, common law as well as positivist, can be traced to a period of fierce competition for power in England, raising issues of who controlled the law and how. Whence did judges derive the authority to discover law? On what grounds do so-called common law judges decide, if not directly from the text of the relevant law or authoritative legal materials? And why do they defer to previous decisions (the practice called *stare decisis*) even where they might be persuaded that convincing authority, textual or otherwise, is opposed?

In Holmes's reconceptualization, common law was not strictly "judge-made," as commonly characterized.[35] This ignores the importance given by Holmes to the broader experience taken into account by judges in their retrospective adjustments of legal rules, and even of the crucial role of consensus among judges, lawyers, and litigants that is implied in Holmes's 1870 comment that "a well settled legal doctrine embodies the work of many minds, and has been tested in form as well as substance by trained critics whose practical interest it is to resist it at every step." A caricature of common law has been the notion that judges, in resolving even the most difficult cases, are specially equipped to divine from within the "preexisting" law of that situation – appealing to what Holmes mocked as a "brooding omnipresence in the sky." He rejected this in favor of a naturalistic theory of inquiry, in which intractable legal disputes were viewed as bearing a certain degree of unforeseen novelty or originality, and the legal profession, in concert with the community at large, worked out a gradual resolution through progressive abstraction from specific cases.

Much of his early research drew on the traditional domain of private law, wherein statute making had yet to make substantial inroads by the mid-nineteenth century. One might assume that Holmes was developing a theory for that part of the law alone, irrelevant to the growing body of legislation, to which positivism could better apply. A powerful movement toward legislative reform and codification of the common law was already under way while Holmes was engaged in this work.[36] Holmes would retain the traditional continuity between common and statute law.

[35] Postema, *Bentham and the Common Law Tradition*, 588.
[36] Horwitz, *The Transformation of American Law 1870–1960*, 123.

Taken as a whole, his effort was aimed toward encompassing statute law, and was framed with the comprehensive positivist theory of John Austin in mind. It was an extended criticism of Austinian positivism, and an effort to present a unified theory of all law, accounting for the judicial role in interpreting and applying all forms of law, precedent, statute, and constitution. In this it has had an incomplete and uneven reception.

The early scholarship includes an effort to make a rough analytical map of two quite different things: first, of the categories of the law, organized around its putatively innate conceptual elements, drawing in particular from an elaborate scheme set forth earlier in the century by John Austin. Next, to better understand the difficulties he encountered in settling on anything *innate*, the analysis turns to the historical development of legal conceptualization itself. The first project was undertaken in an essay on codification: it began as a critical examination of possible schemes of *legislative* organization of law as a whole.

Thus did Holmes become engaged by 1870 with the relation of legal classification, legal history, and codification. Within this threefold relation lie important issues concerning the nature and sources of authority, law, and justice. Is law a natural entity? Is its inherent nature (presumably consisting in certain basic conceptual elements) discoverable? If not natural, then is that nature entirely subject to legislative fixation? What, in this context, are we to make of the legal conception of justice, especially in relation to morals? Two centuries earlier, in an England riven by the clash of crown and rising professional classes, the same threefold relation had been at the center of opposing theories of law put forth by Hobbes and the common law judges.

The positivist project, begun with Hobbes's defense of the central state, was undertaken with an implicit commitment to the belief that law is a definable entity. This has two meanings: definable in clear language, the dictionary sense, and *actually* defined by a real and identifiable boundary – having a distinct *ontology*, a term denoting concreteness. The two are easily confused; both fit the spirit and purpose of reform better than the notion that law cannot be universally defined or that it has an open, or *nonexistent*, boundary. In contrast is the tradition of common law as an acentric legal order better explained by history than static analysis. Insofar as its nature had been revealed, it was through such sweeping historical theories as Henry Maine's notion of the evolution of legal relations from status to contract. Clearly influenced by Maine, Holmes proposed his own sweeping theory, a movement from moral to external standards of conduct and liability. Consistent with a skeptical outlook, this implied a retreat from moral certainty, and the attribution of a degree of moral skepticism to the emergent common law itself.[37]

Although critical of Maine, Holmes's theory was similarly developmental, perceiving legal concepts in the context of their emergence and growth. Pure positivism and its textualist simplification leave little room for such developmental talk. Holmes could talk on both sides of the divide because the appearance of some empirical aspects of positivism were part of the historical shift. By 1894 he had come to welcome legislation, indeed the application of utilitarian reform, as the legal enterprise coming to control its own destiny: "The time has gone by when law is only an unconscious embodiment of the common will. It has become a conscious reaction upon itself of organized society knowingly seeking to determine its own destinies."[38]

More significant is the resilience of the attitudes of early common law theorists and Holmes's resistance to the most basic elements of what has now become hard-core positivist doctrine.[39] Pure positivism, the analytical version that Holmes challenged in detail during the formative period of his research, has itself encountered problems, not least among them the twentieth-century critiques of Ronald Dworkin. Since Hobbes it has wrestled continually, and less than successfully, with the boundary question: in what fundamental elements, precisely, does "law" consist? Hart's effort to unify positivist thinking by moving away from the command definition favored by Hobbes and Austin toward an analytical arrangement of "primary" and "secondary" rules, governed by a Rule of Recognition, has fallen into scholastic wrangling.[40]

A leading topic during the last century has been the status of moral principles and abstract rights. Lon Fuller, and later Dworkin, undermined positivist confidence by pressing the case that they must fall *within* the

37 For a comment on the relation of the Scottish Enlightenment to common law theory, see chapter 3, n. 31.

38 Holmes, "Privilege, Malice, and Intent," in *Collected Legal Papers*, 129–30.

39 "A classic form [of legal positivism] holds that a community's law consists only of what its lawmaking officials have declared to be the law, so that it is a mistake to suppose that some nonpositivist force or agency – objective moral truth or God or the spirit of an age or the diffuse will of the people or the tramp of history through time, for example – can be a source of law unless lawmaking officials have declared it to be." Ronald Dworkin, *Justice in Robes* (Cambridge, Mass.: Belknap Press, 2006), 187.

40 Id., 188.

boundary.[41] Debate about law in the mid-twentieth century took on an ideological element, informed by experience with "immoral" Nazi laws and the Cold War. It was later influenced by the intervention of federal courts, led by the Supreme Court, to end state-sponsored racial segregation as well as to assert new rights of personal privacy and fair criminal procedures under the authority of the Constitution. The status of "principles" – the question of whether they lie inside or outside the definition of law – was engaged with these developments.

For his skepticism about principles Holmes was posthumously criticized as an amoral authoritarian positivist, obscuring his true position.[42] The same theme has more recently been sounded by Alschuler and others as a condemnation for promoting "law without values."[43] His conception throughout, consistent with classical common law theory, has been antithetical to a strict boundary. He maintained that morals and values work their way into the law, but this did not provide judicial license for sitting judges to import their own subjective values under the abstract language of rights.[44]

While sounding like a positivist separation of law and morals, this is distinct from legal ontology. It is a critique of abstraction and a criterion of interpretation. While analytical in character, it is grounded in both analytical and historical research. Through a combination of analytical and historical methods, Holmes came to deny the positivist assumption that law can be understood through taxonomic analysis, as a static or synchronic entity.[45]

The early research papers are dense and often awkwardly written, but they are necessary to a full understanding of Holmes's intellectual path. It is not a direct linear progression, but jumps from topic to topic and doubles back to earlier insights. Nor is it obvious that Holmes always had a clear goal in mind during this period, beyond absorbing and abstracting as much information as possible. His work during the formative period

[41] Lon L. Fuller, *The Morality of Law* (New Haven: Yale University Press, 1969); Dworkin, *Taking Rights Seriously*.

[42] Fuller, *The Law in Quest of Itself* (Boston: Beacon Press, 1966), 62, 117.

[43] Alschuler, *Law without Values*.

[44] Holmes, "The Path of the Law," in *Collected Legal Papers*, 170.

[45] We should distinguish the legal positivism growing out of John Austin's command definition from the original and much broader "positivism" of Auguste Comte, whose cause Holmes had supported from college days. It is undeniable from the early essays that Holmes hardly viewed himself as a strict follower of John Austin.

gives the impression of a record of explorative self-education, writing out his thoughts as the most effective means of achieving an understanding of his subject as a whole.

Harvard Law School, which he entered in the fall of 1864, did not hold his attention; he left in December 1865 for private practice in Boston, commuting back and forth from an active intellectual life in Cambridge. He soon took upon himself a major responsibility, revising and updating the leading four-volume treatise, *Kent's Commentaries on American Law.* Amidst this formidable task, which obliged him to spend every spare hour reading cases and textbooks covering the entire field of law, he drafted a series of essays published over the decade 1870–80 in the *American Law Review*, of which he served as an editor from 1870 to 1874.[46]

In editing *Kent's Commentaries* while simultaneously reading and re-reading Austin's extended treatise, Holmes was undertaking an account of the actual common law of his time, as seen beneath the shadow of the most influential theoretical analysis of law since Hobbes. The essays are unified by this comparison in two phases. Holmes's attention was first engaged by topics that provided him with historical and analytical background for testing Austin's basic assumptions and conclusions. It then shifted to seeking a groundwork for an alternative theory of his own, in which major positivist precepts were rejected. The resulting conclusions were embodied in *The Common Law*, but there was to be more development in his thinking while on the highest appellate courts of Massachusetts and the United States, especially in constitutional law.

46 White, *Justice Oliver Wendell Holmes*, 87–147.

5

Holmes and Legal Classification

> [E]very positive law, or every law strictly so called, is a direct or circuitous command of a monarch or sovereign number to a person or persons in a state of subjection to its author. And being a command (and therefore flowing from a determinate source), every positive law is a law proper, or a law properly so called.
>
> Besides the human laws which I style positive law, there are human laws which I style positive morality, rules of positive morality, or positive moral rules. (134)
>
> In consequence of the frequent coincidence of positive law and morality, and of positive law and the law of God, the true nature and fountain of positive law is often absurdly mistaken by writers upon jurisprudence. (162)
>
> John Austin, *The Province of Jurisprudence Determined* (1832)

The decade of the 1870s, the first part of which Holmes took up the subject of legal classification, demonstrated a seriousness of purpose that seems incongruent with the blithe spirit who half a century later would write to his friend Frederick Pollock:

> [Justice] Brandeis the other day drove a harpoon into my midriff with reference to my summer occupations. He said you talk about improving your mind, you only exercise it on the subjects with which you are familiar. Why don't you try something new, study some domain of fact? Take up the textile industries in Massachusetts and after reading the reports sufficiently you can go to Lawrence [Mass.] and get a human notion of how it really is. I hate facts. I always say the chief end of man is to form general propositions – adding that no general proposition is worth a damn. Of course a general proposition is simply a string for the facts and I have little doubt that it would be good for my immortal soul to plunge into

them, good also for the performance of my duties, but I shrink from the bore – or rather I hate to give up the chance to read this and that, that a gentleman should have read before he dies. I don't remember that I ever read Machiavelli's *Prince* – and I think of the Day of Judgment.[1]

Here in private correspondence is an unserious and somewhat misleading Holmes. Although he may have been honest about a bumpy motorcar trip to Lawrence from his summer home in Beverly Farms to study factory conditions, he could not have hated facts to accomplish what he had done in the 1870s. The reference to general propositions alludes to those earlier days. Holmes had discussed the relation of facts and abstractions, particulars and generals, with Wright, Green, James, Joseph Warner, Peirce, and other amateur philosophers of Cambridge, contemporaneously with his examination of the relation of specifics and generalizations in the law.[2]

His close friend "Will" James had written from Berlin in 1868, "When I get home let's establish a philosophical society to have regular meetings and discuss none but the very tallest and broadest questions – to be composed of nothing but the topmost cream of Boston manhood. It will give each one a chance to air his own opinion in a grammatical form, and to sneer and chuckle when he goes home at what damned fools all the other members are – and may grow into something very important after a sufficient number of years." Evidence of meetings is fragmentary and comes mainly from Peirce's later recollections.[3] A letter from Henry James to Charles Eliot Norton in early 1872 mentions that Holmes, along with his brother James "& various other long-headed youths have combined to form a Metaphysical Club, where they wrangle grimly & stick to the question. It gives me a headache merely to know of it."[4] Had Holmes continued to keep the daily record of appointments and discussions that he kept only from 1866 to late December 1867 (noting the philosophical "palavers" with Wright and James), we might have a clearer picture.[5]

[1] Holmes to Pollock, May 26 1919, *Holmes–Pollock Letters*, vol. 2, p. 14.

[2] Fisch, "Metaphysical Club," 20.

[3] Id., 3–29.

[4] Id., 4–5.

[5] Although the original club may have died in late 1872, we know from correspondence that it was revived in 1876; Francis Ellingwood Abbot received a letter from William James in January of that year inviting him "to join a Club for reading and discussing philosophical authors, which meets once a week at present and is composed of C. C. Everett, N. St. John Green, O. W. Holmes, Jr., John Fiske, Thos. Davidson. J. B. Warner, Prof. Bowen, and one or two others [Peirce was in Europe until August]. We have begun with Hume's Treatise on Human Nature and the next meeting is at this house, next Sunday evening at ½ past seven promptly." Holmes's copious diary of his reading records Hume's *Treatise* in April

The term "pragmatism" was not formally applied to the thoughts of these contemporaries until 1898, and Holmes never heard it applied to such discussions.[6] Certainly addressed was the nature of generals and their relation to the particulars for which they served (in Holmes's apt phrase) as a "string." Pragmatism is characterized as the view that theories must be linked to experience or practice,[7] and as such the validity of a proposition is made dependent on both its past and its future, in its success as a reflection of experience and a guide to practice.

The historical context tells us much. Religion and Continental philosophy were formative influences on the currents of thought in nineteenth-century Cambridge, and thence on the emergence of pragmatism.[8] A leading issue was the status of empirical science in religious belief. Descartes, Locke, Berkeley, and Hume were familiar authorities. Unitarianism, a liberal belief that accommodated the more commercial and secular culture of post-Calvinist New England, had found a defense against Transcendentalist and other challenges in Scottish realism, a "philosophy of common sense."[9] After Kant, debates over empiricism became increasingly troubled over the status of supra-empirical knowledge.[10] The Scot William Hamilton, who influenced the young Chauncey Wright, had expounded an empiricism acceptable in Harvard and Cambridge, one that left room for God and scripture without too much extra space for Transcendentalist obscurantism.[11]

1876, presumably in finishing it. See Little, "Early Reading," 192; Fisch, "Metaphysical Club," 7–8.

When Charles Hartshorne began preparing Peirce's *Collected Papers* in 1927, he wrote to Justice Holmes, at eighty-six the only surviving member of the original club, to inquire about it and received this reply: "I am afraid that I cannot help you much in the way of recollections of Charles Peirce. I think I remember his father saying to me, "Charles is a genius," and I remember the august tone in which, at one of the few meetings at which I was present, Charles prefaced his opinion with '*Other* philosophers have thought.' Once in a fertilizing way he challenged some assumption that I made, but alas I forget what. But in those days I was studying law and I soon dropped out of the band, although I should have liked to rejoin it when it was too late. I think I learned more from Chauncey Wright and St. John Green, as I saw Peirce very little." Fisch, "Metaphysical Club," 10–11.

6 See Sami Pihlstrom, "Peirce's Place in the Pragmatist Tradition," in Cheryl Misak, ed., *The Cambridge Companion to Peirce* (Cambridge: Cambridge University Press, 2004), 27–48. In 1908 Holmes called pragmatism an "amusing humbug" in a letter to Pollock. Holmes to Pollock, June 17, 1908, *Holmes-Pollock Letters*, vol. 1, p. 139.

7 Cheryl Misak, "Charles Sanders Peirce (1839–1914)," in *Cambridge Companion to Peirce*, 1.

8 See Kuklick, *Rise of American Philosophy*, 5–27.

9 Id., 10–16.

10 Id., 16.

11 Id., 16–18.

This accommodation was disrupted by two developments, noted in chapter 3, not long before Holmes returned from the Civil War: John Stuart Mill's skeptical attack on Hamilton, and Darwin's *Origin of Species.* While Asa Gray, Harvard professor of natural history, would claim with contemporary fundamentalists, "To us a fortuitous Cosmos is simply inconceivable. The alternative is a designed Cosmos," no one could postpone the destruction of the philosophical basis of Unitarian orthodoxy, with its brittle understanding of empiricism, extending to its account of the status of and basis for scientific knowledge, including "general propositions."[12] Concern with this problem was a main current energizing Wright, Peirce, James, Green, Holmes, and other members of the club that James had proposed in 1868.

There appear to be three main interests brought to the conversations: Wright's evolutionary theorizing, Green's esteem for Alexander Bain's definition of belief as that on which one is prepared to act, and the legal theories of Green and Holmes. Green urged the others to look to "the practical significance of every proposition," and claimed that "every form of words that means anything indicates some sensible fact on the existence of which its truth depends."[13]

Another current of special concern to Holmes at this time was the context of John Austin's revolutionary jurisprudence. After deciding on a career in law rather than philosophy,[14] the status of *legal* concepts – general propositions in the law – occupied his attention. Austin had brought a new approach to expository jurisprudence in England.[15] Holmes saw at once that Austin's search for a uniform universal classification, if successful, might transform law into a distinctive kind of empirical science. If unsuccessful, it might oblige a different hypothesis on the relation of facts to general concepts.

His objections to Austin would emerge in the essays covering the period between 1870 and the Lowell Lectures in 1880. They have much to do with the attempt to establish a coherent logical arrangement for law that would place a discrete boundary around it with the objective of a universal comprehensive analysis. These elements, the notion of boundary and of internal analysis, were not as important for Hobbes, and they had

[12] Id., 20–26.
[13] Id., 49; Fisch, "Metaphysical Club," 20, 26.
[14] Novick, *Honorable Justice*, 95–96.
[15] Herget, *American Jurisprudence*, 12–22.

never been attempted with Austin's scope and detail. Hobbes had led the way with his identification of law as sovereign commands, but with Austin, legal positivism fully adopts the characteristic that it has maintained to the present: the ideal of law, and of a philosophy of law, as (in the words of Ronald Dworkin) an "autonomous, analytic, and self-contained discipline."[16]

The issue most allied with the debate over legal reasoning in the late tracts of Hobbes and Hale is that of sovereignty. The importance of a clear location and identity for sovereign power was plain to Hobbes, although given the nature of parliamentary participation in the sixteenth century he could not solve the problem cleanly. Much debate was devoted by Hobbes and his critics to defining the locus of supreme power to make the laws.[17] Hale in the *Reflections* takes issue with certain aspects of this account reflected in Hobbes's late *Dialogue*, in particular with his lack of attention to the historical consensual limitations attributable to the unwritten English constitution.[18] Similar issues would be taken up by Holmes in response to Austin's definition of the sovereign power two centuries later. To Holmes, writing in 1870, the command definition simply solved one definitional problem by creating another: "In the first place, who has the sovereign power, and whether such a power exists at all, are questions of fact and of degree."[19]

The center of the debate had begun to shift away from the source of raw power toward identification of the conceptual framework and boundary of law, a movement that would develop considerably further by the time of Fuller's challenge to Hart at mid-twentieth century, becoming still more extended today. Indeed, the two matters, the source of power and the boundaries of positive law, are alike in important respects. Both appear as matters of empirical fact from which important conclusions must arise. They offer an identifible and authoritive character to law, as well as the prospect of understanding what is most basic in it.[20] Confidence in such essentials would presumably promote the effectiveness of the legal order itself, its beneficial operation and improvement. It

[16] See Dworkin, *Justice in Robes*, 188.

[17] Yale, "Hobbes and Hale," 135–50.

[18] Hale, *Reflections*, 507–12.

[19] Holmes, "Codes, and the Arrangement of the Law," in *Formative Essays*, 80, and in 1 *Collected Works*, 214.

[20] See Roger A. Shiner, *Norm and Nature: The Movements of Legal Thought* (Oxford: Clarendon Press, 1992), 5–9.

should expose vulnerabilities and increase the prospect of fulfilling the law's purposes, the promotion of a more coherent system of justice.

With Austin, sovereignty and boundary are still linked by the command definition, but there is an important new element: logical arrangement. This had not seemed imperative to Hobbes in his defense of the sovereign prerogative. But if there is a weakness in Hobbes's position it is to be found in the remark made by the Philosopher in response to the Lawyer's insistence on reason inherent in the common law: "There is not amongst men a universal reason agreed upon in any nation, besides the reason of him that hath the sovereign power. Yet though his reason be but the reason of one man, yet it is set up to supply the place of that universal reason." Hobbes's sovereign reason drew on the image of a discrete monarch and was vulnerable to the charge of arbitrariness. It demanded elucidation by later theorists interested in the Hobbesean project, fortifying and rationalizing the legal authority of the state. Addressing this deficiency in the seventeenth century was the reformer Jeremy Bentham, with the theory of utility.[21]

Austin was a loyal disciple of Bentham, and there is a lengthy treatment of utilitarianism in his *Lectures*.[22] There is also a direct connection between that discussion and Austin's choice of logical arrangement, based on various types of right and duty found throughout the law.[23] While recognizing the close relationship of duties and rights, Austin apparently preferred the latter out of concern to emphasize the positive scope of action necessary to maximize utility:

> But the final cause or purpose for which government ought to exist, is the furtherance of the common weal to the greatest possible extent. And it must mainly attain the purpose for which it ought to exist, by two sets of means: *first*, by conferring such rights on its subjects as general utility commends, and by imposing such relative duties (or duties corresponding to the rights) as are necessary to the enjoyment of the former: *second*, by imposing such absolute duties (or by imposing

[21] As Friedrich observes, Hobbes sought to mitigate the arbitrariness of sovereign power by assigning judges the task of interpreting a "law of nature," and his legal philosophy is based on a principle of utility. Friedrich, *Philosophy of Law in Historical Perspective*, 87, 89.

[22] Austin, *Lectures*, vol. 1, pp. 109–70.

[23] Id., 412: "A monarch or sovereign body expressly or tacitly *commands*, that one or more of its subjects shall do or forbear from acts, towards, or in respect of, a distinct and *determinate* party. The person or persons who are to do or forbear from these acts, are said to be subject to a *duty*, or to lie under a *duty*. The party towards whom those acts are said to be done or forborne is said to have a *right*, or to be invested with a *right*" (emphasis in original).

such duties without corresponding rights) as tend to promote the good of the political community at large, although they promote not specially the interest of determinate parties.[24]

Holmes too was drawn to the prospect of logical arrangement, for reasons that would later appear ambivalent. Bentham's earlier call for codification, as a precondition for the reform of society and legal institutions, was still much discussed in England and America, and codification was a live issue in several states after the Civil War.[25] Holmes's mistrust of the codification project is evident in remarks made in the 1870 article, "Codes, and the Arrangement of the Law," opening as it does with the reference to Lord Mansfield and the case-specific reasoning of the common law. It is followed by the remark, "These [aspects of common law method] are advantages the want of which cannot be supplied by any faculty of generalization, however brilliant, and it is noticeable that those books on which an ideal code might best be modeled avowedly when possible lay down the law in the very words of the court."[26]

Holmes appears from the outset suspicious of the Hobbesean or Austinian position in the debate over sovereign reason. Nevertheless, he proceeded in 1870 to experiment with his own logical arrangement, preferring a classification under the rubric of duty rather than right, as duty was empirically closer to the proscriptive nature of the law:

Duties precede rights logically and chronologically. Even those laws which in form create a right directly, in fact either tacitly impose a duty on the rest of the world, as, in the case of patents, to abstain from selling the patented article, or confer an immunity from a duty previously or generally imposed, like taxation. The logical priority of duty in such instances is clear when we consider that in its absence any man might make and sell what he pleased and abstain from paying for ever, without assistance from law. Another illustration is, that, while there are in some

[24] *Lectures*, vol. 1, p. 282; see also 290–91: "Every legal right is the creature of a positive law: and it answers to a relative duty imposed by that positive law, and incumbent on a person or persons other than the person or persons in whom the right resides. To every legal right, there are therefore three parties: The sovereign government of one or a number which sets the positive law, and which through the positive law confers the legal right, and imposes the relative duty: the person or persons on whom the right is conferred: the person or persons on whom the duty is imposed, or to whom the positive law is set or directed."

[25] Horwitz, *Transformation of American Law 1870–1960*, 117, 123.

[26] Holmes, "Codes, and the Arrangement of the Law," in *Formative Essays*, 77, and in 1 *Collected Works*, 212.

cases legal duties without corresponding rights, we never see a legal right without either a corresponding duty or a compulsion stronger than duty.[27]

His criticism of the "rights" system was that it was not close enough to the actual operation of law and legal sanctions. It presented an image of an envelope of protection, emphasizing the scope of conduct made permissible by law, whereas that of duties was of conduct merely prohibited or required. Holmes concluded that the latter was closer to the true picture. This is nearer the vision of Coke and Hale than of Hobbes and Austin; the scope of possible social conduct had no necessary relation to the phenomenon called law. It could be engaged in anyway, and was neither created by nor dependent on state sanction, nor any hypothetical legitimating concept, such as rights.

While Holmes was writing this critique, Green was boiling down certain legal concepts to their practical essence. In "Proximate and Remote Cause," also published in 1870, he concluded that liability for personal injury was not the physical remoteness from the defendant's conduct but the degree of certainty with which injury might have been anticipated. After Green's early death in 1876, a year after Wright's, Holmes would take this insight to its fullest extension.[28]

In his earlier writings of the decade 1870–80, Holmes experimented with what he called the "philosophical" organization of the different branches of law seen as classifications of duty (see the Appendix). In the course of so doing, his initial doubts concerning sovereign command and sanction gradually matured in a manner that was to transform his ultimate perspective into an evolutionary one. By 1872, using a review of an article by Frederick Pollock to summarize a series of lectures he had given to undergraduates at Harvard College, Holmes reached a more explicit critique of Austin's command definition, specifically in response to Austin's rejecting custom as part of law. As pure custom was neither commanded nor sanctioned by the sovereign, Austin considered it but a "motive for decision," becoming law only when its adoption by the legislature or the courts demonstrated the tacit consent of the sovereign. To this Holmes replied:

Austin said, following Heineccius (*Recitationes*, §72), that custom only became law by the tacit consent of the sovereign manifested by its adoption by the courts; and that before its adoption it was only a motive for decision, as a doctrine of

[27] Holmes, "Codes, and the Arrangement of the Law," in *Formative Essays*, 79–80; 1 *Collected Works*, 214.

[28] Kuklick, *Rise of American Philosophy*, 49–50.

political economy, or the political aspirations of the judge, or his gout, or the blandishments of the emperor's wife might have been. But it is clear that in many cases custom and mercantile usage have had as much compulsory power as law could have, in spite of prohibitory statutes; and as to their being only motives for decision until adopted, what more is the decision which adopts them as to any future decision? What more indeed is a statute; and in what other sense law, than that we believe that the motive which we think that it offers to the judges will prevail, and will induce them to decide a certain case in a certain way, and so shape our conduct on that anticipation?[29]

While this passage has frequently been interpreted as an early statement of the attitude later characterized as legal realism, it is noteworthy for the comment that "custom and mercantile usage have had as much compulsory power as law could have, in spite of prohibitory statutes." This too is an extension of the approach of Hale and Blackstone, quite at odds with that of Hobbes and Austin. Custom is already at work with a "compulsory power." Law is not objectified as separate from the factors motivating decision, and custom is indeed placed on the same footing as statutory law, even as Blackstone had equated the *lex scripta* with the *lex non scripta.* Austin, on the other hand, had drawn a sharp distinction between custom and statutes, holding that unsanctioned custom was merely a rule of morality:

Now a merely *moral*, or merely customary rule, may take the quality of a legal rule in two ways: – it may be adopted by a sovereign or subordinate legislature, and turned into a law in the direct mode; or it may be taken as the ground of a judicial decision, which afterwards obtains as a precedent; and in this case it is converted into a law after the judicial fashion. In whichever of these ways it becomes a legal rule, the law into which it is turned emanates from the sovereign or subordinate legislature or judge, who transmutes the moral or imperfect rule into a legal or perfect one.[30]

Holmes then takes up the question that, since Hobbes, has connected sovereignty with the boundary of law: the definition of law as the command of the sovereign:

Passing to the sufficiency of Austin's definition for determining what sovereign commands are to be called law . . . the specific penalty or sanction which Austin seemed to tacitly assume as the final test, could not always be relied on.

The notion of duty involves something more than a tax on a certain course of conduct. A protective tariff on iron does not create a duty not to bring it into the country. The word imports the existence of an absolute wish on the part of the

[29] Holmes, "Book Notice," in *Formative Essays*, 91–92, and in 1 *Collected Works*, 294, 295.
[30] Austin, *Lectures*, vol. 2, p. 553.

power imposing it to bring about a certain course of conduct, and to prevent the contrary. A legal duty cannot be said to exist if the law intends to allow the person supposed to be subject to it an option at a certain price. The test of a legal duty is the absolute nature of the command.[31]

Here the criticism by Hale, of the dubious location by Hobbes of the sovereign power and its problematic identification, is given a still further elaboration. Addressing the overall character of the law itself, Holmes argued that various manifestations are not of the nature of commands. It is not just the difficulty of establishing a clear identification of the sovereign that undermines positivist analysis; Holmes now points to aspects of law that are empirically antithetical to the analytical project.

While Holmes's emphasis on the concept of duty reflects the centrality Austin gave to both duties and rights in his systematic account of jurisprudence, he had begun to challenge the project of any such logical arrangement. H. L. A. Hart would make a criticism similar to that of Holmes nearly a century later: "Legal rules defining the ways in which valid contracts or wills or marriages are made do not require persons to act in certain ways whether they wish to or not. Such laws do not impose duties or obligations."[32] But whereas Hart would restructure legal positivism by placing the concept of law within a new boundary consisting of primary and secondary rules and a Rule of Recognition,[33] Holmes would proceed in a direction that would lead him to abandon the quest for an analytical system for all law and to question whether any determinate boundary could be established at all.

Before addressing this, we should note the occasion for the short 1872 article in which Holmes reviewed an article by Frederick Pollock. The title of Pollock's piece was "Law and Command," and it was an extended criticism of the command definition:

It will be my aim to show that this definition, if exclusively insisted on, errs by elevating what is at most one characteristic of law into its essence, that contrariwise, by losing sight of what is really an essential constituent, it narrows the proper scope of law and tends to an unsatisfactory view of its operation, and that by putting forward the arbitrary and suppressing the necessary aspect of legislation it seriously obscures the organic relation of law to the community.[34]

[31] Holmes, "Book Notice," in *Formative Essays*, 92, and in 1 *Collected Works*, 296.
[32] Hart, *Concept of Law*, 27.
[33] Id., 77–96.
[34] Pollock, "Law and Command," *Law Magazine and Review*, new series, no. 3 (1872), 191.

Arguing against a strictly analytical approach, Pollock emphasized the continuing influence of custom on the law – the same point that custom is already at work independent of sovereign command with its own compulsory power. Pollock urged an alternative theory recognizing that law evolves, a point that Holmes would emphasize in the later phase of his own research:

> Law in the widest sense is a condition, or assemblage of conditions, under which the evolution of things proceeds, . . . and the determination of which is part of the collective consciousness of that society.[35]

In 1873 Holmes published "The Theory of Torts," in which the common law model was enhanced with the previously quoted (in chapter 3) depiction of decisions accumulating around opposing poles. Although apparently moving away from the notion of arranging or schematizing all law around the concept of duty, and toward a theory of liability more like that of Green's, he would again publish a revised "expository" table of duties (see the Appendix). The connection between the early and later articles has not been altogether clear.[36] If the direction of the early articles is difficult to fathom now, it presented difficulty when first written to no less a scholar than Frederick Pollock.

Holmes had been introduced to Pollock during a visit to England in the summer of 1874, and the two became lifelong friends. There is much evidence in their fifty-eight-year correspondence of common views about law. Yet Pollock in 1877 asked whether Holmes thought a codified arrangement was undesirable "*in itself*" (Pollock's emphasis) or only "that there is no advantage in doing it by legislative authority." He confessed, "I am not really in possession of your view" and suggested it be made plainer in a future article.[37] Holmes's reply, if any, has not survived, but his published writing had already begun to move beyond this issue. By 1876 he had satisfied himself that a comprehensive philosophical arrangement was impossible and had shifted his attention from right and duty to the evolving nature of legal concepts in general. Though he had already sent

35 Id., 205.

36 See Herget, *American Jurisprudence*, 41: "But Holmes' flirtation with the expository tradition was short-lived. He became convinced in the latter part of the 1870s that the pursuit of jurisprudence in this direction would lead to deadends, or worse. A perceptive biographer of Holmes, Mark DeWolfe Howe, suggests that Holmes perceived the mystical hand of German metaphysics behind the expository paradigm, and this ran counter to his empiricist and pragmatic leanings."

37 Pollock to Holmes, July 26, 1877, *Holmes-Pollock Letters*, vol. 1, pp. 7–8.

Pollock all the articles published through 1876, Pollock failed to see the shift, which is found in a close critique of Austin.

Austin had in his *Lectures on Jurisprudence* stressed the relation between the critical concepts of rights and duties to the status of persons affected by them:

> There are certain *rights* and *duties*, with certain *capacities* and *incapacities* to take rights and incur duties, by which *persons*, as subjects of law, are variously determined to certain *classes*.
>
> The rights, duties, capacities, or incapacities, which determine a given person to any of these classes, constitute a *condition* or *status* which the person occupies, or with which the person is invested.
>
> One and the same person may belong to *many* of the classes, or may occupy, or be invested with, *many* conditions or *status*. For example, one and the same person, at one and the same time, may be son, husband, father, guardian, advocate, or trader, member of a sovereign number, and minister of that sovereign body. And various *status*, or various conditions, may thus meet or unite in one and the same person, in infinitely different ways. (emphasis in original)[38]

To understand his focus, it is important to remember that Austin had in mind the creation of a table that would effectively and comprehensively display the arrangement of the essential classifications of the law. Austin's published lectures contained various tables, but none are dispositive in detail or vindicate his project.[39] Holmes, in an article published in 1872 that still experiments with the duty scheme, "The Arrangement of the Law: Privity," set forth his own table (see the Appendix) suggesting that the task is impossible. His claim is that, because rights and duties "may be succeeded to by another who cannot fill the situation" (on which the original status was based), the task of organizing the law around the concepts of right and duty is impossible. "It is obvious," notes Holmes of his own table, "that this scheme does not exhaust the whole body of the law."[40]

Holmes's second attempt to arrange the law under categories of duty in 1872 encountered a distinct threat to the prospective comprehensiveness of the overall project of logical arrangement. To see whether his system of duties could be applied across the board, Holmes, yet focusing on the methodological implications of Austin's *Lectures*, developed a chart

38 Austin, *Lectures*, vol. 2, p. 706.

39 Austin, *Lectures*, vol. 1, p. 79.

40 Holmes, "The Arrangement of the Law: Privity," in *Formative Essays*, 96, 97, and in 1 *Collected Works*, 304, 305; see Appendix.

dividing the law by reference to the classes of persons on whom burdens were imposed as well as to those in favor of whom they are imposed. Holmes's six divisions were "duties of all the world to the sovereign," "to all the world," and "to persons in particular situations," and also "duties of persons in particular situations to the sovereign," "to all the world," and "to other persons in particular situations." When he proceeded to test the arrangement, it became apparent that the conceptual scheme ascribed a primary importance to what Holmes called "the situation of fact" or the "definition of the situation."[41]

> The duties to persons in a particular situation begin with their beginning, and end with their ceasing, to fill that situation. When you describe the situation, that is, the facts, to which the duties are incident as a legal consequence, you describe the beginning and end of the duties as to a given individual.[42]

A problem arose in considering legal succession. If classifying duties depended on the situation of fact creating such duties, then succession of others to those duties should in theory depend on succession to the situation of fact. But while this might be true in the majority of actual instances, it was by no means true of all:

> Some continuing rights are incidents to a situation of fact, which can only be filled by the first person entitled to the rights in question. A certain individual and no other is the person with whom a certain contract was made, or to whom a certain franchise or monopoly was granted; yet the continuing rights incident to the situation of contractee or grantee may be succeeded to by another who cannot fill the situation, and the same is true of ownership as distinguished from bare possession.[43]

This led Holmes to ask how the law had made possible succession by others not party to the original situation and the ascription of the original duties to or for the successor. Another way of putting the question was to ask how the law had been able to continue using the absolute terminology of duties, which implied a relationship between the individual and the situation, in instances where the original defining relationship did not exist. His answer was that it had succeeded in doing so through the

[41] *Formative Essays*, 114, and 1 *Collected Works*, 316. See Appendix. These concerns apparently originate with Austin's lectures on the relation of rights to status; see *Lectures*, vol. 2, pp. 718–59.

[42] Holmes, "The Arrangement of the Law: Privity," in *Formative Essays*, 98, and in 1 *Collected Works*, 304.

[43] *Formative Essays*, 98, and 1 *Collected Works*, 304–6.

creation, at an earlier time, of a fictitious identification of the successor with the original person.

The aggregate of the ancestor's rights and duties or total *persona* sustained by him was easily separated from his natural personality, and regarded as sustained in turn by his heir, in view of the fact that it was originally his only as head of the family, and consisted of the aggregate of the family rights and duties. If we start here with succession to the entire situation of an individual in the community, on the assumption of his entire *persona*, we shall find the other and more usual examples of succession in privity easier to understand. . . . The first succession in privity was the universal succession of the Roman law; then privity in the succession to specific things occurs when the notion of ownership was originally subordinate to a personal relation with the right over a thing as an incident, then it is extended to successions generally.[44]

In the course of researching this issue, Holmes found the history of the relation between master and servant to be particularly illuminating of the phenomenon, although constituting a special case:

We have thus far dealt with clear cases of substitution where a successor assumes a *persona* to the exclusion of the individual who had sustained it until then. There is another class, where the new comer is introduced under a *persona* without excluding his predecessor.[45]

While a servant eventually assumed a legal status independent of his master, this was not originally true:

Under the early Roman law the wife, children, and servants of a citizen were his slaves. They could not be said to stand in a legal relation to him, for they had no standing before the law except as sustaining the *persona* of the family head.[46]

It was here that Holmes observed that the fictitious identification of servant and master might also elucidate the origin of the doctrine of vicarious liability:

It will be observed, moreover, that as the master's right to benefits acquired by his servants is general, and as he is liable for the latter's torts wherever a liability is imposed, the slave may be said to sustain his master's *persona* for purposes indefinite not only in number but in kind.[47]

44 *Formative Essays*, 100, and 1 *Collected Works*, 307. The early family had been identified with its head, and the heir's assumption of the family headship with its rights and obligations led to the fiction that a grantee assumed the grantor's identity in the same manner, eventually spreading to the law of chattels and other rights and obligations.

45 *Formative Essays*, 110, and 1 *Collected Works*, 313.

46 *Formative Essays*, 110, and 1 *Collected Works*, 314.

47 *Formative Essays*, 111, and 1 *Collected Works*, 314.

This amplification of the essay on privity was to become the connecting link to Holmes's next essay, "The Theory of Torts," published in July 1873. While in form it sought to set forth a new arrangement of duties implicit in the branches of tort law consistent with the overall duty scheme, the essay devotes much of its attention to bringing together the strands of earlier doubt and weaving the outline of a new theme – the growth of case law through the gradual articulation of standards of conduct. Through the master-servant example Holmes first confirmed the connection between his early demonstration of the lack of coextensivity of duty and sanction with its corollary that liability to a civil action does not import culpability. The continuity with the previous essay is revealed in Holmes's reference to it:

> I do not owe my butcher a duty not to buy his meat, because I must pay for it if I buy. And as liability to a civil action for the amount of the plaintiff's detriment is quite different from a punishment proportioned to the defendant's guilt, so, conversely, liability to such an action does not necessarily import culpability, as it has been thought to do by some of Bentham's followers. The liability of a master for his servant, which is one of the instances illustrative of this proposition, and which Austin tried to account for by the notion of remote inadvertence, has been explained heretofore.[48]

On securing this connection, Holmes set the stage for one final approach to classification based on duty, now by dividing torts into categories of duties in which the consciousness of the party liable is an element and those in which it is not. In the latter category Holmes distinguished between duties determined by acts or events exactly defined and those not exactly defined. Into the latter category he placed "negligence *latiori sensu*." The majority of the essay is devoted to explaining how negligence came to be put there, and it marks a turning point.

Negligence *latiori sensu* meant negligence in the broadest sense, covering all the cases in which it might be pleaded, not necessarily involving proof of a particular state of mind. In dividing torts into duties wherein consciousness was and was not an element, "negligence" cases in the broad sense at first posed a dilemma. It had become clear from the master-servant example that there were at least some within this group – master-servant cases having been treated as negligence by lawyers as well as by the Austinian school of jurisprudence – that did not involve any proof of the defendant's lack of care. What then was to be done with the entire group?

[48] Holmes, "A Theory of Torts," in *Formative Essays*, 117, and in 1 *Collected Works*, 326.

> Half-way between the two groups which have been indicated [requiring and not requiring consciousness] lie the great mass of cases in which negligence has become an essential averment, since Bentham's ideas have gotten into the air, and the abolition of the old forms of action has allowed pleaders to state their case according to their own views of its essential elements. What does this modern negligence mean? Austin, following his general notion that liability imports culpability, analyzed negligence as the state of the defendant's mind. This seems to us unsatisfactory; and to show why, we must begin at a little distance from the subject.[49]

Presenting the question in this manner led Holmes to examine the entire group from the standpoint of the development of legal precedents in negligence cases, and it brought him to the position that the entire group should be placed in the latter category, those not requiring consciousness of the defendant. Looking behind the practice of lawyers, and the assumptions of analytical jurisprudence that were based on it, the law had to be seen as a process of constant change:

> The growth of the law is very apt to take place in this way: Two widely different cases suggest a general distinction, which is a clear one when stated broadly. But as new cases cluster around the opposite poles, and begin to approach each other, the distinction becomes more difficult to trace; the determinations are made one way or the other on a very slight preponderance of feeling, rather than on articulate reason; and at last a mathematical line is arrived at by the contact of contrary decisions, which is so far arbitrary that it might equally well have been drawn a little further to the one side or the other.[50]

The critical observation was that the submission of a case to the jury for trial on the issue of negligence was, as a practical matter, simply part of the process of the evolution of explicit standards of conduct in areas where they had not been settled on by either statute or the growth of precedent. Hereupon Holmes cited the *Beadel v. Perry* decision, for the proposition of making explicit a rule emerging from prior cases by holding that "a building cannot be complained of unless its height exceeds the distance of its base from the base of the ancient windows."

Thus he concluded that negligence was not a hybrid class between conscious and unconscious tort but was governed generally by external standards of conduct. Having reached this generalization, Holmes was able to avoid an ambiguous place for negligence. This led to his threefold division of tort law into the categories of "duties of all to all," "persons in

[49] *Formative Essays*, 118, and 1 *Collected Works*, 327.
[50] *Formative Essays*, 119, and 1 *Collected Works*, 327.

particular situations to all," and conversely of "all to persons in particular situations." And, one final time, Holmes was to allude to the original focus that had launched his research:

> Indeed it is believed to be one of the evils of not having a comprehensive arrangement of the law that we lose the benefit of such generalizations as a philosophical system would naturally suggest, and cases are discussed only on the foot of the particular relation out of which they arise dramatically, but of which they are legally independent.[51]

This may be part of the answer Pollock might have found to his question concerning Holmes's purpose in exploring arrangement. Pollock asked the question four years after this essay was published, having received a copy of it along with the other papers that Holmes had sent from America. Pollock's puzzlement is in the movement of Holmes's theory. Holmes made no effort to illuminate it, or even to call attention to it in his ongoing correspondence with Pollock. Presumably, the alternative theory that lay at the end of his exploratory path was a sufficient legacy. The earlier essays read today almost like an intellectual diary, written for himself alone as he explored philosophical aspects of classification.

The full answer to Pollock's question is found in context. Professor James Herget, who in his recent study of American jurisprudence looks back on the quest for universal legal categories, which continued long after Austin and which he likens to the search for a "holy grail," astutely asks:

> Are these concepts empirical generalizations or are they inherent mental structures or inherent social structures? If they are none of these, as it turns out, then the alternative is that they are simply convenient word usages, technical terminology no different from that of the plumber or the cook, and, hence, having nothing to do with science.[52]

Early on in this quest, which continues today with analytical positivism, Holmes had tested the deeper level of significance to Austin's system of classification, concluding that a better path to philosophical understanding lay in history. By 1873, classification was still useful to him as an analytical tool, but was in the process of being downgraded to an ancillary role. While still engaged in testing the merit of organizing the law around duties, he would finally conclude, after exploring every aspect, that an

[51] *Formative Essays*, 125, and 1 *Collected Works*, 332.
[52] Herget, *American Jurisprudence*, 116.

analytical scheme, from a philosophical standpoint, was undesirable "in itself."[53]

An irony may be found in the fact that this last exercise in solving the problems of arrangement introduced a new principle that was to supplant the original undertaking and gain a powerful life of its own. The principle of evolution toward external standards of liability would tie together the leading strands of his criticism of analytical jurisprudence and lead to a new synthesis, emerging after he published again nearly three years later.

The early period of his scholarship, in which Holmes tried mightily to test various duty-based schemes of arrangement, could be reflected in his casual comment to Pollock in 1919 that "no general proposition is worth a damn." In part this refers to the false sense of universality that Austin had presumed and Holmes would deny. A further meaning would be added as Holmes moved toward a general theory of liability and judicial responsibility: general propositions do not decide concrete cases.

In an earlier letter from Pollock dated July 3, 1874, there appears a comment challenging Holmes's citation of *Beadel v. Perry* for the key principle that would occupy a central place in his thought: "As to the case which professed to lay down a mathematical rule about rights to light and air, I think you will find that notion has been exploded by several later decisions in the Appeal Court. (N.B. Our equity cases in courts of first impression are for various reasons to be used with great caution as authorities on questions of pure law.)"[54]

Holmes chose to ignore this relevant criticism. He would go on to use the same argument, still citing *Beadel*, in *The Common Law*.[55] The report

[53] That is to say, as providing self-explanatory universal categories. Herget provides an illuminating summary of the post-Austinian quest for universal categories in *American Jurisprudence*, 82–116. Much interest was inspired by the scheme advanced by Wesley N. Hohfeld in two famous articles published in 1913 and 1917. Ironically, Holmes's critique of Austin years before was barely recognized and never retrieved by critics of the project itself. As Herget notes, there is a remarkable tendency toward ignoring previous relevant scholarship throughout the history of American jurisprudence. Id., ix. While most critics of the project have mustered analytical reasoning against it, probing inconsistency and incoherence, Holmes is unique in arguing from the historical derivation of legal terms and language. One reason for ignoring Holmes's critique of fundamental universals may be his failure to elucidate the relevance of it to *The Common Law* and later writings.

[54] Pollock to Holmes, July 3, 1874, in *Holmes–Pollock Letters*, vol. 1, p. 4.

[55] Holmes, *The Common Law*, 128. However, Holmes now cites three additional cases, *City of London Brewery Co. v. Tennant*, L. R. 9 Ch. 212, 220; *Hackett v. Baiss*, L. R. 20 Eq. 494; and *Theed v. Debenham*, 2 Ch. D. 165.

of this decision, on which Holmes relied, is surprisingly bereft of support for the underlying proposition that English common law courts had moved with deliberate consideration toward a final consensual rule. He had nevertheless become convinced of the accuracy of his own unique vision of the emergence and growth of specific standards of liability.[56]

[56] In a note to Holmes's edition of *Kent's Commentaries*, written shortly after *Theory of Torts*, he enlarges as follows:

> Furthermore, when the facts are admitted, or capable of exact statement, it is simply a question of policy, not here discussed, whether the function of the jury shall not cease after a rule suggested by their finding has been applied to the satisfaction of the court, and whether that rule shall not be adopted thereafter by the court as a precedent in like cases, on the principle mentioned at the beginning of this note, and in accordance with the tendency of the law to work out exact lines through the region of uncertainty always to be found between two opposite extremes, by the contact of opposite decisions. As has been done, for instance, in the rule against perpetuities, or as to what is a reasonable time for presenting negotiable paper, as is happening with regard to sales, by successive decisions as to what are differences in kind, and what are only differences of quality; as has partially taken place with regard to ancient lights, where the former rule, that an infraction of a prescriptive right of light and air, to be illegal, must be substantial, a question of fact for the jury (Back v. Stacey, 2 C. & P. 465), is giving place to the exact formula that, in ordinary cases, the building complained of must not be higher than the distance of its base from the dominant windows. Beadel v. Perry, L. R. 2 Eq. 465.

James Kent, *Commentaries on American Law*, vol. 2 (Boston: Little Brown, 1873, O. W. Holmes, ed.), 561 n. 1; 2 *Collected Works*, 198.

6

The General Theory of Liability

> If, within the bounds which I have set myself, any one should feel inclined to reproach me for a want of greater detail, I can only quote the words of Lehuerou, "*Nous faisons une theorie et non un specilege.*"
>
> O. W. Holmes, conclusion of Preface to *The Common Law* (1881)

> Holmes must be one of the very few theorists of modern times who have argued for a general theory of liability embracing both the criminal and the civil law, and the contemporary English lawyer is certain to be deeply suspicious of his suggestion that "the general principles of criminal and civil liability are the same."
>
> P. S. Atiyah, 1981 Holmes Lecturer at Harvard Law School

These two brief remarks, by Holmes and the British legal scholar P. S. Atiyah, separated by a century, bracket the transit of what may be called Holmes's general theory, the historical hypothesis that he wedded to his common law conception after an absorbing period of work in the years 1873–76.

Holmes had joined George Shattuck and William Adams Munroe in a full-time Boston law practice, and pursued his research at night and on weekends. The intensity of effort, leading to eventual publication of *The Common Law* in 1881, is reflected in letters and later remarks.[1] By 1881 Holmes's intellectual path had gone from critique to construction – toward "*une theorie et non un specilege*" – but long before its hundredth anniversary the theory had fallen prey to the "deep suspicion" of which Professor Atiyah would speak in his 1981 Holmes Lecture.

[1] Howe, *Justice Oliver Wendell Holmes: The Proving Years*, 11–25, 96; White, *Justice Oliver Wendell Holmes*, 130.

The journal of his reading, which he kept from 1865 until the end of his life, reflects a new focus during the three years preceding his next publication in 1876–77, the two-part essay "Primitive Notions in Modern Law."[2] This hiatus in writing and redirection of attention mark a major turning point. One result was the gradual abandonment of the subject of legal classification with its illuminating critique of defects in Austin's scheme and approach, a topic that appears hardly at all in *The Common Law*. The book, on which scholarly attention has mainly been focused, is missing a substantial piece of the intellectual path toward its eventual theme, the historic shift from moral to external standards of liability.

The Common Law, following Holmes's prefatory comment, begins with material drawn from the essays on "Primitive Notions" and sets forth on its journey toward a general theory of liability. The only remaining evidence of the earlier interest in classification is the surprisingly perfunctory dismissal of any concern for "*specilege*" – an obscure French term for taxonomy – as if a good part of the past decade had not been obsessed with it.

The question posed by Pollock in 1877, and several related questions, are still relevant for anyone who has worked through the early essays: whether Holmes was concluding that a systematic arrangement was merely undesirable or actually impossible, and how then to explain and interpret legal concepts in a coherent and comprehensive way. Answers are to be found, some only by implication. But absent the context of such fundamental questions, *The Common Law*, preoccupied as it is with advancing a universal theory of liability, has been a baffling and vulnerable treatise.

Pollock should be recognized as more than a foil. Both he and Holmes were questioning premises of analytical jurisprudence. Questions Pollock had raised in "Law and Command," the 1872 article in *Law Magazine and Review*, prompted Holmes to stake his own claim by publishing the notes to his course in jurisprudence.[3] He would pursue them into new territory, with an attitude perhaps less collegial than may appear from their correspondence. Holmes has paid for the failure to explain himself fully with a century of misreading. David Rosenberg has shown how easily scholars have been misled regarding a key point in *The Common Law* – his analysis of liability for personal injury.[4]

2 Little, "The Early Reading of Justice Oliver Wendell Holmes," 186–91.

3 See chapter 5, n. 34.

4 Rosenberg, *Hidden Holmes*, 8–10, 163–69. Rosenberg finds it almost inexplicable that so many scholars have strained against Holmes's plain language or ignored a substantial part

The three 1981 Centennial Holmes lecturers, Atiyah, Benjamin Kaplan, and Jan Vetter, declined to counter what Vetter referred to as "the marked tendency, which has gained strength over the last generation, to revise sharply, if not to reverse, the formerly dominant appraisal of Holmes."[5] If indeed the early work on Austin is an important part of his legacy, he has himself to blame for burying it, or at least putting it out of sight, with the offhand quote from Julien Marie Lehuerou, a French historian, dismissing the import of analytical classification.[6]

With the turn to history there is evidence of an effort to confirm the rejection of classification and reconceptualize the nature of legal classes and concepts. The renewed drive of writing after 1876 reveals a zest for confirming the historical process that trumps the search for innate relationships, a gradual process that may offer a better clue to the fundamental nature of concepts, further undermining any claim that might be made for the permanence of any conceptual system. With this agnostic perception arrives a constructive one that finally overwhelms it, the extension of the historical insight into a general theory of liability, the theme that takes over *The Common Law* and that has given rise to such broad disapproval. A good part of that derives from confusion in interpreting the term "moral"

of his writing to find a "lax negligence standard" providing nascent American industry with a "covert subsidy," characteristic of a putative nineteenth-century trend. Id., 8. This may well be connected with the widespread failure to find a connection between the earlier focus on classification and the later theory of external standards. Without the purpose of framing an alternative to Austin's categories, scholars have looked for other motives such as political or economic preference.

5 Jan Vetter, "The Evolution of Holmes: Holmes and Evolution," in *Holmes and the Common Law: A Century Later*, occasional pamphlet no. 10 (Cambridge, Mass.: Harvard Law School, 1983), 76.

6 G. Edward White, in *Justice Oliver Wendell Holmes*, asks perspicuously whether Holmes's alteration of his scholarly perspective was a "fully conscious one," noting that his later accounts were usually varnished and patently misleading, such as the letter to Harold Laski in 1922:

> You ask me what started my book. Of course I can't answer for unconscious elements. I don't think Maine had anything to do with it except feed the philosophic passion. I think the movement came from within – from the passionate demand that what sounded so arbitrary in Blackstone, for instance, should give some reasonable meaning – that the law should be proved, if it could be, to be worthy of the interest of an intelligent man. . . . I don't think of any special book that put me on the track – though the works that I cited such as Lehuerou helped. I rooted around and made notes until the theory gradually emerged. (Holmes to Laski, June 1, 1922, in *Holmes-Laski Letters*, vol. 1, pp. 429–30)

in Holmes's hypothesis of an evolution from moral to external standards. Where does this usage come from?

Holmes's journal shows a burgeoning interest in historical studies of English, French, German, and Roman law, as well as studies in the emergent discipline of cultural anthropology. The first part of the essay, appearing in April 1876, indicates that the early law of surrender had reached the center of his attention. This essay concentrates on documenting the influence of primitive notions of vengeance on strict and vicarious liability as well as the limitation of liability in admiralty law. In a passage near the beginning, Holmes relates how, in developing his previous perspective in "The Theory of Torts," his interest became focused on the primitive origins of modern standards of liability. This bears careful reading, as it witnesses elation at finding an interpretation of history that he believes "has not been attempted before" and (a propos the subject of judicial restraint) the root of his later attitude toward "policy" in law:

> To lay the foundation for the discussion to which we have referred [the essay on torts] we were led to glance incidentally at the historical origin of liability in some cases which Austin, following the jurists of the mature period of Roman law, had interpreted on grounds of culpability; and to point out that it sprung from the much more primitive notion, that liability attached directly to the thing doing the damage. This suggestion will be found to have occurred to earlier writers who will be quoted. But we shall endeavor in this article to explain that primitive notion more at length, to show its influence on the body of modern law, and to trace the development from it of a large number of doctrines which in their actual form seem most remote from each other or from any common source; a task which we believe has not been attempted before. If we are successful, it will be found that the various considerations of *policy* [emphasis added] which are not infrequently supposed to have established these doctrines, have, in fact, been invented at a later period to account for what was already there, – a process familiar to all students of legal history.[7]

It should be remembered that Holmes's use of the master-servant example entered the essay on torts to buttress the corollary to the proposition that duty and legal sanctions are not coextensive, first demonstrated in the lectures at Harvard College summarized in July 1872. The corollary was that legal liability is not coextensive with culpability, an idea that had emerged as a working assumption through the work on tort law. In a footnote to the essay on torts we find evidence of Holmes glancing

[7] Holmes, "Primitive Notions in Modern Law," in *Formative Essays*, 129, 130, and in 3 *Collected Works*, 4–5.

"incidentally" at the origin of liability in the primitive notion that it "somehow attached upon the thing doing the harm." Yet the same footnote refers back to Holmes's use, in the essay preceding, of the master-servant example to elucidate the incompleteness of the duty scheme when applied to succession. The footnote in the essay on torts thus bears witness to the acquisition of a key piece in the puzzle from which he would assemble an evolutionary legal philosophy.[8]

It was not until the first part of "Primitive Notions" that this piece assumed its preeminent place. There, as announced in the passage just cited, Holmes ascribed to the primitive desire for vengeance a formative influence on a number of doctrines, including strict and vicarious liability, as well as to the limitation of liability in the law of admiralty. The same examples were to be prominent in *The Common Law.* From Holmes's reading between 1873 and 1876 was drawn the original documentation for this proposition. Here is a major clue to his meaning of "moral": vengeance is the primitive "moral" standard of liability, later replaced by externality, or the prevailing community standard of prudent conduct under the relevant circumstances.

Holmes traced various modern forms of liability back to a common foundation in ancient systems of law – principally drawing on early Greek, Roman, German, and Anglo-Saxon sources, with a variety of others from the Old Testament to recent anthropological studies of primitive tribes. All demonstrated an interest in "getting at" the offending instrumentality, whether person, animal, or object, as in Exodus: "If an ox gore a man or a woman that they die, then the ox shall surely be stoned, and his flesh shall not be eaten; but the owner of the ox shall be quit."[9] He noted that in Plato if a slave caused harm, he was to be given up to the injured person if the owner failed to remedy the mischief himself. In early German and English law, even in the customs of primitive tribes, the injured party or his relatives might seek redress against the offending animal or thing.

> The rude Kukis of Southern Asia were very scrupulous in carrying out their simple vengeance, life for life; if a tiger killed a Kuki, his family was in disgrace till they retaliated by killing and eating this tiger, or another; but further, if a man was killed by a fall from a tree, his relatives would take their revenge by cutting the tree down, and scattering it in chips.[10]

[8] Holmes, "The Theory of Torts," in *Formative Essays,* 117 n. 1, and in 1 *Collected Works,* 326 n. 1.

[9] Holmes, "Primitive Notions in Modern Law," in *Formative Essays,* 134, and in 3 *Collected Works,* 7.

[10] *Formative Essays,* 136; 3 *Collected Works,* 9.

Thus if early law were to intervene, it was through a cause of action against the owner, as the instrumentality was not subject to legal process. The only alternative to surrender lay in the payment of "composition," the value of the offending thing. Hence the early action was not based on the fault of the owner. When payment of money originated as an alternative to surrender, liability of the master or owner for the acts of his servant or animal had been created not from the logic of fault later ascribed to them but from these early practices to effect revenge. So also the limitation of liability to the value of the offending instrumentality, insofar as it remained in the law of admiralty after damages had otherwise assumed a relation to harm, is originally explained by ancient history, not a post hoc rationale.

Neither installment of the new essay carries any update of Holmes's duty scheme of classification, which has now lost its prominent focus. What appears to account for this change of emphasis, and for the renewed drive of his writing that would culminate in *The Common Law*, is the attitude that there is an overriding lesson to be learned from the primitive origins of modern standards of liability greater than the analytical doubts Holmes had developed regarding analytical classification. This lesson is that the framework of modern law, notwithstanding gradual accommodation of considerations of public policy, is generated from origins that must by its own standards be considered nonlogical.

Thus emerged a further argument for the elevation of experience over abstract reason, articulated two centuries earlier by Hale. Like Hale, who affirmed this insight in obscurity against the thesis of Thomas Hobbes, Holmes reaffirmed it in the teeth of the Austinian project. Despite the fanfare he gave it in 1876, its relation to Austin's philosophy would recede virtually out of sight as he moved toward the more distinctive destination of his grand theory in *The Common Law*.

A further and parallel move can be seen in the second part of the essay, which begins with the following statement of purpose: "The object of the following investigation is to prove the historical truth of a general result, arrived at analytically in the pages of this *Review* five years ago."[11] The result to which Holmes alludes is the explanation he developed to account for the manner in which the law had been able to accomplish the passage of special rights to successors to whom the original situation of fact did not apply:

[11] Holmes, "Primitive Notions in Modern Law. No. II," in *Formative Essays*, 147, and in 3 *Collected Works*, 21.

> How does this happen? How can a man who has not used a way for twenty years acquire a right by prescription? How can a man sue or be sued on a contract to which he was not a party? The article referred to [the October 1872 essay on privity] furnished further examples, and the answer there given was that in such cases there is a fictitious identification of distinct persons for the purpose of transferring or completing the right. We have now to consider what light history will throw on the same question.[12]

Hereupon Holmes took pains to document the earlier point from Roman, German, and early English sources, reaching the conclusion that "the question propounded at the beginning of this article has now been answered by history in a way which confirms the results of analysis."[13] This passage directly addresses Dicey's confusion in 1882 over the relation of historical and analytical method. Dicey had read *The Common Law* as equivocating between the two, while Holmes enlisted both in reconstructing common law theory. There is no evidence that Holmes ever responded to him. Clearly, he assumed that his contribution was amply displayed in the final treatise.

Holmes now went further, tracing the intrusion of nonlogical elements into the law of succession. Identification of the successor with the grantor could not explain the emergence in the law of the notion that a given right could become associated with the object of possession itself.

> But, although it would be more symmetrical if the above analysis exhausted the subject, another case will show that something still remains to be accounted for. It has been stated above, that a disseisor would not be allowed to join the time of his disseisee to his own. If the change of hands is wrongful, there is no room for the analogy just explained. But, suppose a right of way had been already acquired before the disseisin, how would it be then? Would the disseisor have an action against a person, other than the rightful owner of the dominant estate, for obstructing the way? Very little authority has been found in the books of the common law; but it is believed that such an action would lie.[14]

The reason that had come to be given for the existence of such an action was that the easement ran with the land. The attribution of possessory rights and duties to inanimate objects could only be a development parallel to the influence of the law of surrender on the development of tort liability, indicating again the proclivity of the law to permit the "language of personification," drawn from primitive notions, to "cause confusion." This example gave still greater strength to Holmes's historical argument

[12] Id.

[13] *Formative Essays*, 159; 3 *Collected Works*, 30.

[14] *Formative Essays*, 159–60; 3 *Collected Works*, 30.

against any attempt to comprehend the law as a logical system: "How comes it, then, that one who neither has possession in fact nor title, is so far favored? The answer is to be found not in reasoning, but in a failure to reason."[15]

In tracing these multiple historical connections to seal the doom of philosophical classification, the two-part essay on primitive notions culminated a period in Holmes's research that might be characterized as explorative, while the later writings mainly involve extension and exposition. After 1876 occurred a synthesis within the overall progression, consolidating doubts about Austin's static system into the evolutionary theory of liability.

This grand theory has preoccupied critics, and is so commonly mistrusted that its origins are ignored. The terminology, suggesting an inevitable shift from "moral" to "external" standards, leads to contemporary confusion. One aspect is the association of his final position with Austin's strict separation of law and morals. The fact that Holmes took no pains to disclaim that association after early reviews of *The Common Law* suggests that it was not on his agenda openly to confront the formidable Hobbesian tradition. The better explanation is what I have cautiously called a proto-Hegelian move – recasting the Hobbesian ethos as a product of history – although in detail it was quite unlike Hegel. It was rooted not in *Zeitgeist* or the innate force of ideas but in a maturation of the process of resolving concrete and particular conflicts. Compared with Hobbes, Holmes's theory provided a more naturalistic historical foundation for the objective rule of law, without which a coherent and robust order was inconceivable.[16]

Hobbes and Austin had separated law from morals for at least one major reason sympathetic to Holmes: the removal of confusion. Yet the nature of the confusion was quite different. We have seen that Hobbes was troubled by individual moral notions at odds with interests of the state ("all violence proceed[s] from controversies that arise between men concerning *meum* and *tuum*, right and wrong, good and bad, and the like"), and Austin focused on definitional precision in the interest of utilitarian reform ("In consequence of the frequent coincidence of positive law and morality, and of positive law and the law of God, the true nature and

15 *Formative Essays*, 160; 3 *Collected Works*, 30.

16 Thus, such remarks as "If a man is on a plank in the deep sea which will only float one, and a stranger lays hold of it, he will thrust him off if he can. When the state finds itself in a similar position, it does the same thing." *The Common Law*, 38.

fountain of positive law is often absurdly mistaken by writers upon jurisprudence"). For Holmes the problem lay in misreading the contemporary import of legal terms that had been passed down through generations, carrying moral nuances that were no longer – if they ever truly had been – in effect. This did not, as with Hobbes and Austin, draw an inviolable barrier separating contemporary ethical standards of conduct from law.

Such would be made plain in the final synthesis leading directly into *The Common Law.* Holmes returned in 1880 to the notion of successive approximation, and described more distinctly its historic role in the generation of legal doctrine. This early insight, having first appeared with Mansfield's description of the "business man suddenly appointed judge," had been irreconcilable from the outset with positivist legal analysis. Now Holmes placed it at the center of his theory of liability, the evolution toward "objective standards."

By 1880, when the last of the preliminary essays, "Trespass and Negligence," was published, Holmes had returned to the problem of defining the actual grounds on which judges and juries act in tort cases. Traditional analysis, he had noted in 1873, offered but two alternatives. It was either because, as Austin contended, the harm caused was based on the fault of the defendant or it must be the opposing view, that the defendant would be held strictly liable for any harm regardless of fault ("if the act was voluntary, it is totally immaterial that the detriment which followed from it was neither intended nor due to the negligence of the actor").[17]

Holmes reaffirmed his earlier conclusion that this traditional dichotomy was a false one. Now he elaborated a third alternative: negligence "does not mean the actual state of the defendant's mind, but a failure to act as a prudent man of average intelligence would have done." The test of liability was the measure of foresight. If the average reasonable man could or should have foreseen the consequences of the act, then the defendant would be held liable. Austin's view was that "the guilt or innocence of a given actor, depends upon the state of his consciousness, with regard to those consequences, in the given instance or case."[18] This

[17] Holmes, "Trespass and Negligence," in *Formative Essays*, 226, and in 3 *Collected Works*, 76.

[18] 1 *Lectures*, 440. Austin uses the terms "guilt" and "innocence" even in discussing liability for negligence. He confesses some confusion: "Now a state of mind between consciousness and unconsciousness – between intention on the one side and negligence on the other – seems to be impossible. The party thinks, or the party does *not* think, of the act or consequence. If he think of it, he *intends*. If he do not think of it, he is *negligent* or

struck Holmes as wrong because no evidence of the defendant's mind appeared to be requisite. The opposing view, that "a man acts at his peril," was equally wrong because "if the intervening events are of such a kind that no foresight could have been expected to look out for them, the defendant is not to blame for having failed to do so, and therefore his act was innocent."[19]

This is crucial, as it is repeated almost verbatim in *The Common Law* and has been at the center of much later criticism. Its emergence in Holmes's writing suggests strongly that it does not derive from an attitude drawn from personal preference or social bias regarding the distribution of costs arising in personal injury cases. Rather, we find two old themes, successive approximation and the problems of logical classification, joined in a new mission. Austin's classification project, which had led to the assumption that negligence liability must be described as either fault or no-fault, a form of *x* or *not-x*, was displaced first by Holmes's tentative placement in his own arrangement of legal duties,[20] and ultimately by the observation that the term "negligence" referred to a "cause of action," the legal term signifying a form or class of *inquiry*. The legal process had as yet *no answer* to the question of liability in an original case, and it would have to seek one through a process of case-specific inquiry, leading to eventual "specification."

The exposition of this process in *The Common Law* has understandably thrown many readers off the trail. Holmes refers to negligence as *a form of not-x*, that is to say, as a unique form of liability without fault, or strict liability. What he clearly means is that the specific circumstances of a new case brought to the courts under the rubric of negligence – say, a trolley operated in a certain manner on a busy thoroughfare – are bound to be repeated with slight enough variations to the point where jury verdicts eventually find a line where the pattern of trolley operation is deemed unsafe enough to fail the "prudent man" standard.[21] Thereafter, a rule

heedless." Yet he concludes that "Intention is always separated from Negligence, Heedlessness, or Rashness, by a precise line of demarcation. The state of the party's mind is always *determined*, although it may be difficult (judging from his conduct) to ascertain the state of his mind." Id., 441–44.

19 Holmes, "Trespass and Negligence," in *Formative Essays*, 234, and in 3 *Collected Works*, 82.

20 Discussed in "The Theory of Torts," which included the final table of legal duties. See Appendix.

21 A possible origin of the "prudent man," noted in Holmes's reading diary for 1865–66, is William Jones, *An Essay on the Law of Bailments* (London: J. Nichols, 1781), 5–6.

may be laid down by the courts, defining precisely which conduct will thenceforth create liability "as a matter of law" – without regard to the state of the defendant's mind. Once specified, the rule of liability becomes "strict" in that conditional sense.

While it is understandable to attribute a Hobbesian character to his emphasis on the constant seeking of an external standard, it further establishes Holmes's kinship with traditional or "classical" common law theory. It connects law deeply with custom and practice; indeed, it finds a new way to do so, opening a continuing – cumulative though piecemeal – window on custom as reflected in jury determinations. The interests of the sovereign state benefit from the fact that community-derived standards are becoming externalized and objectified, though in Holmes's account they were the product in the first instance of a localized and basically decentralized process.

Holmes had tried to show, with respect to negligence, that cases were submitted for individual consideration only where a clear rule did not exist, that the general rules were applied equally without regard to state of mind, and that even the individual jury determination was made without any need for subjective evidence of the thoughts of the party accused but rather by comparison of his or her conduct to the hypothetical "prudent man." In close cases the issue would revolve around the degree to which common sense would suggest that injury was likely under the circumstances – the foreseeability of harm. Simply stated, the point was that legal negligence, despite what Holmes considered the "moral" overtone of the term, comprised a process developing a set of categories of action rather than abstract logic. Defendants would be held to a community-wide norm, and liability for injury occasioned to others would be determined by apparent circumstances – by the visible environment of conduct rather than the subjective consciousness of the actor.

This generalization, focusing as it did on the requisite facts surrounding a cause of action in a major area of law, would soon appear applicable across the board, even to criminal and contract law. All forms of litigation, it would seem, are initiated by general terms that proceed toward specification in particular cases. This is the nature of the courtroom process, carrying many disputes into trial and a portion of them on to appeal, where specific questions of liability must be abstracted. In moving toward this thesis, Holmes was able to abandon his 1873 category of torts "in which the Consciousness of the Party liable is an element" – such as "fraud" or "maliciously causing breach of contract" – as the same practical observation could be applied to the legal usage of "malice" and "fraud."

As a general observation it fitted Holmes's long-held doubt concerning the uncertainty of fundamental legal concepts implying moral absolutes, such as rights and duties, and tied his earlier analytical criticism with the evolutionary theme into a uniform perspective.

As in his earlier treatment of the concept of duty, the argument applied strict scrutiny to the moral overtones of legal terminology. The word "malice" in ordinary language, he noted while extending the argument to criminal law, includes something more than mere intentionality. It means "not only that a wish for the harmful effect is the motive, but also that the harm is wished for its own sake."[22] But in contemporary practice intention alone was enough to constitute legal malice, and intention itself he demonstrated to be reducible to sheer foreseeability of the likely consequences of the act, not judged by any attempt to look inside the mind of the individual offender. This was arguable even in criminal prosecutions where one would most expect to find concern with the subjective state of mind. "The test of foresight is not what this very criminal foresaw, but what a man of reasonable prudence would have foreseen." An example made this clear:

> For instance, if a workman on a house-top at mid-day knows that the space below him is a street in a great city, he knows facts from which a man of common understanding would infer that there were people passing below. He is therefore bound to draw that inference, or, in other words, is chargeable with knowledge of that fact also, whether he draws the inference or not. If then, he throws down a heavy beam into the street, he does an act which is likely to cause death, or grievous bodily harm, and he is dealt with as if he foresaw it, whether he does so in fact or not. If a death is caused by the act, he is guilty of murder. But if the workman has reasonable cause to believe that the space below is a private yard from which every one is excluded, and which is used as a rubbish-heap, his act is not blameworthy, and the homicide is a mere misadventure.[23]

Once having demonstrated the role of external standards even in criminal and tort rules that seemed specifically to impose an element of intent,[24] and adding for the Lowell Lectures an argument extending objective standards to contract, Holmes's evolutionary philosophy was firmly in place.[25]

[22] Holmes, *The Common Law*, 44.

[23] Id., 55–56.

[24] See Introduction to *Formative Essays*, 45–6.

[25] For a critical view of Holmes's extension of the external standard of liability into the criiminal law, see Atiyah, "The Legacy of Holmes Through English Eyes," in *Holmes and the Common Law: A Century Later*, 27–73.

Unlike the analytical jurisprudence of John Austin, Holmes's final perspective saw law as neither a closed nor logical system. Nor was it an essentially static formulation: it was process-oriented, and stressed three elements. First, that legal analysis must be guided by the fact of historical development:

> What has been said will explain the failure of all theories which consider the law only from its formal side, whether they attempt to deduce the *corpus* from *a priori* postulates, or fall into the humbler error of supposing the science of law to reside in the *elegantia juris*, or logical cohesion of part with part. The truth is, that law hitherto has been, and it would seem by the necessity of its being is always approaching and never reaching consistency.[26]

Second, that modern rules of liability spring from vengeance, which he sees as a "moral basis":

> My aim and purpose have been to show that the various forms of liability known to modern law spring from the common ground of revenge. In the sphere of contract the fact will hardly be material outside the cases which have been stated in this Lecture. But in the criminal law and the laws of torts it is of the first importance. It shows that they have started from a moral basis, from the thought that some one was to blame.[27]

And third, that this "moral basis" has gradually been supplanted by external standards:

> While the terminology of morals is still retained, and while the law does still and always, in a certain sense, measure legal liability by moral standards, it nevertheless, by the very necessity of its nature, is continuously transmuting those moral standards into external ones, from which the actual guilt of the party concerned is wholly eliminated.[28]

This, in brief, summarizes Holmes's path through the year 1880, at the eve of delivery of the Lowell Lectures that would become *The Common Law.* The early chronology provides a context for understanding different aspects of the overall theory, a relation that is not at all clear from his later exposition. It demonstrates the connection between the earlier focus on classification and the later interest in historical sources. It casts light on the controversial move whereby the theory was extended beyond

[26] Holmes, "Common Carriers and the Common Law," in *Formative Essays*, 159, and in 3 *Collected Works*, 75–6; repeated in *The Common Law*, 32.

[27] *The Common Law*, 33.

[28] Id.

negligence into criminal and contract law. It demonstrates a strong connection between his theory of liability and mode of textual interpretation, emphasizing "objective" meaning over subjective intent.[29] Indeed, it resolves much of the subsequent dissatisfaction with *The Common Law*, considered by itself.

On the occasion of the centennial of *The Common Law*, Massachusetts Supreme Judicial Court Justice Benjamin Kaplan, who followed Holmes's footsteps from Harvard law faculty (where he taught this writer) to the high court of Massachusetts, found the theory unpersuasive and, from the podium of the annual Holmes Lectures, ruled it largely irrelevant to the work of modern state courts.[30] The second lecturer, P. S. Atiyah, an authority on English common law, said of the evolutionary hypothesis, "It is not wholly clear whether Holmes regarded this as a contingent historical fact or as some kind of necessary truth, but whichever alternative is taken, this position has few defenders today."[31]

In the following decade, Morton Horwitz found *The Common Law* "obscure and inaccessible in addition to being rarely read," and Holmes biographer G. Edward White, reflecting the criticism of Albert Venn Dicey in his 1882 review, found it to suffer from "lack of thematic and methodological consistency," noting that "its central theory is elusive and cryptically rendered."[32] Patrick J. Kelley, in his painstaking 1992 study of Holmes's Massachusetts decisions, saw Holmes urging a quirky hypothesis on his colleagues with mixed success, and stretching to reach unsatisfactory results in order to prove the overall principle.[33]

There is some corroboration to all these criticisms. Rather than addressing their grounds in detail, I have offered an alternative reading that is, I suggest, internally consistent and manifestly relevant to the history of legal philosophy and to the issues before us today.[34]

[29] Holmes, "Legal Interpretation," in *Collected Legal Papers*, 203.

[30] Benjamin Kaplan, "Encounters with O. W. Holmes, Jr.," in *Holmes and The Common Law: A Century Later*, 16–18.

[31] Atiyah, "The Legacy of Holmes through English Eyes," 30.

[32] White, *Justice Oliver Wendell Holmes*, 179, 195.

[33] See Kelley, "Holmes on the Supreme Judicial Court: The Theorist as Judge," in *The History of the Law in Massachusetts: The Supreme Judicial Court 1692–1992*, ed. Russell K. Osgoode (Boston: Supreme Judicial Court Historical Society, 1992), 283–84, 298–99, 302.

[34] The aspect of his formulation that has undergone most criticism is not fatal to the entire conception. The extension of Holmes's insistence on external standards is not integral

The pattern of research as a whole conveys a distinctive view of the nature of law and civil society. The underlying conception of society is closer to Hobbes than the utilitarianism of Austin and Bentham. It reflects Holmes's exposure to the struggle of Darwinian evolution, much discussed in the Metaphysical Club and confirmed in some respects by the American Civil War, both of which reinforced doubts concerning the prospects for law-based liberal or utilitarian reform.[35]

to the theory of successive approximation nor to the notion of conflicts resolved through line drawing in case-specific decisions.

Nevertheless, the process of specification, by which objective rules are eventually settled in a given class of controversy, appeared doubtful to Benjamin Kaplan:

> Holmes . . . was mistaken in thinking that, after repeated jury verdicts on given fact situations, judges would feel free to hold as a matter of law that there was or was not negligence. That was a false dream of hope. For example, the "stop, look, and listen" rule for the grade crossing situation, laid down by Holmes in 1927, was in substance annulled by an opinion by Cardozo in 1934. Facts have an irreducible fluidity. (Kaplan, "Encounters With O. W. Holmes, Jr." at 5)

In fairness to Holmes, I do not think he would have disagreed about the "fluidity of facts," especially if that implies that economic or technological circumstances, and even community standards of prudence, might change so as to make earlier judicial formulations obsolete. Kaplan does not consider Holmes's notion of specification in the larger context of transgenerational community inquiry through the common law.

35 An account of the influences leading Holmes toward an evolutionary theory is that of Philip P. Wiener in *Evolution and the Founders of Pragmatism*. Wiener notes, "The linkage of Holmes with the Metaphysical Club lies in the fact that Wright's arguments for the ethical neutrality of science and evolution appear in scarcely modified form in Holmes's separation of ethical ideals from the science of law, which uses only external standards of social expediency and the public force." Id. at 174. This is supported by Holmes's own favorable comments about Wright in later correspondence. Sheldon Novick, one of Holmes's biographers and editor of Holmes's *Collected Works*, has suggested the appeal of a rationalist morality that Holmes shared with other Victorian intellectuals, such as Leslie Stephen: the call to discover a scientific replacement for religion. In a 1919 letter to Morris R. Cohen, Holmes (responding to a query about whether Voltaire had influenced his skepticism) emphasized the importance of science in his thinking:

> My father was brought up scientifically – i.e. he studied medicine in France – and I was not. Yet there was with him as with the rest of his generation a certain softness of attitude toward the interstitial miracle – the phenomenon without phenomenal antecedents, that I did not feel. The Origin of Species I think came out while I was in college – H. Spencer had announced his intention to put the universe into our pockets – I hadn't read either of them to be sure, but as I say it was in the air. . . .

This helps to account for Holmes's ultimate choice of an evolutionary theory and perhaps also his need to fortify it with some concept of a uniform natural progression toward a single general principle, the external result. The intellectual climate a century later became inimical to such sweeping theorizing, and the multiform growth of the law does not lend supporting evidence to a monolithic explanation. See Holmes to Cohen,

Despite his exposure to social conflict, he was not inclined, given the weight of historical evidence in the working of the law, to join Hobbes or Austin in building a centralized view of law or of the state. He looked backward to common law as the archetypal decentralized model, modified in the spirit of public inquiry, parallel to the Peircean model of scientific inquiry and problem solving, balanced with a comprehensibility and predictability derived from the spread of external standards. It is a historically based approach to the questions posed by analytical theory. Holmes drew his historical inspiration from Henry Maine and Frederick Maitland, as well as from his friend Frederick Pollock.[36]

Unlike Hobbes, Holmes's conception does not originate from a paradigm of man in the state of nature but draws on the operation of law in resolving conflict. It distinguishes Holmes in this respect as an empirical legal, rather than an abstract political, theorist. Both writers concur on the prevalence of conflict, but Holmes's depiction is rooted in intensive legal research, and he provides a distinctly un-Hobbesian response, more accepting of an implicit and ongoing set of diverse conflicts and skeptical of an overriding assumption of the *Leviathan*: that public safety and civil society turn on an *analytical* order imposed by the sovereign.

Holmes's order is radically opposed to the extreme forms of centralization conceptualized and experienced in the twentieth century. It is decentralized, supple, and unfinished; it is constantly under construction and revision.[37] This attitude understandably sets up a tension between the opposing demands of freedom and order, of local and central – a tension that is, after all, implicit in the United States Constitution. The centralizing pull of this tension is evident in Holmes's emphasis on objective standards and in his deference to legislation and "sovereign prerogative."[38] In the other direction, the pull of freedom is implicit in the openness to developing and changing standards of conduct, even in the interpretation of legislation, and (as will become evident) in his constitutional restraint. This background underlies what Richard A. Posner has identified as a tension between flexibility and strictness in Holmes's approach to interpretation as a judge.[39]

February 5, 1919, in F. S. Cohen, ed., "The Holmes-Cohen Correspondence," 10 *Journal of the History of Ideas* 14–15 (1948).

[36] See Holmes to Pollock, March 4, 1888, in vol. 1, *Holmes-Pollock Letters*, 30–31.

[37] Holmes, "Common Carriers and the Common Law," in *Formative Essays*, 222–23, and in 3 *Collected Works*, 75–6.

[38] Holmes, *The Common Law*, 38.

[39] Posner, Introduction to *The Essential Holmes*, xii.

In contrast, the order of John Austin found its origins in three sources: the enclosed, analytic, command vision of law proposed by Hobbes, Bentham's vision of utilitarian reform through legal command and sanction, and (not least) the quest for a systematic understanding of law as a universal phenomenon. Like Holmes, Austin was driven by powerful personal ambition, fed by his association with preeminent intellectuals. He saw himself as the pioneer of a new scientific jurisprudence. In the spirit of his time, he adopted political economy as a model, recognized as the first successful model of social science, and his driving ambition was to establish jurisprudence as a second such science, exhibiting similar scientific features.[40]

Holmes too had been impressed as an undergraduate with the expansion of science, nurtured by his years at Harvard and extensive reading after the Civil War,[41] but his eventual picture of science was different, focusing less on a speculative or Aristotelian model and more (like Wright and Peirce) on the process of communal inquiry.[42]

The analytical positivism of Hobbes, Austin, and Hart has had surprising vitality, still remaining (as Ronald Dworkin now calls it) the "ruling theory of law." Its bias against history is deep. Modern positivism and its contemporary critics have been intent on finding essential truths in the abstract debate over the relation of law and morals.

H. L. A. Hart's separation of law and morals, inherited from Austin, presumed that there are features of the two that are permanent, and thus permanently distinguishable. Insofar as legal positivism has become "merely a series of elaborations, emendations, and clarifications of H. L. A. Hart's work,"[43] Holmes is clearly not a legal positivist in the contemporary sense, though if positivism were given a broader definition, as an effort to establish a study of law's nature (as Brian Bix puts it)

[40] W. L. Morison, *John Austin* (Stanford, Calif.: Stanford University Press, 1982), 1: "John Austin believed that the first 'moral' (now, it would be called social) science to be established was political economy, as expounded particularly by David Ricardo and epitomized by James Mill. It was Austin's own ambition to establish a second such science, jurisprudence, exhibiting the scientific features which he admired in political economy. These features were, firstly, its presentation of its subject matter as patterns of observed mental and physical events. It was an empirical science. Secondly, it presented its patterns of events by reference to the universal features which all events have: their logical features as these are discerned by the traditional logic associated with Aristotle. It was a logically systematic science."

[41] See Howe, *The Shaping Years*, 17–18, 206–207, 209, 221–22, 256–58.

[42] See n. 35 and chapters 3 and 5 supra.

[43] Brian Bix, "Legal Positivism," 32.

"in the scientific spirit,"[44] Holmes can be considered within the positivist tradition.

Another nuance of the term "legal positivism," hardly a formal theory, is the notion that "might makes right," and it has often been suggested that Holmes's occasional offhand remarks reflected a harsh version of this viewpoint. While he may have believed that stronger interests generally prevail in socio-legal conflicts, he recognized that strength lay not just in wealth but in organization, and his overall theory runs contrary to any suggestion of judicial subservience or premature assistance to the repositories of power.[45]

Holmes departs from Hart in one salient respect. Hart's overriding concern is to preserve a domain of study and understanding in which contemporary law may be effectively defined and, in a sense, confined. Bix, in the recent *Blackwell Guide to the Philosophy of Law and Legal Theory*, describes it as "a study of the nature of law, disentangled from proposals and prescriptions for which laws should be passed or how legal practice should be maintained or reformed."[46] The key word here is "disentangled," a term that can imply the separation of real entities. As with the semantics of texture, the quest for conceptual distinction has led to ontological separation.[47]

The device through which Hart's separation is maintained is his "Rule of Recognition," claimed to be a necessary feature of all law, implying a stable set of social and professional conventions. By this device Hart took the study of law a critical step further than a domain of understanding to a domain of operation, a step that Holmes declined at an early stage of his research. That step is implied by the tendency of analytical positivism toward interpretive closure, giving the impression that a systematic understanding may permit answers to new legal questions. This has reinforced the assumption of judicial determinism, that judges are

44 Id., 30.

45 The best explanation of Holmes's view can be found in his own words: "It is perfectly proper to regard and study the law simply as a great anthropological document. It is proper to resort to it to discover what ideals of society have been strong enough to reach that final form of expression, or what have been the changes in dominant ideals from century to century. It is proper to study it as an exercise in the morphology and transformation of human ideas." Holmes, "Law in Science – Science in Law," in *Collected Legal Papers* at 212.

46 Bix, "Legal Positivism," 30.

47 This may be compared to Alfred North Whitehead's criticism of "misplaced concreteness." Paul F. Schmidt, *Perception and Cosmology in Whitehead's Philosophy* (New Brunswick, N.J.: Rutgers University Press, 1967), 84.

primary and final actors, whether in the "interpreting" or the "making," of law.

Holmes first rejected this step in 1870 when he wrote that "it is the merit of the common law that it decides the case first and determines the principle afterwards." New questions enter the domain of law as yet undefined and unclassified. They are decided individually, guided by a sense of prevailing standards of prudent conduct, drawn in the first instance from jury determinations. Arrangement takes place gradually, as repeated instances lead to judicially abstracted rules. By the ongoing contribution of lawyers, judges, legal scholars, and legislators, the law over time takes on the likeness of an organized system, informing and guiding most activity. Nevertheless, it is in the nature of difficult cases, rising to the higher levels of appeal, to contain some degree of novelty and originality such that the existing system of understanding does not provide an answer in precedent or authoritative text.

At this stage, Holmes's account of the judicial role differs from that of Hart and the positivists. For Hart, the judge alone is the primary actor in resolving the matter. Either the answer can be found within the system of legal understanding, permitting the judge to decide according to legal reasoning, or it cannot, obliging the judge to "legislate," that is, to create new law. For Holmes, the judge should recognize the yet-uncertain relation of the case to the law as it is presently understood, and act accordingly, deciding the case on particular grounds, as a tentative, perhaps experimental, step in the application of prior experience and precedent toward an eventual general resolution. While Holmes sometimes referred to this as "interstitial legislation," it has in his context an entirely different meaning from that of Hart.[48]

Holmes's position stands apart from the entire line of development of contemporary legal philosophy. This literature has been heavily influenced by Ronald Dworkin's challenge to Hart's concept of law, first developed in essays leading to *Taking Rights Seriously* (1977). There, Dworkin famously claimed that Hart's Rule of Recognition could not account for the apparent operation of rights and principles in judicial decisions, a subject I take up in the next chapter.

Morals in general – the moral values and concerns of society – are distinguished by Holmes from moral propositions and arguments, in a

[48] See Rosenberg, *Hidden Holmes*, 43; Posner, *Problems of Jurisprudence*, 20. I address this at greater length in chapter 8, in the context of Holmes's limited view of the judges' role in making "policy."

way that they are not by Dworkin and the positivists. While the former are permitted, indeed required, as a vital force in the development of law, moral arguments are disqualified by Holmes as grounds for legal decisions. For Holmes, morals are not ontologically separate from law. Words denoting them are, however, treated with the skepticism born of his overall conception of law and the legal process. This attitude permits us to take a new and more critical look at Dworkin's theory itself.

7

Morals and Skepticism in Law

> And in this activist climate (in which the government of faith seems so preeminently relevant), the skeptical style must appear as an unintelligible piece of sophistication. Government in this style is, we have seen, primarily a judicial activity; and where men are intent upon achievement, either individual or communal, judicial activity is easily mistaken for a hindrance. It abdicates exactly at the point where the activist expects an assertion of authority; it withdraws where he expects it to proceed; it insists upon technicalities; it is narrow, severe and unenthusiastic; it is without courage or conviction. Here is a style of government which recognizes a multiplicity of directions of activity, and yet expresses approval of none; which assumes imperfection and yet ventures upon no moral judgement. It sets a high value on precedent, but does not believe that the path of precedent leads to any specific destination.
>
> Michael Oakeshott, *The Politics of Faith and the Politics of Scepticism*

The above passage is taken from a manuscript found after Michael Oakeshott's death in 1990 and published in 1996.[1] Oakeshott used footnotes sparingly, but employed one here to cite a passage from Holmes. Criticizing the effort to perfect society through government power, Oakeshott referred to a speech in 1899 to the New York State Bar

[1] The manuscript appears to have been written shortly after World War II. Oakeshott's politics of faith refers to the perfectibility of human beings and their institutions through their own efforts. The prime condition of the emergence of the politics of faith was a "remarkable and intoxicating increase of human power" making its appearance at the beginning of modern history and stimulating the hope of salvation through politics, and the promise of prosperity, abundance, and welfare. This faith corresponds to that disposition Oakeshott calls "rationalism in politics" or the "ideological style of politics." Oakeshott, *The Politics of Faith and the Politics of Scepticism* (New Haven and London: Yale University Press, 1996), xi, 46.

Association in which Holmes doubted the value of "eternal principles" in defining the limits of judicial policy making.

> Precisely because I believe that the world would be just as well off if it lived under laws different from ours in many ways, and because I believe that the claim of our special code to respect is simply that it exists, that is the one to which we have become accustomed and not that it represents an eternal principle, I am slow to consent to overruling a precedent, and think that our important duty is to see that the judicial duel shall be fought out in its accustomed way.[2]

Holmes has recently been held responsible for what Professor Albert W. Alschuler calls a "downward path" of American law. Alschuler claims that Holmes led the "revolt against natural law" that ended the "moral realism" of the "golden age" of American law prior to the final third of the nineteenth century. This set it on its current relativistic course, opposed to lofty abstraction and moral principle – a condition in which "[j]ustice is nothing else but the interest of the stronger."[3]

There is in the doubting of eternal principles an implied deference to prevailing powers, but language here is treacherous, and care is required in distinguishing between methods and outcomes. Oakeshott has helped us to see that Alschuler's conclusion does not follow from Holmes's observation. Acknowledging the powers embodied in precedents, whether social, economic, or the forgotten roots of taste and tradition, is not a surrender to relativism or rank injustice.

The way that social progressives, such as the young Felix Frankfurter, were drawn to Holmes despite his deeply unprogressive grounds for deferring to legislation,[4] shows how mightily Holmes has defied easy characterization. An older Frankfurter, appointed to the Court by the next President Roosevelt, was to all appearances more conservative, with acquired traits of a Holmesean skepticism. Part of the mix – and here I must defer to G. Edward White and refer the reader to him – is to be found in the biases of time, class, and personality, just as we bring these to the table in reassessing Holmes today. His skeptical mindset was complex and arguably often inconsistent,[5] but remains susceptible to an overall understanding.

[2] The passage is from Holmes, "Law in Science – Science in Law," originally written as an address to the New York State Bar Association on January 17, 1899; in *Collected Legal Papers* at 239.

[3] Alschuler, *Law without Values*, 8, citing Thrasymachus.

[4] White, *Justice Oliver Wendell Holmes*, 378–411.

[5] White notes, for example, that Holmes "simultaneously attacked the jurisprudential soundness of a body of 'federal common law' and unabashedly contributed to developing it in negligence cases," and "was disinclined to defer to the verdicts of juries in common

In his common law–based theory, the state is not, as in Hobbes's *Leviathan*, the exclusive source of all law and legal rationality. The causal relation of law and conduct is reversed: law largely follows the values of society, it does not dictate them. Its principal elements are critical rather than affirmatory: critical of legal ontology, system building, and uniform taxonomy. It is critical even of the most conservative positivist legacy, that of extreme textualism in legal interpretation. Holmes's skepticism reflects a distinctive understanding of society and its relation to the legal process.

As noted in previous chapters, Holmes's notion of the historical transformation of standards of blame served to mark the common law as embodying a skepticism of moral terminology, of deontological concepts such as right and duty, and thus of ideology. His skepticism has frequently been identified – most recently by Louis Menand – as a personal and emotional component of his thought, whether deriving from his Civil War experience or innate social Darwinist leanings.[6] But skepticism, as Gerald Postema has shown, was part of the strategy of traditional common law theory in challenging the defenders of the centralized state in their problematic reliance, like that of Hobbes, on sovereign natural reason.[7]

Coke employed this strategy in his *Institutes*: "The Common Law is nothing else but reason.... But this is an artificial perfection of Reason gotten by long study, observation, and experience, and not every mans natural reason," concluding, "No man (out of his private reason) ought to be wiser than the law, which is the perfection of reason."[8] A similar point was advanced by Hale in the *Reflections*, questioning the existence of a uniform faculty of reasoning and stressing the difficulty of ministering with transparent rationality to the "diseased body" of human affairs.

law subjects but inclined to tolerate the views of legislatures on constitutional questions" (381, 409). He was remarkably quick to accept uncritically the bias toward eugenics in upholding the compulsory sterilization of "mental defectives" in *Buck v. Bell*, 274 U.S. 200 (1927).

6 Professor Howe also saw Holmes's skepticism as a product of his Civil War experience, a theme popularized by Edmund Wilson in *Patriotic Gore*. Howe, "The Positivism of Mr. Justice Holmes," 64 *Harv. L. Rev.* at 536. See also Touster, "Holmes a Hundred Years Ago," 688–90; Louis Menand, *The Metaphysical Club* (New York: Farrar, Straus & Giroux, 2001), 61–67; Alschuler, *Law without Values*, 29.

7 Postema, *Bentham and the Common Law Tradition*, 60–71.

8 Coke, *Institutes*, vol. 1, sec. 21, p. 138.

Common law skepticism was tied to a notion that the collective wisdom in rules of long standing is more reliable than the logical judgment of any particular individual. It is more reasonable, Hale writes in the *Reflections*,

> to preferre a Law by wh[i]ch a Kingdome hath been happily governed four or five hundr[e]d yeares then to adventure the happiness and Peace of a Kingdome upon Some Theory of my owne tho' I am better acquainted w[i]th the reasonableness of my owne Theory than w[i]th that Law.[9]

Implicit in this argument is the idea that long experience has afforded ample opportunity to adjust the common law to peculiar and unforeseen circumstances. Thus Coke speaks of the process of *refinement*:

> [O]ur days upon the earth are but as a shadow in respect of the old ancient days and times past, wherein the laws have been by the wisdom of the most excellent men, in many successions of ages, by long and continual experience, (the trial of light and truth) fined and refined, which no one man, (being of so short a time albeit he had in his head the wisdom of all the men in the world), in any one age could ever have effected or attained unto.[10]

Of these two passages Postema comments:

> The argument seems to rest on two related claims. First, it is argued that the law has been subjected to "the trial of light and truth" and has been constantly, though incrementally, readjusted to the complexities of civil life and the common good. The perfection of any art, it is argued, is the product of time and this is no less true of the art of fashioning a body of law to fit a nation and its needs. . . . Second, it is claimed that, for the fashioning of civil arrangements, there is no alternative to the test of time and history; in particular, no single person or generation, however sagacious and far-seeing, can hope to match the record of history. "[L]ong and iterated experience . . . is the wisest expedient among mankind," Hale insists, because it "discovers those defects . . . which no wit of man could either at once foresee or aptly remedy".[11]

Similarities to Holmes are plain enough. What Holmes described in 1870 as the case-specific method of decision making, which he there calls "successive approximation," is not far from what Postema describes as legal rules being "constantly, though incrementally, readjusted to the complexities of civil life and the common good." It is a skepticism of first impressions, and also of the allure of doctrinal certainty. The former is

9 Hale, *Reflections*, 504.

10 Coke, "Calvin's Case," 7 *Coke's Reports*, quoted in J. A. G. Pocock, *The Ancient Constitution and the Feudal Law* (Cambridge: Cambridge University Press, 1957), 35.

11 Postema, *Bentham and the Common Law Tradition*, 64, citing Hale, *Reflections*, 505.

found as early as 1870 in the comment that "[a] well settled legal doctrine embodies the work of many minds, and has been tested in form as well as substance by trained critics whose practical interest it is to resist it at every step." It is only strengthened by Holmes's later conclusion that moral terminology in the law hides the operation of external standards of liability, and his discernment of the nonlogical origins of settled legal doctrines.

In the extended critique of Austin, Holmes did more than simply criticize the project of analytical classification. The vast inheritance of legal concepts and relationships demanded an alternative explanation. Holmes devised an understanding based on observation of the legal process, from historical research as well as from his own intimate knowledge of the law as it was practiced and catalogued. He developed an awareness of the contingency of concepts in relation to the real events to which they are related – an awareness of a reality far more complex than formulaic relationships.

Nearly sixty years later, in 1929, Holmes would recall the early influence of Chauncey Wright in a letter to Frederick Pollock:

> Chauncey Wright a nearly forgotten philosopher of real merit, taught me when young that I must not say *necessary* about the universe, that we don't know whether anything is necessary or not. So that I describe myself as a *bet*abilitarian. I believe that we can *bet* on the behavior of the universe in its contract with us. We bet we can know what it will be. That leaves a loophole for free will – in the miraculous sense – the creation of a new atom of force, although I don't in the least believe in it.[12]

Wright was nine years older than Holmes, had graduated in 1852 from Harvard, and lived in Cambridge not far from the college and Holmes's birthplace. He is the only one of a number of brilliant Holmes friends in Cambridge – including William James, Charles S. Peirce, and N. St. John Green – whom Holmes credits as an influence. According to Peirce, these five would with a few others in 1872 form the discussion group called "The Metaphysical Club," in which Peirce reports that Wright had a leading role.[13] While Holmes is recalled by Peirce as attending this group, there are no such meetings recorded in Holmes's post-1867 diaries, which became mere lists of his reading.

It is clear that Holmes engaged in something like a round-robin of philosophical discussions with these and other Cambridge intellectuals,

[12] Holmes to Pollock, August 30, 1929, in *Holmes-Pollock Letters*, vol. 2, p. 252.
[13] Flower and Murphey, *A History of Philosophy in America*, vol. 2, p. 537.

before and after 1872,[14] and their writings suggest a mutual influence. Philip Wiener has noted the powerful impact of evolutionary theory on all these young intellectuals. Particularly influenced by Wright, who corresponded with Charles Darwin, an essential commonality was the notion "that the meaning of a theory *evolves* with its experimental application, that all claims to truth have to be publicly verifiable and withstand the competition of prevailing ideas, and that the function of ideas is to adjust man to a precarious and changing world."[15]

The name itself, "The Metaphysical Club," is an ironic reference to their abhorrence of metaphysical absolutism; Peirce described it as implying "that almost every proposition of ontological metaphysics is either meaningless gibberish . . . or else is downright absurd."[16]

In a paper Peirce claims to have circulated to the members, he set forth what is referred to as the Pragmatic Maxim: "Consider what effects, that might conceivably have practical bearings, we conceive the object of our conception to have. Then, our conception of these effects is the whole of our conception of the object."[17] An example is the concept of force in physics; Peirce contends that it must be limited to the actual motions of particles or bodies from which force is inferred. We may find a parallel with the method used by Holmes to analyze legal concepts; an example is found in his 1878 essay on "Possession." First, here is Peirce:

> In a recent admired work on Analytical Mechanics it is stated that we understand precisely the effect of force, but what force itself is we do not understand! This is simply a self-contradiction. The idea which the word force excites in our minds has no other function than to affect our actions, and these actions can have no reference to force otherwise than through its effects. Consequently, if we know what the effects of force are, we are acquainted with every fact which is implied in saying that a force exists, and there is nothing more to know. The truth is, there is some vague notion afloat that a question may mean something which the mind cannot conceive; and when some hair-splitting philosophers have been confronted with the absurdity of such a view, they have invented an empty distinction between positive and negative conceptions, in the attempt to give their non-idea a form not obviously nonsensical.[18]

Similarly, Holmes saw the intrusion of Kantian notions into the law of possession as carrying the concept of *intention* beyond its practical bearing

[14] Menand, *The Metaphysical Club*, 201–35.
[15] Wiener, *Evolution and the Founders of Pragmatism*, 26.
[16] Peirce, *Collected Papers*, vol. 5, p. 282.
[17] Id., 258.
[18] Id., 264–55.

in legal proceedings. As he was to summarize in *The Common Law*, "The theory has fallen into the hands of the philosophers, and with them has become a corner-stone of more than one elaborate structure."[19] Holmes saw this as not only false but self-reinforcing:

> Possession was for [Kant] an extension of the ego, a setting of the will into somewhat external to it, and thus an appropriation of that somewhat, or, as Hegel would have said, possession is an objective realization of free will; and the realized free will of the individual can only be restrained when in opposition to the freedom of all, to the universal will expressed by the state. The natural operation of this view on the minds of German lawyers has been to lead them to consider the intent necessary to possession as primarily self-regarding. . . . The will of the possessor being conceived as self-regarding, the intent with which he must hold is thereupon treated in the same way: he must hold for his own benefit.
>
> [T]he direct operation of the law is to limit freedom of action or choice on the part of a greater or less number of persons in certain specified ways; while the fact that the power of removing or enforcing this limitation is generally confided to certain other private persons is not a necessary or universal correlative. Again, the law does not enable me to use or abuse this book which lies before me. That is a physical power which I have without the aid of the law. What the law does is simply to prevent other men to a greater or less extent from interfering with my use or abuse. Such being the direct operation of the law in the case of possession, one would think that the animus or intent most nearly parallel to its movement would be the intent of which we are in search. If what the law does is to exclude others from interfering with the object, the intent which the law should require would seem to be an intent to exclude others.[20]

Both papers were published in the same year, 1878.

If there is a version of the pragmatic maxim implicit in the Holmes article, it is a resistance to an expanded idealist or deontological interpretation of general legal terms by reducing them to their effects in determining liability. This form of skepticism revealed the danger of importing ideology into the grounds for decisions, and would later be used by Holmes to resist the introduction of laissez-faire economic theory into constitutional due process. A legal concept, including a constitutional "right," was denied any inherent abstract content and was limited in meaning to its effects in shaping the particular form of legal liability. The embodiment of those effects was to be sought in prior precedent. Precedent, meanwhile, had been reinterpreted in Holmes's early articles as a consensus growing out of the gradual sifting of case-specific decisions.

[19] Holmes, *The Common Law*, 163.
[20] Holmes, "Possession," in *Formative Essays*, 180, and in 3 *Collected Works*, 46–7.

Considered in light of the rest of Holmes's theory, skepticism was part of a broader perspective. It was connected to an understanding of the formation of concepts in the process of communal or social inquiry. Peirce's formulation, applicable to his scientific interests, was that inquiry began with doubt and sought belief, and that it took place in an ongoing community of the inquirers who worked on the given problem, experimenting and addressing new findings or circumstances as the inquiry progressed. This "community" was not singular and temporary, its work might require several generations of cognate studies, and any consensus could be gradual and transgenerational – a notion suited to the common law. Belief was expressed in general formulations that were themselves subject to revision as the inquiry progressed.[21]

For Holmes the growth of legal rules began with doubt surrounding an emergent problem and emerged from separate case-specific proceedings, exploring common forms of dispute-engendering conduct, each instance displaying varied circumstances. The outcome sought was a general rule, believed to address the relevant conditions, but necessarily open to revision or refinement.

The skepticism growing out of this perspective reflects several kinds of uncertainty. There is no single supreme matrix of law dictating answers to close questions. Rules and principles emerge gradually; at an early stage no single observer is in a position to know the outcome, or perhaps even the direction, of inquiry. In a scientific context, the direction of inquiry might be roughly specified; but in legal disputes, even that may be subject to derailment by the influence of doctrine or ideology. This was a particular threat in close or difficult cases, where competing rules came into play and judges were tempted to choose a direction by reference to a sweeping maxim or "eternal principle," rather than working their way through the relevant case law, the historical background and applicability of competing precedents.

Both Holmes and the common law tradition drew on the notion of a collective insight, which Postema describes as "that reason itself – or at any rate, the sort of practical reason called for in human civic affairs, – is essentially social, that the collective wisdom reposited in the historically evolved Common Law provides the context within which alone the exercise of civic practical reason is possible."[22] But for Holmes there are important departures from that tradition.

[21] Peirce, *Collected Papers*, vol. 5, p. 231.

[22] Postema, *Bentham and the Common Law Tradition*, 70.

In his challenge to Austin, Holmes implicitly raises the question of whether to characterize the common law tradition as entirely one of *reason* at all. The presumption of a pervasive collective wisdom throughout the common law is undermined by the apparent nonlogical origins of legal rules and conceptions, and the use of fictions to hide surviving vestiges. Even if Holmes was not a canonical legal realist, equating law with the decisions of legal officials, he maintained a realistic awareness of the persistence of capricious rulings by individual judges, and as a judge he would witness at first hand the operation of the intellectualist fallacy. His formulation recognizes the importance of novelty in the nature of conflicts that work their way up through the courts, as well as their embodiment of struggles among opposing interests seeking to impose their will on the eventual rules.

This should counter the impression that Holmes's skepticism grows mainly out of cynicism. Given the impediments to "reason" in the growth of the law, there is a sense in which his unvarnished realism is illuminating. Insofar as law is the result of centuries of collective responses to social disputes and conflicts, imperfectly refined and rationalized by judges, legislators, and scholars, it is the residue of the actual historical reasoning process of society, warts and all: vestiges, fictions, intellectualisms, and unresolved struggles in a retrospectively camouflaged display. Despite emergent and changing patterns of conduct, struggles among competing interests, and flawed individual judgments, the depiction leaves ample room for a gradual and revisable formation of consensus.

In the early article "The Theory of Torts," juries appear to play a critical role in legal development. Their decisions are depicted as providing the raw data, the case-specific decisions, indicating the relevant community standard of conduct from which judges eventually abstract rules. Jury decisions have the effect of influencing the legal articulation of standards of conduct, drawn as much from outside as from inside the legal profession and its body of doctrine. They help to shape general standards of ordinary prudence, using the standard of the "reasonable" or "prudent" man. In deciding where the cost of an injury should be born, juries are depicted as knowledgeable interpreters of the customs of the usual types of litigants, and judges refrain from rule making until a clear pattern of decisions has established the standards and expectations indigenous to a given practice.[23]

[23] As a depiction of the origin of earliest rules of liability, this model would have little support. Juries began not as independent assessors of fact, but as recognitors, attestors to the oaths of parties. It was at a late stage, after much doctrine was established, that

It seems clear that the traditional depiction of common law inquiry as social in nature acquires an original definition and importance in Holmes's reconstruction. Its sense of reason is more naturalist than that of Coke; Holmesean reason is but an ideal, never fully realizable, but arguably made more attainable by an accurate map of flaws and misconceptions both past and present. Its authority is not to be found in a final embedded collective wisdom, for this too is a chimera; constant reconsideration is under way. In this sense, reconsideration – when appropriate – is itself a source of authority. The authority for revision is to be found not in detached abstract or sovereign reason, but rather in a consultative partnership with the affected community and its practices, seeking reasons not in pure logic but in what he would call "public policy."

In this reconstruction, the method of the common law might almost be understood as conforming the legal order to a process of rule formation and revision that is, if not democratic in the majoritarian sense, nevertheless neither fundamentally autocratic nor surreptitiously countermajoritarian. Holmes's initial formulation of common law rules, derived by the community-oriented process of "successive approximation" and strikingly parallel to the process Peirce attributed to the development of scientific principles, prefigures Dewey's theory of democratic inquiry.[24] The function of a community of inquirers was as central to the legal theory of Holmes as to the scientific and philosophical theory of Peirce. This picture could have political as well as philosophical significance. The generalizing element of law – the process of rule making and the analysis that goes along with it – could be seen not as imposed from above but as

the fact-finding function became distinct. Early case reports were sketchy and not generally careful to report facts, focusing rather on the subjective interests of reporters. See S. F. C. Milsom, *Historical Foundations of the Common Law* (London: Butterworths, 1969), 34, 36–8. Holmes certainly knew this – his diaries reflect exposure to enough legal history to cast doubt on his model as a historical account. See Little, "The Early Reading of Justice Oliver Wendell Holmes," 8 *Harvard Library Bulletin* 168–80. Yet even as a later development of common law in America, the account is questionable; Professor Horwitz argues at length that judges had far more influence than juries on the transformation of liability. See Morton J. Horwitz, *The Transformation of American Law 1780–1860* (Cambridge, Mass., and London: Harvard University Press, 1977). Nevertheless, the model appears to emerge from the research done by Holmes on his edition of *Kent's Commentaries*; *Commentaries on American Law*, vol. 2: 561, n. 1; 2 *Collected Works*, 198 n. It may have been supported by an awareness of the practice of Lord Mansfield in relying on "special juries" chosen to determine standards of conduct in specialized matters, and first inspired by generalizing from the historical account of the growth of the prudent man standard in *Jones on Bailments*, which appears in Holmes's diary of reading for 1865–66. Little, supra, 169; Jones, *An Essay on the Law of Bailments*.

24 See Robert B. Westbrook, *John Dewey and American Democracy* (Ithaca, N.Y.: Cornell University Press, 1991).

subservient to indigenous custom and practice, indeed to the distinctive practices of the new American society. The community of observers that governed Peirce's conception of scientific inquiry would translate into a vast community of living actors determining the continuing growth of the law and making it responsive to emerging social practices.

Moreover, subjective legal theory making could be reined in by such a conception. The fixation of legal concepts and classifications would await the deliberate and fair assessment of the actual consequences of specific decisions. Hence in the legal context can be seen the practical importance of the so-called Pragmatic Maxim, whereby concepts are to be tested by their consequences.[25] If this maxim is not strictly observed in the legal arena, loose abstraction does more than cloud or distort theory making; it impinges on freedom of action, as the abstractions of law in the hands of judges carry coercive power.[26]

The notion of restraint is thus not located strictly within the legal or political domain, as a condition of the proper operation of a putative system of governance. Nor is law seen as separate and autonomous, as in the dominant school of theory still prevailing in England and America. Instead, judicial restraint is seen as a limiting condition of collective inquiry into the conditions of social ordering, of which law and governance is a contributing, but not the only, factor, its extent and operation to be determined according to the overall success of the project

[25] The best known version of the pragmatic maxim is "consider the effects, that might conceivably have practical bearings, we conceive the object of our conception to have. Then, our conception of these effects is the whole of our conception of the object." 5 *Collected Papers*, 258. In one version of the pragmatic maxim Peirce writes that "if we know what the effects of force are, we are acquainted with every fact which is implied in saying that a force exists, and there is nothing more to know." 5 *Collected Papers*, 265.

[26] For classical pragmatism, generalizing was tested by consequences and connected to the solution of human problems. In law, this highlights the degree of inclusion; yet not just in law, but in science and (a then revolutionary notion) in philosophy itself, meaning can be described as the best consensus of all those confronted with a practical stake in the outcome. Fallibilism, the attitude that no formulation of any principle can be comprehensively final, originated in the discussions of the Metaphysical Club as a reference to the inherent element of uncertainty and ambiguity in forming and translating that consensus through language. We should note how different this is from the Continental associations of the more recent version of pragmatism, which has been given currency under the name of "neopragmatism." Both have emphasized a critique of the foundationalist tendency of Western philosophy. But nineteenth-century pragmatism came to this view less from a sense of exhaustion of the Enlightenment tradition and more from a democratic reconceptualization of Western scientific and political culture. See generally Kellogg, "Who Owns Pragmatism," *Journal of Speculative Philosophy* 6, no. 67 (1992).

of an ordered society. How this is to be managed is a question that runs throughout Holmes's judicial career, albeit often obscured by his willingness to exercise judicial authority in settling difficult issues – when he viewed them as ripe – and his evident pride in doing so.[27]

Holmes observes near the beginning of *The Common Law* that "the life of the law has not been logic, it has been experience." While anticipated in Hale's *Reflections*, that insight takes on a new meaning. In cutting away the presumptively precise and self-determining character of law and replacing it with human exigency, control over the generalizing and rule-making element was detached from its traditional location in the state and rooted in society at large. His was a revolutionary, presumptively classless society dedicated to the radical principles of 1776. Hence it was necessary to recognize the breadth of the community with a stake in the outcome of debate, including philosophical debate, which might affect legal theory and in turn the exercise of sanctions affecting everyone.

Holmes's critique of moral language stands in sharp contrast to the abstract and ahistorical separation of law and morals in contemporary positivism. Morals, in the sense of community standards of conduct, are for Holmes inseparable from the legal process, as they affect its growth and development. But appeals to moral principle by lawyers and judges are to be treated with the utmost caution when they attempt to steer the outcome of a case away from the more concrete and distinctive paths of precedent, outside the established or enacted framework of conduct and association. The historical dimension, and the location of morals in a subtle and dynamic relationship to law, is an essential part. As noted in the preceding chapters, this dimension is profoundly missing from contemporary theory.

Also missing is the reality of ongoing social conflict, fully recognized in Holmes's depiction of law. Although positivism originally recognized the prominence of conflict in the works of Thomas Hobbes, its contemporary successor is relatively unconcerned with any broader vision of law in society; it is now preoccupied with the abstract definition of law. The legal order of John Austin found its origins in the three sources mentioned earlier: the enclosed, analytic, command vision of law first proposed by Hobbes, Bentham's vision of utilitarian reform through legal command and sanction, and the quest for a systematic understanding of law as a universal phenomenon.

[27] See Mark Tushnet, "The Logic of Experience: Oliver Wendell Holmes on the Supreme Judicial Court," 63 Va. L. Rev. 975 (1977); White, *Justice Oliver Wendell Holmes*, 312ff.

Positivism, as modified by H. L. A. Hart and his followers, retains only a weak interest in the third of these considerations. It has given up the command definition, since defining the sovereign in modern democratic society has proven problematic and the notion of law as command overly simplistic.[28] It is detached from utilitarianism and maintains only a loose association with political philosophy. It makes no effort to detail the law's overall classification, as Austin did, content instead to appeal only to broad abstractions in addressing whether law and morals are separate. That question, devoid of historical and political context, is what principally remains of the positivist tradition, now holding a defensive rhetorical line whose original purpose retains only a dim resonance.

Hart's major work, *The Concept of Law,* is a contribution markedly different from Austin's *Lectures in Jurisprudence.* There is little interest in mapping the various forms of liability across the body of the law. Instead, Hart argues in favor of conceiving of law as a system of rules. There are two main types, primary rules, or specific directives, and secondary rules, those that govern the conditions and validity of the primary ones. His central purpose in defining law as such a system is to maintain the notion of a pedigree; in the words of his chief critic, Ronald Dworkin, legal rules "can be identified and distinguished by specific criteria, by tests having to do not with their content but with their *pedigree* or the manner in which they were adopted or developed" (emphasis in original). As Dworkin further notes, "The set of these valid rules is exhaustive of 'the law,' so that if someone's case is not clearly covered by such a rule (because there is none that seems appropriate, or those that seem appropriate are vague, or for some other reasons) then that case cannot be decided by 'applying the law.'"[29]

Dworkin argued from two famous common law cases, *Riggs v. Palmer* and *Henningsen v. Bloomfield Motors, Inc.*, that moral principles can "trump" clear rules of law in legal decisions. In *Riggs* a judge ruled that the beneficiary in a will could not inherit by murdering his benefactor, due to the principle that "No one shall be permitted to . . . acquire property by his own crime." In *Henningsen* the purchaser of a defective car was permitted to recover for injuries after an accident under a warranty limited only to replacement of defective parts. According to Dworkin, the contract was overridden by the "principle" that "courts generally refuse to

[28] Hart, *The Concept of Law,* 18–22.
[29] Dworkin, *Taking Rights Seriously,* 17.

lend themselves to the enforcement of a bargain in which one party has unjustly taken advantage of the economic necessities of [an]other."[30]

Armed primarily with these examples, Dworkin attacked Hart's concept of law with the claim that "when lawyers reason or dispute about legal rights and obligations, particularly in those hard cases when our problems with these concepts seem most acute, they make use of standards that do not function as rules, but operate differently as principles, policies, and other sorts of standards."

Such a claim should have considered the objections to moral argument that Holmes had articulated throughout his career, but given the confusion over Holmes's relation to analytical positivism, Dworkin was never pressed to do so. The objection, reflected in the expression "general propositions do not decide concrete cases," was aimed at the tendency of sheer statements of "principle" to evade the painstaking task of locating the new case within competing lines of prior decision and precedent. That task would engender a judicial opinion explaining why one line of precedent should prevail over another – why, in effect, the rule found in prior cases would govern the murder of a benefactor rather than the standard testamentary laws. A principle might be articulated, but it would be tied to the specific circumstances, not freely available for trumping other settled rules.

Hart, in a 1994 postscript to a later edition of *The Concept of Law*, conceded Dworkin's characterization of the operation of principles in cases such as *Riggs* and *Henningsen*, and found a way to include them within his concept of law, as part of the hierarchy of rules governing a legal system. This argument, called "soft positivism" or "inclusive positivism," uncritically accepts the status of arguments from principle within law, and incorporates them into a revised account of law's fundamental nature.[31]

Contemporary jurisprudential debate was thus framed in terms sufficiently flexible that they could accommodate either side of the debate over the relation of law and morals. With the concept of secondary rules and the rule of recognition, Hart met the arguments of both Lon Fuller and Ronald Dworkin to the effect that moral principles may be considered within the boundary defining law. While Dworkin has further advanced his argument in ways not considered here, the debate has failed to recognize Holmes's distinction between the values and beliefs

[30] Id., 23–24.

[31] For a excellent summary of the arguments, see Bix, "Legal Positivism," 36–38.

embedded in society and sweeping generalizations in legal arguments or judicial opinions. Focusing on professional conventions of argumentation, in which lawyers are presumed to enunciate moral values and principles on behalf of their clients, judicial power to choose among them is implied. For anyone sharing Holmes's concern, there is little practical difference between the positions of Hart and Dworkin.

Dworkin's position has led to a division among analytical positivists into two camps: "inclusive" and "exclusive" legal positivists. The former agreed (with Hart, based on the postscript) that while there is no necessary moral content to a legal rule (or a legal system), a particular legal system may, by conventional rule, make moral criteria necessary or sufficient for validity in that system.[32] The latter have denied there can be any necessary connection; moral criteria can be neither sufficient nor necessary conditions for the legal status of a norm.

All sides have accepted Dworkin's account of the process whereby *Riggs* and *Henningsen* were decided: "morals," in the form of the two principles enunciated by the deciding courts, overrode otherwise established rules of law that would have led to a different result. No one has considered the possibility that the trumping principles enunciated by the deciding courts in both cases can be understood as opposing common law grounds of decision, both entitled to consideration in Holmes's model. In fact, the court in *Riggs* explicitly follows Holmes, not Dworkin, referring not to a trumping "moral principle" but, citing applicable precedent, to a "fundamental maxim of the common law."[33]

[32] Id.

[33] *Riggs v. Palmer*, 115 N.Y. 506, 511, 22 N.E. 188, 190 (1889). It is evident in both cases that abstract "principles" are not the sole or even primary motivating reasons for decision. In *Riggs v. Palmer* the statement of principle is drawn from a decision of the Supreme Court in *New York Mutual Life Insurance Co. v. Armstrong*, 117 US 591 (1886), invalidating payment under a life insurance policy to the murderer of the insured, where the policy was taken out with the expectation of profiting from the murder. The *Riggs* court further cites precedent to the effect that "[a] will procured by fraud and deception, like any other instrument, may be decreed void and set aside, and so a particular portion of a will may be excluded from probate or held inoperative if induced by the fraud or undue influence of the person in whose favor it is" (Allen v. M'Pherson, 1 H. L. Cas. 191; Harrison's Appeal, 48 Conn. 202.), as well as direct authorities in the civil law invalidating a bequest in the event of murder by the beneficiary. The opinion in *Henningsen* is lengthy and complex, and here as well it appears that the particular facts of the case, in the light of other relevant prior decisions, are far more persuasive on the court than the broad statement of "principle," in this case taken verbatim from language in a dissent by Justice Frankfurter in *United States v. Bethlehem Steel Corp.*, 315 US 289, 326 (1942) (denying relief to the federal government for inordinate profits from wartime contracts): "the courts generally refuse to lend themselves to the enforcement of

As Holmes wrote in 1870, "New cases will arise which will elude the most carefully constructed formula. The common law, proceeding, as we have pointed out, by a series of successive approximations – by a continual reconciliation of cases – is prepared for this, and simply modifies the form of its rule."[34] Modification is not always smooth; *Riggs* and *Henningsen* are cases in which opposing grounds of decision obliged a difficult choice. We may recall what Holmes said in *Northern Securities v. United States*: "Great cases like hard cases make bad law. For great cases are called great not by reason of their real importance in shaping the law of the future but because of some accident of immediate overwhelming interest which appeals to the feelings and distorts the judgment. These immediate interests exercise a kind of hydraulic pressure which makes what previously was clear seem doubtful, and before which even well-settled principles of law will bend."[35]

Brian Bix has recently wondered whether contemporary positivism helps with any real problem.[36] It has not been notably successful in addressing the core problem of contemporary law, deciding difficult and controversial cases, as it removes legal difficulty into the innately intractable category of legal *indeterminacy*. If Dworkin is right about Hart's attempt to fix a comprehensive formula, then indeed there is such a thing as sheer legal indeterminacy, and judges in problematic cases are forced

a 'bargain' in which one party has unjustly taken advantage of the economic necessities of the other."

By Holmes's account, such statements are aspects of the reconcilation of decisions, while the result is reached from facts of the particular case in light of available precedent. He would maintain this understanding even where courts explicitly state otherwise, which they do not in either *Riggs* or *Henningsen*. Dworkin does not claim that principles are direct or primary reasons in such cases, only that lawyers and judges "make use of" them. *Taking Rights Seriously*, 22. Nevertheless, Dworkin's argument rests on a strict inductive model of legal decisions, seen in isolation – what Frederick L. Will called the "positive view of induction" – which assumes that philosophical scrutiny of justification questions can be carried out putting aside all considerations of how such questions came into existence. Will, *Induction and Justification* (Ithaca and London: Cornell University Press, 1974), 164–68.

34 Holmes, "Codes, and the Arrangement of the Law," in *Formative Essays*, 80, and in 1 *Collected Works*, 213.

35 193 U.S. 197, 400 (1903). "Hard" cases, in this context, maintains its original meaning as "cases that tug at the heartstrings." Posner, *Problems of Jurisprudence*, 161 n. 1.

36 See Bix, "Legal Positivism," 31: "If legal positivism is not about the importance of the separate and 'scientific' study of law, or at least not about that *today*, one might wonder what its purpose and meaning is. One suspects that legal positivism's distinctiveness and its point have become more elusive, even as it has become more established within English-language analytical jurisprudence – perhaps *because* it has become more established in analytical jurisprudence."

to "legislate" in the strong, absolute sense of the term. Hart has conceded this point, affirming (in his famous postscript) a "picture of the law as in part indeterminate or incomplete and of the judge as filling the gaps by exercising a limited law-creating discretion," while insisting that judges' powers "are *interstitial* as well as subject to many substantive constraints."[37]

> None the less, there will be points where the existing law fails to dictate any decision as the correct one, and to decide cases where this is so the judge must exercise his law-making powers. But he must not do this arbitrarily: that is he must always have some general reasons justifying his decision and he must act as a conscientious legislator would by deciding according to his own beliefs and values.[38]

For the crucial problem of resolving difficult cases, we are left with but two alternatives in contemporary analytical theory: either there is "no answer" within the law or there must be an appeal to moral principle, inevitably influenced by the judge's own "beliefs and values."

In a recent comment on the state of contemporary legal philosophy, Dworkin bemoans that the strategic retreat of "inclusive" positivism has reduced the appeal of positivism to maintaining an academic elite or guild, separate and distinct from legal practice and the substantive fields of law, "a discipline that can be pursued on its own with neither background experience nor training in or even familiarity with any literature or research beyond its own narrow world and few disciples."[39] I suggest that positivism does exercise continuing influence beyond academia, and on contemporary modes of legal thinking. Its long shadow is cast over the problem of constitutional interpretation, where text is viewed as supreme and exhaustive.

When cases arise that defy any clear solution by reference either to the text or its putative "original understanding," there is an inescapable tendency to endow constitutional language with "principle." Holmes stands virtually alone among major legal theorists in emphasizing that general principles do not decide cases, they hide other motives for decision. They hide a failure to confront the disentangling of specific considerations in

37 Hart, *The Concept of Law*, 272–73.

38 Id., 273.

39 Dworkin, *Justice in Robes*, 213. Kuklick, in *The Rise of American Philosophy*, notes that the professionalization of philosophy at mid-twentieth century radicalized the shift toward technical specialized research whereby philosophy lost the synthesizing, comprehensive function more characteristic of the period in which Holmes and his intellectual peers flourished. Id., 565.

the continuum of related disputes, and the cautionary policy of restraint when no clear consensus can be found.

In the following chapters I turn to a condensed consideration of Holmes's judicial career. This is not intended as a comprehensive analysis; major topics, such as free expression, are left out.[40] Rather, I wish to show the continuity between the theory and its application, even where it has been subject to modification and change. Holmes was a confident judge, quick to impose his own view of the bearing of precedent. But despite his frequent mention of "policy," he remained attached to a theoretically limited judicial role with regard to making it. Articulations of policy by judges were fundamentally retrospective and connected to an evaluation of prevailing community standards. Second, Holmes's skepticism of general propositions diverted him from the contemporary practice that has come to be known as judicial "interest balancing." He was aware that competing social interests were increasingly involved in litigation, but he sought to avoid choosing between them and remained faithful to the early vision of case-specific line drawing. Finally, he carried his method into constitutional cases under the Fourteenth Amendment, and applied it *mutatis mutandis*, despite the very different context. Holmes's constitutional restraint was rooted in his theory of the common law.

The idealized picture Holmes brought from his research was largely retrospective; in that sense the law is "behind the times." Judges were engaged in looking backward to evaluate the relation between established patterns of conduct to the general formulations of the emerging common law. If this attitude sounds quaint in light of the current Court's engagement with contemporary issues, we find Holmes reassessing it soon after his appointment to the bench. Many of the claims he would confront on the Massachusetts high court were framed with an eye on the future, not the past, and the courtroom struggle would become less concerned with careful assessment of precedent and more with future "desires and interests." This would require a method of distinguishing precedents from interests, established patterns from proposed ones. It would often give rise to his refrain that "general propositions do not decide concrete cases."[41]

[40] I have addressed this in an article on Holmes and Learned Hand, "Learned Hand and the Great Train Ride," 56 *American Scholar* 471 (1987).

[41] E.g., *Lochner v. New York*, 198 U.S. 45, 76 (1905) (Holmes, dissenting).

8

Judges, Principles, and Policy

> Questions of policy are legislative questions, and judges are shy of reasoning from such grounds. Therefore, decisions for or against the privilege, which really can stand only upon such grounds, often are presented as hollow deductions from empty general propositions like *sic utere tuo ut alienum non laedas*, which teaches nothing but a benevolent yearning, or else are put as if they themselves embodied a postulate of the law and admitted of no further deduction, as when it is said that, although there is temporal damage, there is no wrong; whereas, the very thing to be found out is whether there is a wrong or not, and if not, why not.
>
> O. W. Holmes, "Privilege, Malice, and Intent" (1894)

At the end of the anxious carriage ride with Fanny Holmes and George Shattuck across East Cambridge on December 8, 1882, lay Holmes's appointment to the Supreme Judicial Court of Massachusetts – the "SJC," as lawyers call it. It would present him with a large workload and broad, basically unlimited appellate jurisdiction, ruling on all appeals, criminal and civil. Much of the work was as mundane as any state court of its era, ranging through crimes, injuries to body, property, and land, business and domestic relations, and local regulation.

Holmes soon wrote Pollock, "No very great or burning questions have been before me although a good many fairly interesting ones." Their correspondence reveals that "interesting" to Holmes meant capable of testing or confirming "some theories of [his] book."[1] The next decade, as Morton Horwitz has noted,[2] brought social and economic

[1] Holmes to Pollock, November 2, 1884, in *Holmes-Pollock Letters*, 26.
[2] Morton J. Horwitz, *The Transformation of American Law 1870–1960*, 65.

turbulence that would be reflected in the cases before Holmes's court and influence aspects of his theory, in particular, the battle between business and organized labor, in which his intervention – dispassionate, driven entirely by his theoretical concerns – would earn him the favor of Theodore Roosevelt and a seat on the Supreme Court of the United States.

During his twenty years on the SJC, Holmes was constantly attuned to the application of his theory to the cases before him. Eager for a large share of the workload, he was keen to demonstrate its immediate relevance and to test and revise the theory where necessary.[3] Such engagement is consistent with the spirit of the theory. Holmes had become an actor in the script he originally drafted in the decade of the 1870s, a script that calls for ongoing editing; the law "is always approaching and never reaching consistency. It is for ever adopting new principles from life at one end, and it always retains old ones from history at the other which have not yet been absorbed or sloughed off."[4]

In one sense, Holmes entered this continuum as a component of the law seeking to comprehend itself, a cog in the great engine, capable of transformation as it gathered its destiny through self-reflection. In another sense, he was in pursuit of an ever clearer understanding of the correct judicial role and of its limitations. He was driven by an extraordinary dual quest, for influence over his colleagues and the verdict of history as well as for objectivity and transparency in understanding and exemplifying the judge's proper place in historical context.

A conundrum for scholars has arisen from Holmes's frequent remarks about the influence of "policy" on judicial decisions. Citing his extrajudicial writings, especially *The Common Law* and his essay "The Path of the Law," scholars have characterized Holmes as holding that "courts decide '[q]uestions of policy'" by choosing among competing "considerations of what is expedient for the community concerned."[5] They have concluded from this that he believed judges could do this in each case. But as Mark Tushnet noted in 1976 after an exhaustive perusal of the entire body of Massachusetts opinions, there is in his judicial writings hardly any explicit weighing of competing policies and little evidence of Holmes carrying out this putative program.

[3] Patrick J. Kelley, "Holmes on the Supreme Court; The Theorist as Judge," 275–352.

[4] Holmes, "Common Carriers and the Common Law," in *Formative Essays*, 223, and in 3 *Collected Works*, 75–6.

[5] Rosenberg, *Hidden Holmes*, 43.

This is another example of the need to keep in mind the entire flow of Holmes's thinking. Policy referred to the long-run effect of applying community standards to congenital disputes, not to any immediate judicial rationale for a particular decision. The point originated with the challenge to the legacy of John Austin. The emphasis on policy, or more precisely "social advantage," derived from the early attack on analytical classification, which he saw as supporting the practice of what has subsequently been called "mechanical" jurisprudence, or the notion that logic dictates the answers to judicial questions. This is the theme with which *The Common Law* begins: "the life of the law has not been logic but experience."

Just as it was inevitable to Holmes that meanings change over time in the language of the law, it is apparent to us that meanings have changed for terms used by Holmes. Teasing out the drift and import of his use of words such as "moral," "policy," and "principle," and his own attitude toward our present understanding of them, will occupy scholars as long as Holmes's words are considered apart from the entire development of his thought. The passage at the head of this chapter carries an insight to his evolving thought regarding policy and general propositions. It is from an article written in 1894 as a revision to the general theory of external standards, which he urged his fellow justices to study at the height of their dispute over the struggle between business and labor.

The first prominent mention of policy is found in Holmes's brief 1872 book notice, which was discussed in chapter 4. This was a review of the article entitled "Law and Command" by Frederick Pollock, critical of John Austin, and Holmes sought to establish his own share of credit for launching a challenge to analytical jurisprudence. Here he summarized a course of lectures in jurisprudence given to Harvard undergraduates in the spring of 1872, engaging his own criticism of the Austinian scheme of classification.

In these lectures Holmes elucidated his challenge to Austin's project of defining all law as a system of duties or rights, terms that gave it a false normative concreteness. Examples such as protective tariffs did not create a duty, because "[t]he notion of duty involves something more than a tax on a certain course of conduct." He concluded with the observation that would be developed in his 1873 essay, "The Theory of Torts," that legal liability derives not from logical inferences from a scheme of rights and duties but from the gradual drawing of lines in litigation, such that "[p]ublic policy must determine where the line is to be drawn. The rule of the common law, requiring the owner of cattle to keep them on his land at his peril, has been very properly abandoned in some of the western states, where the enclosure of their vast prairies is necessarily for a long time out of the question."[6] Public policy is, in this context, the local community standard applied reflexively by the jury, which might differ from region to region depending on prevailing conditions.

The 1873 article would take the subject further in explaining the judge's role in abstracting such policy from jury decisions. A comment appears in the essay on common carriers that Holmes wrote six years later in 1879, repeated in *The Common Law*, with a pointed reference to "policy":

> [I]n substance the growth of the law is legislative. And this in a deeper sense than that that which the courts declare to have always been the law is in fact new. It is legislative in its grounds. The very considerations which the courts most rarely mention, and always with an apology, are the secret root from which the law draws all the juices of life. We mean, of course, considerations of what is expedient for the community concerned. Every important principle which is developed by litigation is in fact and at bottom the result of more or less definitely understood views of public policy; most generally, to be sure, under our practice and traditions, the unconscious result of distinctive preferences and inarticulate convictions, but none the less traceable to public policy in the last analysis.[7]

This passage has derailed many commentators. At first glance it appears to support the worst fears of Justice Scalia, handing an unlimited law-making license to the common law judge. Many scholars have taken these comments as promoting the judge as autonomous policy maker. Mark Tushnet's reading is that judges could base their judgments on broad considerations of policy,[8] such that he found it odd that Holmes consistently refrained from engaging policy himself.[9] For Tushnet, Holmes was not following his own script: "[H]is opinions do not carry out *The Common*

[6] "To leave the question to the jury for ever, is simply to leave the law uncertain." Holmes, "The Theory of Torts," in *Formative Essays*, 119–20, and in 1 *Collected Works*, 328.

[7] Holmes, "Common Carriers and the Common Law," 631; in *Formative Essays*, 222–23, and in 3 *Collected Works*, 75.

[8] Tushnet, "The Logic of Experience: Oliver Wendell Holmes on the Supreme Judicial Court," 63 *Virginia L. Rev.* 975, 1012 (1977); "Once external standards are acknowledged as controlling, a judge will find it easier to articulate reasons for choosing one such standard rather than another. Since individual quirks of litigants no longer matter, only competing questions of public policy remain and the judge can address them directly." Id. at 1013.

[9] "Holmes believed judges to be capable of deciding questions of policy. But in his own opinions, if two principles of public policy competed for recognition, and both seemed reasonable, Holmes refrained from making explicit choices between the policies and resorted to technicality and history of a very conceptual sort. Because Holmes knew that these cases of conflicting policy were the hardest and most significant, his opinions do not carry out *The Common Law*'s implicit program of exposing the policies that justify judicial decisions." Id. at 1017.

Law's implicit program of exposing the policies that justify judicial decisions."[10]

The explanation is that such policy is "the unconscious result of distinctive preferences and inarticulate convictions," something different from judges weighing policy preferences and consistent with Holmes's understanding of judicial restraint. The same passage continues:

> And as the law is administered by able and experienced men, who know too much to sacrifice good sense to the syllogism, it will be found that when ancient rules maintain themselves in this way, new reasons more fitted to the time have been found for them, and that they gradually receive a new content and at last a new form from the grounds to which they have been transplanted. The importance of tracing the process lies in the fact that it is unconscious, and involves the attempt to follow precedents, as well as to give a good reason for them, and that hence, if it can be shown that one half of the effort has failed, we are at liberty to consider the question of policy with a freedom that was not possible before.[11]

In a conservative reading, Holmes wants to show that judges do respond to policy, but by following community-approved standards and precedents, and where precedents derive from ancient rules, judges could and should update the reasoning. He does not argue here that they should *set* the policy so much as be aware of it and give it the expression that a jury – and successive jury determinations – cannot. A footnote to the end of this paragraph refers the reader to the 1876 essay, "Primitive Notions In Modern Law," which Holmes had written as he sharpened his turn away from Austin's system. He follows the above passage, and concludes the 1879 essay, with a tacit reference to Austin:

> What has been said will explain the failure of all theories which consider the law only from its formal side, whether they attempt to deduce the *corpus* from *a priori* postulates, or fall into the humbler error of supposing the science of law to reside in the *elegantia juris*, or logical cohesion of part with part. The truth is, that law hitherto has been, and it would seem by the necessity of its being is always approaching and never reaching consistency.... It will become entirely consistent only when it ceases to grow.[12]

Well before 1880 he was opposing what Horwitz calls the conceptualist tradition,[13] an approach that found support in the Austinian presumption

[10] Id.

[11] Holmes, "Common Carriers and the Common Law," in *Formative Essays*, 223, and in 3 *Collected Works*, 75.

[12] *Formative Essays*, 223; 3 *Collected Works*, 75–6.

[13] Horwitz, *Transformation of American Law 1870–1960*, 54.

of logical cohesion. Instead, he urged that analytical consistency is not found in preexisting structure but worked in piecemeal. There is judicial autonomy here, to be sure, but it is constrained. Before assessing its extent, we should simply keep in mind that "policy," in Holmes's phraseology, has a special meaning. It first appears in opposition to the analytical attachment to logic, and refers to the underlying motivation behind the standard of prudence. It takes shape from the nature of repeated conflicts or controversies. In its mature form it is the expression of an eventual consensus, insofar as one may be found.

By the time of his 1894 article on privilege, Holmes had turned his attention to the common habit of arguing from "empty general propositions," as if an abstract consistency of doctrine were to be found in time-honored legal maxims such as *sic utere tuo ut alienum non laedas.*[14]

As Holmes acquired experience on the state court, there appears a sharpened recognition that in some cases lines must be drawn where there is yet little or no consensus. Here the language of line drawing persists, but in a context that implies a limitation to judicial declarations of policy, one beyond which individual judges should withdraw, indeed one whose outlines may be tantalizingly indistinct and easily hidden by the "benevolent yearnings" of legal discourse mentioned in the article on privilege. In *Patnoude v. New York, New Haven & Hartford Railroad*, decided in 1901, the line drawing analogy can be seen to refer to this sort of indeterminate situation; we find it applied to something called "irreconcilable desires." Disposing of the case on technical grounds, Holmes nevertheless explained in this case why he was disinclined toward weighing alternative policy considerations.

The issue was whether a street railway might be liable when its flapping canvas freight cover startled and injured a passing horse.

> It is desirable that as far as possible people should be able to drive in the streets without their horses being frightened. It is also desirable that the owners of land should be free to make profitable and otherwise innocent use of it. More specifically, it is desirable that a railway company should be free to use its tracks in any otherwise lawful way for the carriage, incidental keeping and final delivery of any lawful freight. A line has to be drawn to separate the domains of the irreconcilable desires. Such a line cannot be drawn in general terms.[15]

[14] Use your own property in such manner as not to injure that of another. Harry N. Scheiber, "Comment: Public Rights and the Rule of Law," 71 *Cal. L. Rev.* 217, 223 n. 26 (March 1984).

[15] 180 Mass. 119, 121–22, 61 N.E. 813, 814 (1901).

The implication is that the judge must recognize that where competing policies are involved in opposing arguments, perhaps drawing on distinct lines of precedent, the decision must not choose conclusively between one or the other: *such a line cannot be drawn in general terms.* It should simply mark the "separation" of alternative public choices, not yet reconciled by consensus (or legislation) into a rule of law.

To draw the line more generally amounts to a practice that has in fact gained wide acceptance, known in contemporary terms as judicial "interest balancing."[16] Professor Horwitz claims that Holmes was the first American legal theorist to articulate a "balancing test," thus introducing an era of "modernism" in American legal thought that would replace logical deduction from general premises.[17] What Holmes meant is quite different from the practice of balancing as it has come to be known; Alexander Aleinikoff has described the recent understanding as follows:

> By a "balancing opinion," I mean a judicial opinion that analyzes a constitutional question by identifying interests implicated by the case and reaches a decision or constructs a rule of constitutional law by explicitly or implicitly assigning values to the identified interests.[18]

[16] It is to be distinguished from an approach to adjudication that has been fashionable ever since Dean Louis Henkin's famous 1978 article on "constitutional balancing." Henkin, "Infallibility under Law: Constitutional Balancing," 78 *Colum. L. Rev.* 1022 (1978).

[17] Horwitz, *Transformation of American Law 1870–1960*, 56–57.

[18] T. Alexander Aleinikoff, "Constitutional Law in the Age of Balancing," 96 *Yale L. J.* 943, 945 (1987): "The customary way in which our contemporary legal system deals with competing interests is through balancing. The conflicting interests are identified, quantified, and compared, and the weightier interest prevails. The process of interest balancing, however, entails so many unconstrained judicial determinations that the subjective values of the judge are necessarily called into play on multiple occasions during the balancing process." Girardeau A. Spann, in "Simple Justice," 73 *Georgetown L. J.* 1041, 1060 (1985), observes: "Judges cannot balance interests without recourse to their subjective preferences. Even judges with the best intentions will balance competing interests according to their views about both the relative importance of those interests and the degree to which each interest will be advanced or frustrated by particular outcomes in the case before the court. Because this activity is essentially unconstrained, however, it is difficult to see how a judge could possibly engage in it without recourse to subjective values. When legal doctrine calls for interest balancing, therefore, it does something that is seemingly counterproductive. Because particular doctrinal applications are utterly dependent upon how the balance is struck, the subjective preferences that doctrine is designed to guard against necessarily drive application of the doctrinal rules. Once again, asking a judge to balance competing interests is a lot like asking a judge to prevent unjust discrimination." See also Mark Tushnet, "Anti-Formalism in Recent Constitutional Theory," 83 *Mich. L. Rev.* 1502 (1985); Stephen E. Gottlieb, "The Paradox of Balancing Significant Interests," 45 *Hastings L. J.* 825 (1994); and Kathleen M. Sullivan, "Categorization, Balancing, and Government Interests," in Stephen E. Gottlieb, ed., *Public Values in Constitutional Law* (Ann Arbor: University of Michigan Press, 1993).

On the contrary, we should take Holmes's observations in the *Patnoude* case, as well as in the 1894 article, to mean that the line between the two competing interests should not be resolved by weighing the competing policies, but rather marked out on a case-by-case basis, "one case at a time," as Cass Sunstein puts it. In the context of a divided appellate court, Sunstein refers to this as deciding close cases on the basis of "incompletely theorized agreements." In essence, the case must be decided, but not on general grounds. Holmes might well have approved what Sunstein elucidates as "agreements on concrete particulars amid disagreements or uncertainty about the basis for those concrete particulars."[19]

Another remark by Holmes follows the last passage from *Patnoude* quoted above: "Most of us regard the question as not too delicate to be within our competence to decide without the aid of a jury." The offhandedness of this comment, like many similar ones sprinkled throughout his Massachusetts opinions, should not hide its pivotal place in understanding his approach to judicial restraint. Holmes, as discussed in the previous chapter, began increasingly to put the experienced judge in the place of the jury, as a connoisseur of prevailing standards of conduct. It is a controversial move, but essential to his method. The idea of common law juries finding the relevant community standard lay behind Holmes's account of the growth of the law. It was the notion of the juries' sense of norms embedded in community practice that permitted Holmes to develop and justify the idea of judicial rule making, not as policy making in the contemporary sense but as "specification" through "successive approximation." This comment is a reference to his sense that the judge is no less a representative of the community who must look to the standard of the "reasonable" and "prudent" person.

A connoisseur is not necessarily an arbiter. It is important to the scheme that a fresh assessment of policy is not wide open to the judge in each individual case, but must take place in a gradual discovery, mediated by the process of litigation, assuring its communal and consensual nature. In this regard the common law is a delayed-action measuring device, discovering and reflecting policy that has become firmly enough settled into the consciousness and conscience of judges and juries to become a reasonably clear standard of dispute resolution. This should explain why Holmes refrains from substantive discussion of policy in his

[19] Sunstein, *One Case at a Time*, 11.

opinions or in anything approaching "assigning values to the identified interests."

It may also explain why, as Patrick J. Kelley demonstrates in his painstaking analysis, Holmes hung on so doggedly to the universal theory of externalizing standards – despite confronting persistent exceptions to that hypothesis, cases involving undeniably subjective standards that persisted in various forms of liability, such as libel and slander and malicious interference with business, and like *Tasker v. Stanley* where an independent wrongdoer intervened between the act complained of and the alleged harm.[20]

To keep the theory intact, Holmes found himself obliged to construct a theory of exceptions, which he did in systematizing a common law of privilege. Privilege had the effect of removing an otherwise plausible claim of injury from the possibility of recovery, like the privilege that protects harmful statements concerning a former employee, given honestly but provable to be false. It translates into justifiable injury, or the various types of harm that a defendant may legally do to a plaintiff because the law has found a policy reason to permit it. This permitted evidence concerning the actual state of a defendant's mind, not translated into an "external" standard of prudent conduct.[21]

Privilege is a feature of the common law process unaddressed in *The Common Law*. Holmes had been aware of the problem, but had not formulated it in terms of privilege; he seems not to have anticipated the impact it might have on his theoretical scheme until repeatedly encountering cases like *Tasker* in the work of the Supreme Judicial Court. This appears to be the main impetus for his publication in 1894 of the article in the *Harvard Law Review* entitled "Privilege, Malice, and Intent." In a letter transmitting a copy to Sir Frederick Pollock, Holmes described the article as "a supplement to the doctrine of the external standard."[22]

Of significance to his later constitutional restraint, the problem of legal privilege forced Holmes not merely to "supplement" his theory, but also

[20] *Tasker v. Stanley*, 153 Mass. 148, 26 N.E. 417 (1891). Kelley notes how Holmes also struggled to reconcile his theory of objective standards with the so-called last wrongdoer doctrine, and wrote to Pollock explaining his theoretical adaptation and noting his efforts to "get it in" the court's opinions. Kelley, "Holmes on the Supreme Court: The Theorist as Judge," 308–13, 324–31. See also Tushnet, "The Logic of Experience: Oliver Wendell Holmes on the Supreme Judicial Court," 63 *Virginia L. Rev.* at 983–84.

[21] Holmes, "Privilege, Malice, and Intent," in *Collected Legal Papers*, 117.

[22] Holmes to Pollock, April 2, 1894, in *Holmes-Pollock Letters*, vol. 1, p. 50.

to address more explicitly the confusion that often arose where judges decided close and controversial cases where the lines of prior doctrine were obscure. Privilege was an area in which the appellate courts often operated without adoption of, or induction from, an accretion of jury determinations, as in the early negligence model. It was also rife with controversies lacking consensus on either side of competing "irreconcilable desires." While its stated purpose is to account for exceptions to the theory of external standards, in this latter respect the article may also be seen as a defense of the original common law line-drawing analogy by extending it as a theory of restraint: as a warning against hiding subjective policy preferences behind "empty general propositions."

Privilege would play a prominent role in the most controversial matter Holmes was called on to decide as a Massachusetts judge: the right of union workers to engage in organized activity designed to persuade other workers to join their cause. *Vegelahn v. Guntner*, decided in 1896, was an early case in which Holmes found occasion to apply the analysis contained in the 1894 article.[23] Employees in a furniture factory had sought higher wages and shorter hours, and their employer, Vegelahn, had refused and responded by firing their agent, Guntner. The employees went on strike, and picketed to persuade others not to do business with Vegelahn. Fights ensued, and Vegelahn sought an injunction.

Trial of the case was assigned to Holmes, sitting in equity session, who enjoined all threats of violence but ruled that the picketing was lawful "so far as it confined itself to persuasion and giving notice of the strike."[24] Vegelahn appealed, and the case was heard by the full court, Holmes and the six other justices. A majority of five held that picketing was "an unlawful interference with the rights both of employer and of employed," rights that were "secured by the Constitution itself," as employers had "a right to engage all persons who are willing to work for [them] at such prices as may be mutually agreed upon," and "persons employed or seeking employment have a corresponding right to enter into or remain in the employment of any person or corporation willing to employ them."[25]

[23] 167 Mass. 92, 44 N.E. 1077 (1896).

[24] White, *Justice Oliver Wendell Holmes*, 287.

[25] "Thus, the picketing was one means of intimidation, indirectly to the plaintiff, and directly to persons actually employed, or seeking to be employed, by the plaintiff, and of rendering such employment unpleasant or intolerable to such persons. Such an act is an unlawful interference with the rights both of employer and of employed. An employer has a right to engage all persons who are willing to work for him, at such prices as

The majority rested their ruling on a constitutional right of contractual freedom. Holmes dissented, and his dissent summarizes key points of his method:

> [I]n numberless instances the law warrants the intentional infliction of temporal damage because it regards it as justified. It is on the question of what shall amount to a justification, and more especially on the nature of the considerations which really determine or ought to determine the answer to that question, that judicial reasoning seems to me often to be inadequate. The true grounds of decision are considerations of policy and of social advantage, and it is vain to suppose that solutions can be attained merely by logic and the general propositions of law which nobody disputes. Propositions as to public policy rarely are unanimously accepted, and still more rarely, if ever, are capable of unanswerable proof. They require a special training to enable anyone even to form an intelligent opinion about them. In the early stages of law, at least, they generally are acted on rather as inarticulate instincts than as definite ideas for which a rational defense is ready.[26]

In this passage Holmes suggests that applicable policy may not be embodied in clearly applicable precedents, but *hidden*, and he criticizes "solutions . . . attained merely by logic and the general propositions of law which nobody disputes." This has seemed to some observers as a new theme, but in fact it is not. It is traceable back to the critique of moral language in his early work on Austin's system of classification, to the rejection of moral language, and to the skepticism of general propositions. The same matter had been explained in greater detail two years earlier in Holmes's article on privilege, which is worth repeating with the addition of its first line:

> But whether, and how far, a privilege shall be allowed is a question of policy. Questions of policy are legislative questions, and judges are shy of reasoning from such grounds. Therefore, decisions for or against the privilege, which really can stand only upon such grounds, often are presented as hollow deductions from empty general propositions like *sic utere tuo ut alienum non laedas*, which teaches nothing but a benevolent yearning, or else are put as if they themselves embodied a postulate of the law and admitted of no further deduction, as when it is said that, although there is temporal damage, there is no wrong; whereas, the very thing to be found out is whether there is a wrong or not, and if not, why not.[27]

may be mutually agreed upon, and persons employed or seeking employment have a corresponding right to enter into or remain in the employment of any person or corporation willing to employ them. These rights are secured by the constitution itself." 167 Mass. 97, 44 N.E. 1077.

26 167 Mass. 105–6, 44 N.E. at 1080 (Holmes, dissenting).

27 Holmes, "Privilege, Malice, and Intent," in *Collected Legal Papers*, 120.

When the full Supreme Judicial Court of Massachusetts overruled Holmes, the majority relied on a general proposition, that constitutionally protected rights of "free contract" between employer and employee were violated by the picketing strikers. Holmes objected that this erected a general principle, albeit drawn from the Massachusetts Constitution, in place of the inquiry of whether "there is a wrong or not, and if not, why not." In doing so the court had failed to reach the ultimate question of whether this particular interference was privileged. This is, I suggest, a form of the practice that Ronald Dworkin has warranted in claiming that judges may appeal directly to rights and principles in difficult cases, interpreting the *Riggs* and *Henningsen* cases as legitimate examples of doing so.

In both the *Vegelahn* dissent and in the article on privilege, Holmes noted the problem of supporting the proposition of "free contract" as a valid common law ground, by citing various common forms of permissible interference with rights of contract – a point he would make again with telling effect in the famous *Lochner* dissent.[28] And he directed the court's attention to precedents establishing the privilege of economic competition: "it has been the law for centuries that a man may set up a business in a country town too small to support more than one, although thereby he expects and intends to ruin someone already there, and succeeds in his intent." The reason, Holmes took care to explain, was that "the doctrine generally has been accepted that free competition is worth more to society than it costs, and that on this ground the infliction of the damage is privileged."[29]

[28] *Lochner v. New York*, 198 U.S. 59, 75–76 (1905).

[29] 167 Mass. at 106, 44 N.E. at 1080. The *Vegelahn* majority had gone on to consider the claim of privilege by the workers in the following manner:

> The defendants contend that these acts were justifiable, because they were only seeking to secure better wages for themselves, by compelling the plaintiff to accept their schedule of wages. This motive or purpose does not justify maintaining a patrol in front of the plaintiff's premises, as a means of carrying out their conspiracy. A combination among persons merely to regulate their own conduct is within allowable competition, and is lawful, although others may be indirectly affected thereby. But a combination to do injurious acts expressly directed to another, by way of intimidation or constraint, either of himself or of persons employed or seeking to be employed by him, is outside of allowable competition, and is unlawful.

To this Holmes replied that the illustration of the man setting up a new business in a country town shows that the policy of allowing free competition justifies the intentional inflicting of temporal damage, including the damage of interference with a man's business by some means, when the damage is done, not for its own sake, but as an

Over the next few years Holmes defended his analytical scheme to his colleagues on the court, urging that they read his privilege article, which some apparently did, as he would note in a grateful comment the next time a similar matter arose. If indeed the majority found it persuasive, it was for judicial method only, not for the union cause. Four years later the court decided *Plant v. Woods*, again involving the lawfulness of combined union activity; there the union combined to strike and boycott for a closed shop. In *Plant* the majority noted Holmes's article and his *Vegelahn* dissent, but ruled again against any right to strike. Dissenting again, Holmes commented that it was on a "difference of degree" as to the court's application of his perspective, rather than a failure of the court to confront the issue at all. "Much to my satisfaction, if I may say so," he wrote,

> the court has seen fit to adopt the mode of approaching the question which I believe to be the correct one, and to open an issue which otherwise I might have thought closed. The difference between my brethren and me now seems to be a difference of degree, and the line of reasoning followed makes it proper for me to explain where the difference lies.[30]

What was the difference, and why was it so important to Holmes? In his new dissent, Holmes defined the issue that now divided him from the majority as that of the legitimacy of the purpose of the threatened union action. For the majority, the purpose was somehow akin to extortion – like obtaining "a sum of money [from the employer] which he is under no legal obligation to pay." For Holmes the purpose of striking for a closed shop went no farther than, and indeed not as far as, the ultimate and judicially acceptable purpose of raising wages. For him the purpose of the union strike was to consolidate the union's organization in order to increase its effectiveness in the struggle for more pay:

> I infer that a majority of my brethren would admit that a boycott or strike intended to raise wages directly might be lawful, if it did not embrace in its scheme or intent violence, breach of contract, or other conduct unlawful on grounds independent of the mere fact that the action of the defendants was combined. A sensible

instrumentality in reaching the end of victory in the battle of trade. Given this, the majority's *ratio decidendi* was faulty, in that it focused on the element of combination and relied on an irrelevant distinction between combinations among persons "to regulate their own conduct" and those "expressly directed to another." The majority view would hold all in the latter category unlawful, including competitive combinations, rather than focus as Holmes would on the purpose and manner in which the damage was inflicted.

30 176 Mass. 492, 504, 57 N.E. 1011, 1016 (1900) (Holmes, dissenting).

> workingman would not contend that the courts should sanction a combination for the purpose of inflicting or threatening violence or the infraction of admitted rights. To come directly to the point, the issue is narrowed to the question of whether, assuming that some purposes would be a justification, the purpose in this case of the threatened boycotts and strikes was such as to justify the threats. That purpose was not directly concerned with wages. It was one degree more remote. The immediate object and motive was to strengthen the defendants' society as a preliminary means to enable it to make a better fight on questions of wages or other matters of clashing interests.[31]

Holmes suggests that method is as important as outcome; the majority had abandoned an abstract constitutional ground and resolved the case as a choice between lines of precedent, openly making the difference a "matter of degree." It was an important matter of degree; the majority opinion, while paying its respects to Holmes's argument in the privilege article and the *Vegelahn* dissent, had failed to come to grips with his concern about the remoteness of purpose, and that failure was now a matter of record. In abandoning the constitutional ground, the majority could not hide its choice of precedents and render its decision, as with all high court constitutional pronouncements, irreversible other than by constitutional amendment. Flaws or inconsistencies in the court's rationale were, by following Holmes's example, made plain.

We might note in passing that Holmes's theory is remarkably cognizant of the phenomenon of judicial reconsideration. With the judicial role openly engaged in marking points in an always somewhat tentative line, a single decision, even by a high appellate court, does not forever foreclose the ongoing consensual process. Eventually, Holmes's dissent in *Plant* would become law. This attitude may appear naïve, or even dangerous, especially when applied to the Supreme Court of the United States, a final venue where controversies of national importance are expected to be resolved and the United States Constitution authoritatively interpreted. Yet even there, Holmes's 1905 dissent in *Lochner*, parallel to the labor cases in many respects, would eventually become law.[32]

If in the article on privilege he appeared to resign himself to the possibility that judges with different economic sympathies might decide cases differently, in both labor dissents Holmes hewed a path independent of his own personal preference. In both he identified the pertinent policy as that of allowing free competition, and noted in *Vegelahn* that "it is plain from the slightest consideration of practical affairs, or the most superficial

[31] Id.
[32] White, *Justice Oliver Wendell Holmes*, 362–66.

reading of industrial history, that free competition means combination." Then, in *Plant*, Holmes made clear his view that this policy must be applied with equal force to employers and workers, notwithstanding his personal skepticism of the wisdom of the union cause.[33]

Cases such as these certainly make the role of the judge emerge as more pivotal than that of the jury.[34] Perhaps with this in mind, Holmes was prompted to articulate a perspective on the question of policy going somewhat beyond that found in the 1894 article on privilege. In "Law in Science and Science in Law," an address to the New York State Bar Association delivered on January 17, 1899,[35] he first restated, and sharpened, his early image of the development of law as an "approach toward exactness [in which] we constantly tend to work out definite lines or equators to mark distinctions which we first notice as a difference of poles." Then he advanced a picture of law as a medium for the working out of urgent conflicts in a far less leisurely manner than the gradual growth of common law rules out of particular jury determinations. In this regard, the address expands on a comment in the 1894 article on privilege: "The time has gone by when law is only an unconscious embodiment of the common will. It has become a conscious reaction upon itself of organized society knowingly seeking to determine its own destinies."

33 Holmes explained as follows:

> Although this is not the place for extended economic discussion, and although the law may not always reach ultimate economic conceptions, I think it well to add that I cherish no illusions as to the meaning and the effect of strikes. While I think the strike a lawful instrument in the universal struggle of life, I think it pure phantasy to suppose that there is a body of capital of which labor as a whole secures a larger share by that means. The annual product, subject to an infinitesimal deduction for the luxuries of the few, is directed to consumption by the multitude, and is consumed by the multitude, always. Organization and strikes may get a larger share for the members of an organization, but, if they do, they get it at the expense of the less organized and less powerful portion of the laboring mass. They do not create something out of nothing. (176 Mass. At 505, 57 N.E. at 1016)

34 This was most likely to take place as cases were taken from trial to appeal, the appellate courts ruled on questions of negligence in specific situations, and such situations were withdrawn from further submission to a jury. See, e.g., *Lorenzo v. Wirth*, 170 Mass. 596, 49 N.E. 1010 (1898), in which Holmes wrote in a personal injury case that it was appropriate for the trial court to decide that no breach of duty had occurred and to direct a verdict for the defendant, rather than leave the question to the jury. Two dissenting justices objected that the question of negligence should have been left for the jury.

35 Holmes, "Law in Science – Science in Law," in *Collected Legal Papers*, 210.

Morton Horwitz sees evidence, especially in writings such as "The Path of the Law," of a major transformation of Holmes's thinking, a reversal of his thesis in *The Common Law*.[36] A change is evident, but it is related less to Holmes's basic vision than to the nature of the controversies flowing

[36] Horwitz, *Transformation of American Law 1870–1960*, 138. Prof. Horwitz argues that the fundamentally new problems brought on by social and economic turbulence in the 1890s caused Holmes to abandon his advocacy of objective standards, adopt the definition of law as prediction of judicial decisions, separate law and morals, and assume an Olympian skepticism leading to judicial restraint. While there is an important transformation during this period, it does not go that far. Holmes had suggested the prediction theory in lectures at Harvard College in the spring of 1872. His distinction of law and morals in the 1890s remains the same as it was in the 1870s, as well as the roots of his famous skepticism. And his restraint would remain closely linked to his theory of objective standards, itself still part of the methodology of line drawing, although exactly what was involved in this methodology would raise new questions for him as the nature of legal controversies evolved.

Horwitz sees this transformation reflected in the famous lecture delivered by Holmes to the students of Boston University Law School in 1896 titled "The Path of the Law." It was published the following year in the *Harvard Law Review*. The essay has been called "the single most important essay ever written by an American on the law" and "the best article-length work on law ever written." It has been cited as seminal for various later schools of jurisprudence, engendered strong views on Holmes, both laudatory and critical, and has usually been at the center of attention for the more occasional writers on Holmes. On its centennial in 1997, it alone was the subject of several symposia of distinguished legal scholars and at least one book-length study.

Examined with care, and in the broad context of Holmes's thought, the essay is consistent with his already established perspective. The essay is organized into two parts, very much reminiscent of the two phases of his research, demarcated by Holmes's remark, "So much for the limits of the law. The next thing I wish to consider is what are the forces which determine its content and its growth." *Collected Legal Papers*, 179. The early years from 1870 to 1873 were devoted to the first topic, the years 1876 to 1880 to the second.

The essay has had the effect of associating Holmes with the school of legal positivism and its strict separation of law and morals. In fact it goes no further in that direction than Holmes had ever gone. The discussion of "limits" is preceded on p. 168 by introductory remarks that note that the separation of rights and duties from their legal consequences exemplifies the confusion between legal and moral ideas. In the ensuing discussion Holmes first demonstrates, as he did in the early essays, that legal rights and duties are not coextensive with their ordinary "moral" meaning, reflecting the initial focus of his critique of John Austin in 1870–72. He then observes that legal malice, intent, and negligence follow an external standard, while "[m]orals deal with the actual internal state of the individual's mind," reflecting his early equation of "moral" with vengeance, and inspiring the evolutionary theme that began to emerge in 1873 with the analysis of negligence.

In the second part of the address, Holmes expands on the latter insight by observing that, while in form the law may appear logical, any conclusion can be given logical form and the law is actually shaped by tradition, tending toward an external standard. Holmes now refers to this as a "general theory . . . of liability." This is summarized as holding that "malice, intent, and negligence mean only that the danger was manifest

into the courts. Disputes in the original model were related to established patterns of conduct, allocating the burden of injury. Patterns were discernible, from which standards of prudence could be inferred to determine outcomes and articulate rules. There the law was an "unconscious," or perhaps intuitive, embodiment of common will. In the new environment, opposing parties were seeking less to redress the past than to control the future. The courts were becoming a forum for the competition among competing interests. Judges were asked not just to work out boundaries between distinct activities, governed by discernible precedents, but to choose among competing interests battling for supremacy. When a doubtful case arose, "with certain analogies on one side and other analogies on the other," it was important to remember

> that what is really before us is a conflict between two social desires, each of which seeks to extend its dominion over the case, and which cannot both have their way. The social question is which desire is strongest at the point of conflict. The judicial one may be narrower, because one or the other desire may have been expressed in previous decisions to such an extent that logic requires us to assume it to preponderate in the one before us. But if that be clearly so, the case is not a doubtful one. Where there is doubt the simple tool of logic does not suffice, and even if it is disguised and unconscious the judges are called on to exercise the sovereign prerogative of choice.[37]

From this it should be evident that the *judicial* prerogative, while "sovereign," was limited. The case must be decided, but not on general grounds.

In the years after 1900, Holmes increasingly worked this observation into his approach to constitutional law. The last sentence resonates with the experience of *Vegelahn* and *Plant*. Judges must decide all cases, even doubtful ones. A case is not doubtful where one "desire" already preponderates, as expressed in prior precedent (he had unsuccessfully argued such a preponderance in *Plant*). Where the case is truly doubtful, it has

to a greater or less degree, under the circumstances known to the actor." This is the formulation finally set forth in *The Common Law* after external standards had been applied across the body of the law.

However, a change of emphasis may be found in such statements as "For the rational study of the law the black-letter man may be the man of the present, but the man of the future is the man of statistics and the master of economics," and the law is "a concealed, half-conscious battle on the question of legislative policy." This refers to Holmes's evolving sense of the nature of cases, discussed in chapter 8, from those involving retrospective analysis of precedent to those entailing battling interests looking to the future.

37 Holmes, *Collected Legal Papers* at 239.

to be decided even if the doubt is "disguised and unconscious." This is a condition reflecting, as the address continues, "the uninstructed and indolent use of phrases to save the trouble of thinking closely" and "the danger of reasoning from generalizations unless you have the particulars they embrace in mind"; "[a] generalization is empty so far as it is general."[38] We may infer an area marked off for restraint: the law should not embody views of policy that are still competing for dominance, but encompass only those views of policy that have already prevailed. It is better that this kind of doubtful case is not disguised by legal language, that the ongoing competition is revealed and left to nonjudicial means for resolution.

Contemporary legal philosophy is blind to this insight. Judges are fully sovereign in doubtful cases, in a sense unlike the limited one described by Holmes. Legal positivism in its stricter "exclusive" mode, presumably precluding argument from morals, must somehow find an answer in the authoritative texts, or let the judges "legislate" in the strong sense. Inclusive positivism, such as Ronald Dworkin's inclusion of rights and principles, *invites* reasoning from generalizations. Conventional theory assumes that there must always be a right legal answer, while Holmes's vision recognizes wide gradations of certainty.

Fourteen years after he delivered these views, and after eleven years on the Supreme Court, Holmes gave the speech to the Harvard Law School Association of New York containing the phrase "time for law." In it Holmes made a mature statement of his position with respect to the problem of judicial interpretation, and implementation, of social desires:

> It cannot be helped, it is as it should be, that the law is behind the times. I told a labor leader once that what they asked was favor, and if a decision was against them they called it wicked. The same might be said of their opponents. It means that the law is growing. As law embodies beliefs that have translated themselves into action, while there still is doubt, while opposite convictions still keep a battle front against each other, the time for law has not come; the notion destined to prevail is not yet entitled to the field. It is a misfortune if a judge reads his conscious or unconscious sympathy with one side or the other prematurely into the law, and forgets that what seem to him to be first principles are believed by half his fellow men to be wrong.[39]

Holmes made this speech when popular discontent with the Court was, as Holmes put it, palpable – the public saw the Court as a tool of "the

38 Id., 239–40.
39 Holmes, "Law and the Court," in Howe, *Occasional Speeches*, 171–72.

money power" and thought the Court had "usurped" the right to declare an Act of Congress unconstitutional. The intense discontent to which Holmes referred grew out of the Court's decisions under the due process clauses of the Fifth and Fourteenth Amendments that no person shall be deprived of life, liberty, or property without due process of law. I now turn to Holmes's application of the principles of his philosophy to due process jurisprudence from the turn of the century, and to the decision of *Lochner v. New York.*

9

Common Law Constitutionalism

All rights tend to declare themselves absolute to their logical extreme. Yet all in fact are limited by the neighborhood of principles of policy which are other than those on which the particular right is founded, and which become strong enough to hold their own when a certain point is reached.

O. W. Holmes, *Hudson County Water Co. v. McCarter* (1908)

In 1901, when the assassination of President McKinley elevated Theodore Roosevelt to the presidency, Holmes had for three years been Chief Justice of the Supreme Judicial Court of Massachusetts. Having sat on that court for two decades, he was now sixty-one, pushing the limit of eligibility for a Supreme Court appointment. Though Justice Horace Gray was ill and expected to resign, creating an opening for another Massachusetts man (a remarkable priority in the politics of the nation), McKinley had promised the appointment to a prominent Boston lawyer, Albert Hemenway. With the President's sudden death, social and family ties came to bear in Holmes's favor.[1] An old Roosevelt friend, Massachusetts Senator Henry Cabot Lodge, intervened on the side of the judge whom he had known from childhood, and made him the leading and ultimately successful candidate.

For almost any other Republican the controversial dissents in the labor cases would have disqualified him. He had written them despite his own doubts about the labor cause, following a theory that, if we take him

[1] Roosevelt had also been impressed by a speech given by Holmes on Memorial Day, May 30, 1895, titled "The Soldier's Faith." Edmund Morris, *Theodore Rex* (New York: Modern Library, 2002), 316; White, *Justice Oliver Wendell Holmes*, 299–307.

at his word, effectively removed his political and economic sympathies. Unaware of that, the President wrote Lodge:

> The labor decisions which have been criticized by some of the big railroad men and other members of large corporations contribute to my mind a strong point in Judge Holmes' favor.
>
> The ablest lawyers and greatest judges are men whose past has naturally brought them into close relationships with the wealthiest and most powerful clients, and I am glad when I can find a judge who has been able to preserve his aloofness of mind so as to keep his broad humanity of feeling and his sympathy for the class from which he has not drawn his clients.[2]

We know from the full record that sympathy and humanity had rather little to do with it,[3] leaving "aloofness of mind" – Holmes's extraordinary intellectual detachment – as an even more impressive force. Shortly after his confirmation Holmes would disappoint Roosevelt with a dissent in *Northern Securities v. United States.* This was the administration's successful challenge under the Sherman Act to the combination of the Northern Pacific and Great Northern railway systems through a holding company, the Northern Securities Company. Roosevelt is said to have

[2] Theodore Roosevelt to Henry Cabot Lodge, July 10, 1902, in Lodge, ed., *Selections from the Correspondence of Theodore Roosevelt,* 2 vols. (New York: C. Scribner's Sons, 1925), I, 517–18.

[3] The very opposite of a broad humaneness has become the contemporary image, fed by a 1977 comment by Professor Grant Gilmore of Yale. Appointed Holmes's official biographer after the death of Mark DeWolfe Howe, and an expert in commercial law, which suited him to understand the period of Holmes's tenure on the SJC, Gilmore was unpersuaded by Holmes's insistent "theory" and formed a profoundly negative opinion of him from letters and the Massachusetts opinions. Gilmore died in 1982 without publishing the expected next volume, having reflected:

> Put out of your mind the picture of the tolerant aristocrat, the great liberal, the eloquent defender of our liberties, the Yankee from Olympus. All that was a myth concocted principally by Harold Laski and Felix Frankfurter about the time of World War I. The real Holmes was savage, harsh and cruel, a bitter, life-long pessimist who saw in the courts of human life nothing but a continuous struggle in which the rich and powerful impose their will on the poor and weak.

But if that mean-spirited vision appealed to him, Holmes in the labor decisions did not succumb to it, apply it to law, or leave it undisputed in the record, especially insofar as something similar might have motivated his fellow justices in reflexively quashing strikes and picketing. His response to conflict, as he had seen it in war, literature, and legal history, is too subtle and important to be easily caricatured. So also his association with liberalism, to which he may not have had a natural affection, but for which he came to find alternative sources of support. The same might be said of his view of the "ordinary man" whom, if not necessarily loved, occupied (in a constructive sense) a pivotal place in his theory and practice. See Grant Gilmore, *Ages of American Law* (New Haven: Yale University Press, 1977), 48–49.

exclaimed of Holmes, "I could carve out of a banana a judge with more backbone."[4]

Like the labor decisions, the *Northern Securities* dissent is another study of intellectual detachment. It is an example of Holmes's common law orientation in reading a legislative text, which will help us to understand his reading of a constitutional text. Similar detachment is a factor in the famous dissents from decisions overruling state regulatory legislation, such as *Lochner v. New York*. As in the revealing second labor dissent, Holmes was in *Lochner* making a point about jurisprudential method.

Despite a prevalent notion to the contrary, Holmes was not averse to all plausible use of the Fourteenth Amendment due process clause to overrule state legislation threatening personal or economic liberty. This too was governed by differences of degree. That is evident from *Pennsylvania Coal Co. v. Mahon*, where he wrote for the majority that, in what he saw as an extreme case, an uncompensated deprivation of property value might constitute an unconstitutional taking.[5] In *Lochner* it was the substitution of a general proposition to cover the true ground for decision that underlay the memorable lines of his dissent.

In both of these instances, the "ordinary man" and the objective standard were a vital force. In *Northern Securities*, Holmes read the Sherman Act as he would all legal texts: by the objective meaning of its words, informed in cases of doubt by the weight of common law precedent. The combination of Northern Pacific and Great Northern was challenged under the terms of the Sherman Act, outlawing "every contract, combination in the form of trust or otherwise, or conspiracy, in restraint of trade among the several states." If these words were to apply to the case at hand, he wrote, they would have to be stretched so as to apply equally to "a partnership between two stage drivers who had been competitors in driving across a state line." To settle this doubt, Holmes confined the words to their meaning in similar context under previous common law precedent. This led to his dissent against applying them to *Northern Securities*, despite the notoriety of the case itself ("Great cases, like hard cases, make bad law").[6]

[4] 193 U.S. 197, 400 (1904); see Morris, *Theodore Rex*, 316; White, *Justice Oliver Wendell Holmes*, 307, 330–32.

[5] 260 U.S. 393 (1922).

[6] 193 U.S. 197, 400 (1903).

His approach to a text began with a comparison of the facts of a case with the plain words of the text in question. While the precise words of a statute were dispositive when their application was objectively clear, where there was doubt the recourse was not to intent or the "spirit" of the act. Precedent and ultimately the line-drawing method must resolve questions of conflict or ambiguity, avoiding appeal to the empty maxim. As a Massachusetts judge Holmes had frequently followed this approach, and we should not be surprised to find that line drawing was applied to cases in which statutes were involved, or even a constitution.[7]

Before he joined the SJC Holmes had seen no reason why an understanding similar to that outlined above could not apply to reading and deciding a constitutional text. Constitutional law did not stand apart in any scheme of classification with which he experimented in the 1870s. It had not assumed the place it has today of a privileged area of legal

7 In *Commonwealth v. Churchill et al.*, argued soon after Holmes arrived on the SJC and decided in November 1883, two defendants, Churchill and Whittemore, were prosecuted under a criminal statute prohibiting keeping and maintaining a tenement used for the illegal sale of liquor. Whittemore had been employed as a salesperson, and Churchill had rented the tenement to Whittemore's employer. The question regarding Whittemore was whether, as a sales employee, he had participated in "keeping and maintaining" the place. The prosecution argued that sales in the presence of the employer, whose guilt was clear, aided the latter in keeping the tenement. "But so do purchases," wrote Holmes, and they had already been ruled exempt from criminal liability:

> The distinction between acts which amount to maintaining the nuisance, and those which do not, is one of degree. We do not think that the misdemeanor of unlawfully selling, committed by a servant, can be said as a matter of law to amount to maintaining a nuisance, unless he has assumed a temporary control of the premises, or in some other way emerged from his subordinate position to aid directly in maintaining it. This limit seems to be indicated by the case upon which the Massachusetts decisions are founded. And none of our cases have gone further than to leave the general question to the jury, whether the defendant aided in keeping the tenement, when it appeared that he did so by exercising some form of control. (citations omitted)

136 Mass. 148, 151 (1883). Here can be found all of the main elements of Holmes's common law model, as set forth in the 1873 article, at work in a statutory context: the existence of opposing lines of precedent, one establishing the reach of statutory language, the other defining a limit to the kinds of conduct that would constitute aiding in the maintenance of the tenement. The case of Whittemore appears to fall somewhere between, obliging the court to mark a point on the line. Moreover, Holmes remarks that "none of our cases have gone further than leaving the general question to the jury." Leaving the general question refers to the fact that in prior cases, after all the evidence had been admitted concerning the employee's sales of liquor in the tenement, the jury would be permitted to decide for themselves whether such evidence constituted "maintenance." No rule governing purely sales employees, such as Whittemore, had yet been arrived at. The case demonstrates that, for Holmes, statutes could indeed leave questions open in virtually the same manner as the common law, for resolution in a parallel way.

doctrine, with special rules of application. It had not yet become the fertile source of jurisdiction for so many areas of heated public controversy. In retrospect, harbingers of such a development were already appearing in decisions under the due process clauses of the Fifth and Fourteenth Amendments.

Provisions limiting government power existed in many state constitutions, including Massachusetts ("no part of the property of any individual can, with justice, be taken from him, or applied to public uses, without his own consent or that of the representative body of the people . . . and whenever the public exigencies require that the property of an individual should be appropriated to public uses, he shall receive a reasonable compensation therefore"[8]). Although constitutional challenges to state statutes were rare, Holmes had occasion as a state judge to interpret such language as early as 1886. In his second due process decision, *Rideout v. Knox*, which involved the constitutionality of regulating the height of a private fence, Holmes noted that

> difference of degree is one of the distinctions by which the right of the Legislature to exercise the police power is determined. Some small limitations of previously existing rights incident to property may be imposed for the sake of preventing a manifest evil; large ones could not be, except by the exercise of the right of eminent domain.[9]

This observation contains clear elements of the common law method. In 1900, with an increase in the number of constitutional challenges to public economic regulation, we may find evidence of the line-drawing analogy applied to due process cases. In *Lincoln v. Dore*, Holmes discussed two earlier due process decisions[10] in the following terms:

> The distinction of constitutional law must be pretty technical if taking a man's money is unlawful in the latter case and is not equally so in the former. It may be that the line between special and general benefits is fixed by a somewhat rough estimate of differences. But all legal lines are more or less arbitrary as to the precise place of their incidence, although the distinctions of which they are the inevitable outcome are plain and undeniable.[11]

Some years later, as a United States Supreme Court Justice, Holmes would in *Hudson County Water Co. v. McCarter* describe the process of

[8] Article 10 of the 1780 Massachusetts Constitution.

[9] 148 Mass. 368, 372–73, 19 NE 390, 392 (1889).

[10] *Harvard College v. Boston*, 104 Mass 470 (1870); *Sears v. Boston* 173 Mass 71; 53 NE 138 (1899).

[11] 176 Mass. 210, 213, 57 N.E. 356, 358 (1900).

drawing a line between permissible state "police power" and constitutionally impermissible deprivations of property without due process of law:

> All rights tend to declare themselves absolute to their logical extreme. Yet all in fact are limited by the neighborhood of principles of policy which are other than those on which the particular right is founded, and which become strong enough to hold their own when a certain point is reached. The limits set to property by other public interests present themselves as a branch of what is called the police power of the State. The boundary at which the conflicting interests balance cannot be determined by any general formula in advance, but points in the line, or helping to establish it, are fixed by decisions that this or that concrete case falls on the nearer or farther side.[12]

As in the common law analysis of tort cases written in 1873, drawing on *Beadel v. Perry*, Holmes went on to illustrate the point with an example of the permissible height of a new building.

> For instance, the police power may limit the height of buildings, in a city, without compensation. To that extent it cuts down what otherwise would be the rights of property. But if it should attempt to limit the height so far as to make an ordinary building lot wholly useless, the rights of property would prevail over the other public interest, and the police power would fail. To set such a limit would need compensation and the power of eminent domain.[13]

From this it can be seen that Holmes was not against reading substantive content into the Fourteenth Amendment.[14] Constitutional rights, like others, could be seen as applied by "matters of degree," even though tending to "declare themselves absolute to their logical extreme." Implicit in this is a view of constitutional rights not as innate or a priori spheres of protected conduct (as in the 1878 article denying that law operated like a natural force) but as causes of action, of which the principal characteristic of interest to Holmes was their operation as avenues of permissible judicial inquiry.

Hudson County Water Co., and other cases in which he raised the analogy with common law line drawing, had less to do with where the line was to be drawn, or how it might be found, than with the danger of failing to recognize that constitutional decisions involve questions of degree. The Court had by 1900 long recognized that claims of constitutional deprivation by

[12] 209 U.S. 349 (1908).

[13] Id.

[14] Bork, *The Tempting of America* (New York: Free Press, 1990), 45; Michael J. Phillips, "The Substantive Due Process Decisions of Mr. Justice Holmes," 36 *American Business Law Journal* 437–77 (1999).

state regulation had to be weighed against the police power, and it had marked out points along the line between them. This did not foreclose the tendency to fall into reliance on postulates formulated in advance. Holmes came to the Supreme Court with a distinct awareness that the inquiry of an appellate court, particularly in constitutional matters, could be short-circuited by abstractions.

The due process clauses of the Fifth and Fourteenth Amendments, protecting against any federal or state laws depriving any person "of life, liberty, or property without due process of law," began shortly after the Civil War to be looked on by parties aggrieved by governmental action much as negligence doctrine in the common law – as a cause of action through which more general grievances might be redressed.[15] Federal due process challenges to state regulations were not new in 1881 when Holmes published *The Common Law.* Four years earlier Justice Samuel Freeman Miller had complained in *Davidson v. Board of Administrators of New Orleans*[16] that, although a strict procedural reading of "due process" had long limited the scope of federal legislation under the Fifth Amendment, passage of the Fourteenth had focused attention on its meaning by inundating the Supreme Court with challenges to state law.

> It is not a little remarkable, that while this provision has been in the Constitution of the United States, as a restraint upon the authority of the Federal Government, for nearly a century, and while, during all that time, the manner in which the powers of that Government have been exercised has been watched with jealousy, and subjected to the most rigid criticism in all its branches, this special limitation upon powers has rarely been invoked in the judicial forum or the more enlarged theater of public discussion. But while it has been a part of the Constitution, as a restraint upon the power of the States, only a very few years, the docket of this court is crowded with cases in which we are asked to hold that State Courts and State Legislatures have deprived their own citizens of life, liberty or property without due process of law.[17]

Miller observed that the character of these cases made it plain that

> the clause under consideration is looked upon as a means of bringing to the test of the decision of this court the abstract opinions of every unsuccessful litigant in a State court of the justice of the decision against him, and of the merits of the legislation on which such a decision may be founded.[18]

15 Freund, *On Law and Justice*, 3–6.
16 96 U.S. 97 (1877).
17 Id. at 103–4.
18 Id at 104.

He added, auspiciously,

> If, therefore, it were possible to define what it is for a State to deprive a person of life, liberty, or property without due process of law, in terms which would cover every exercise of power thus forbidden to the State, and exclude those which are not, no more useful construction could be furnished by this or any other court to any part of the fundamental law.[19]

Within a year, the Supreme Court would decide the case of *Chicago, Milwaukee & St. Paul Railway. v. Minnesota,* holding that due process was violated by a state law making final the decisions of a rate-making commission. From that decision, reflected Judge Charles M. Hough in a *Harvard Law Review* article thirty years later, "I date the flood."[20]

Miller's rumination is the first indication of serious doubt concerning the Court's ability to interpret the due process clause coherently. In early Fourteenth Amendment decisions it had attempted to reconcile the language of the due process clause with the long recognized power of the states to regulate their internal affairs – the "police power." The result was an empty phrase, an *ipse dixit* – the amendment takes up where the police power leaves off. What was the Court to do as new cases arose further and further outside the traditional purview of police regulations? The 1902 decision in *Otis v. Parker,* belonging more to the newer class of economic regulation than to the traditional rubric of "health, safety and morals," marks a new stage in the analysis of the due process clause, cognate with Holmes's prior thinking. This case, held for reargument by a tie vote, awaited Holmes when he joined the Court in 1902.

As Professor Edward S. Corwin and others have noted, in its initial approach to due process the Court had first sought to deal with new controversies through a literal application of the notion of "process." The clause did nothing more than assure procedural safeguards and contained no broader guarantee than that accepted procedures would be followed when the government sought to control the lives, liberties, or properties of citizens.[21] Corwin chronicles the change: Fourteenth Amendment due process was first ignored in the *Slaughter-House*

[19] Id.

[20] Charles M. Hough, "Due Process of Law To-day," 32 *Harv. L. Rev.* 218, 228 (1919); Freund, *On Law and Justice,* 4.

[21] Corwin, "Due Process of Law before the Civil War" and "The Supreme Court and the Fourteenth Amendment," in *American Constitutional History: Essays by Edward S. Corwin,* ed. Alpheus T. Mason and Gerald Garvey (New York: Harper & Row, 1964), 46, 67.

Cases.[22] It was then briefly held at bay with the public purpose doctrine in *Munn v. Illinois,* until the watershed case of *Chicago, Milwaukee & St. Paul Railway v. Minnesota,* in which a state rate-making action was overturned (though on procedural grounds).[23] Although Corwin himself decried the abandonment of a more "procedural" due process, he conceded that the development of "substantive" due process has an inevitable look to it:

> The truth is that, the moment the Court, in its interpretation of the Fourteenth Amendment, left behind the definite, historical concept of "due process of law" as having to do with the enforcement of law and not its making, the moment it abandoned, in its attempt to delimit the police power of the State, its ancient maxim that the possibility that a power may be abused has nothing to do with its existence, that moment it committed itself to a course that was bound to lead, however gradually and easily, beyond the precincts of judicial power, in the sense of the power to ascertain the law, into that of legislative power which determines policies on the basis of facts and desires.[24]

As can be guessed from these sentiments, Corwin would criticize Holmes for what he took to be an unquestioning acceptance of this development; but Holmes's course was dictated by the principles of his own method and the skepticism of empty abstractions.

Corwin identified *Mugler v. Kansas* as the first case in which the procedural view was noticeably absent and replaced by the beginnings of a broader doctrine – what Corwin and the majority of writers have assumed to be the view that due process of law means "reasonable law, in the Court's opinion." These writers often attribute to the Court more certainty of purpose than the record attests, particularly in light of such remarks as those of Justice Miller. Corwin noted the influence of persistent advocates for newly regulated industries, the sheer public pressure of controversies flowing into the judicial arena and demanding consideration at the highest level on more than a strictly procedural basis. He conceded that, if not due process, perhaps other clauses of the Constitution might have been found: "[g]iven a sufficient hardihood of purpose at the rack of exegesis, and any document, no matter what its fortitude, will eventually give forth

22 83 U.S. 36 (1872).

23 94 U.S. 113 (1877); 134 U.S. 418 (1890).

24 Corwin, "The Supreme Court and the Fourteenth Amendment," in *American Constitutional History*, 96.

the meaning required of it."[25] When the flood became irresistible, the Court would fumble for a rationale.

As a theory of public inquiry, Holmes's vision may have embodied a path to restraint, but it was eminently open to the asking of questions – even new ones – that were pertinent to the plain meaning of the relevant text. This double-edged sword of an objective reading is cogently expressed in *Truax v. Corrigan*, where he wrote, "There is nothing that I more deprecate than the use of the Fourteenth Amendment beyond the absolute compulsion of its words to prevent the making of social experiments that an important part of the community desires . . . even though the experiments may seem futile or even noxious to me and to those whose judgment I most respect."[26]

By the turn of the century, Holmes, ever committed to his original common law model, had nonetheless distinguished two types of difficult case. The first was the case caught equidistant from conflicting but established precedents, as in the image of "opposite poles," the "widely different cases" around which cases "clustered" and eventually approached each other as courts marked out points on a line between. On that line "the distinction becomes more difficult to trace," until eventually a definite line is arrived at, which the courts might identify as a settlement of the issues; the cases might then be "reconciled" into a new general rule. Another type was the clash of yet unresolved social interests, suggested in his observations regarding the Patnoude case in 1901, in which the court was confronted with a more indeterminate situation: "A line has to be drawn to separate the domains of the irreconcilable desires. Such a line cannot be drawn in general terms."[27]

In the first the conflict is between maturing lines of precedent, each representing patterns of conduct that have established separate common

[25] Id.: "The value of these dissenting opinions [by Justices Harlan and Holmes in *Lochner v. New York*] is that of most of the other dissenting opinions that we have noted, viz.: that they serve to measure the advance that the law receives in a given direction from the decision dissented from. On the other hand, they are both of them open to criticisms of a rather obvious sort. Thus Justice Harlan was himself the author of *Mugler v. Kansas*, and the line connecting that decision with the one in *Lochner v. New York* is both direct and logical. Much the same criticism has to be levelled against Justice Holmes' dissent also. For it is to be noted that he accepts in toto the present day view of due process of law." But cf. Holmes in *Truax v. Corrigan*, 257 U.S. 312, 344 (1921), n. 26 infra and accompanying text.

[26] 257 U.S. 312, 344 (1921).

[27] *Patnoude v. New York, New Haven, & Hartford Railroad*, 180 Mass. 119, 121–22, 61 N.E. 813, 814 (1901).

law roots and must find an accommodation, as in the *Beadel* example. In the second, the conflict has yet to mature, and involves unreconcilable interests on the opposing sides. Given the prerogative of choice, the judge must decide, but not by choosing between the two more general interests. Here Holmes had come to stress first the necessity of paring away false reasons and, later, the danger of siding prematurely with a view based on beliefs that had yet to prevail.

On December 11, 1902, three days after he took his seat on the Supreme Court of the United States, *Otis v. Parker* was reargued. At issue was whether a provision of the California Constitution, which rendered contracts on margin for the sale of mining stock unenforceable, violated the due process clause of the Fourteenth Amendment of the United States Constitution. Holmes wrote the opinion, and it was issued on January 5. The objection urged in *Otis* was that the restriction on freedom of contract bore no reasonable relation to the evil sought to be cured. Citing *Mugler* for the proposition that a state cannot "interfere arbitrarily with private business or transactions, and that the mere fact that an enactment purports to be for the protection of public safety, health, or morals, is not conclusive upon the courts," he wrote:

> But general propositions do not carry us far. While the courts must exercise a judgment of their own, it by no means is true that every law is void which may seem to the judges who pass upon it excessive, unsuited to its ostensible end, or based upon conceptions of morality with which they disagree. Considerable latitude must be allowed for differences of view as well as for possible peculiar conditions which this court can know imperfectly, if at all. Otherwise a constitution, instead of embodying only relatively fundamental rules of right, as generally understood by all English-speaking communities, would become the partisan of a particular set of ethical or economical opinions, which by no means are held *semper ubique et ab omnibus*.[28]

This passage recognizes that a *subjective* test of reasonableness – in which the justices applied their own views – was inadequate to settle new conflicts between legislative and constitutional rights in controversies arising under the due process clause. In all three categories mentioned by Holmes – laws excessive, unsuited to their ostensible ends, or based on inimical moral notions – it could be said that such laws were "unreasonable" or, in the terms of the *Mugler* opinion, lacking a "real or substantial relation" to one of the purposes within the constitutional power of the states.

[28] *Otis v. Parker*, 187 U.S. 606, 608–9 (1903).

The reason given by Holmes for his reluctance to rely on the *Mugler* test is that "latitude" must be allowed both for differences of view and "possible peculiar conditions" that the Court could know "imperfectly, if at all." This may be regarded as a reappearance, in different garb, of the objective standard of common law liability. If an objective, rather than subjective, test of reasonableness was the correct standard, the Supreme Court must defer when local conditions could be known only "imperfectly."

This would be true of another case, three years later, in which Holmes found himself in dissent: the famous *Lochner v. New York*, holding unconstitutional New York's regulation of hours per day in which bakers could be required to work. That 5–4 majority opinion was written by one of the two dissenters in *Otis*, Justice Peckham, applying a subjective test of reasonableness: "There is no reasonable ground for interfering with the liberty of person or the right of free contract, by determining the hours of labor, in the occupation of baker." The majority clearly felt that a line had to be drawn somewhere short of wholesale regulation of all hours of labor by the state. "It might be safely affirmed that almost all occupations more or less affect the health," Peckham noted, and he observed that the mere excuse of health regulation could warrant intrusion of employment regulation into many businesses:

> In our large cities there are many buildings into which the sun penetrates for but a short time in each day, and these buildings are occupied by people carrying on the business of bankers, brokers, lawyers, real estate, and many other kinds of business, aided by many clerks, messengers, and other employees.[29]

Hence, "[s]carcely any law but might find shelter under such assumptions, and conduct, properly so called, as well as contract, would come under the restrictive sway of the legislature." But Peckham's majority opinion was not content to rest its decision on a relative judgment, nor on the particular facts of the bakers' case.

> It is impossible for us to shut our eyes to the fact that many of the laws of this character, while passed under what is claimed to be the police power for the purpose of protecting the public health or welfare, are, in reality, passed from other motives.... It seems to us that the real object and purpose were simply to regulate the hours of labor between the master and his employees (all being men, *sui juris*) in a private business, not dangerous in any degree to morals, or

[29] *Lochner v. New York*, 198 U.S. 45, 59–60 (1905). Holmes's "objective" reason parallels that of Hale, while Peckham's "subjective" reason echoes that feared by Hobbes. See chapter 4, supra.

in any real and substantial degree, to the health of the employees. Under such circumstances the freedom of master and employee to contract with each other in relation to their employment, and in defining the same, cannot be prohibited or interfered with, without violating the Federal Constitution.[30]

This embodied the same error as the SJC majority had committed in the first labor case, *Vegelahn v. Guntner*: the majority was expressing a view on policy through the guise of a legal right. The Court's focus on a contractual "right" recast the decision from one evaluating specific events into a conflict among general propositions of economic theory: whether it was wise for the state to regulate hours of labor in any profession. In his opening remarks Holmes wrote: "This case is decided upon an economic theory which a large part of the country does not entertain."

If it were a question whether I agreed with that theory, I should desire to study it further and long before making up my mind. But I do not conceive that to be my duty, because I strongly believe that my agreement or disagreement has nothing to do with the right of a majority to embody their opinions in law.[31]

Following this came the same point which he had made in *Otis*, that a policy of permitting state laws limiting absolute freedom of contract was already "settled by various decisions of this court," including Sunday laws, usury laws, prohibition of lotteries, and the like.

The liberty of the citizen to do as he likes so long as he does not interfere with the liberty of others to do the same, which has been a shibboleth for some well-known writers, is interfered with by school laws, by the Post Office, by every state or municipal institution which takes his money for purposes thought desirable, whether he likes it or not. The Fourteenth Amendment does not enact Mr. Herbert Spencer's Social Statics.... Some of these laws embody convictions or prejudices which judges are likely to share. Some may not. But a constitution is not intended to embody a particular economic theory, whether of paternalism and the organic relation of the citizen to the state or of laissez-faire. It is made for people of fundamentally differing views, and the accident of our finding certain opinions natural and familiar, or novel and even shocking, ought not conclude our judgment upon the question whether statutes embodying them conflict with the Constitution of the United States.[32]

Holmes then repeated his earlier refrain – "General propositions do not decide concrete cases" – and stated the judicial approach to policy that

[30] Id. at 64.
[31] Id. at 75.
[32] Id., 75–76 (citations omitted).

finally emerged from the analysis begun a decade before in the 1894 article on privilege:

> I think that the word liberty, in the Fourteenth Amendment, is perverted when it is held to prevent the natural outcome of a dominant opinion, unless it can be said that a rational and fair man necessarily would admit that the statute proposed would infringe fundamental principles as they have been understood by the traditions of our people and our law.[33]

While the memorable phrases in *Lochner* have come over time to be viewed as calling for the end of all interference with state laws impairing freedom of contract, that would be inconsistent with his later remark in *Pennsylvania Coal Co. v. Mahon* that "obviously the implied limitation [the police power] must have its limits, or the contract and due process cases are gone."[34] Reflecting on *Lochner* in 1990, Robert H. Bork praised Holmes's dissent but noted that

> he spoiled it all by adding ". . . unless it can be said that a rational and fair man necessarily would admit that the statute proposed would infringe fundamental principles as they have been understood by the traditions of our people and our law." So Holmes, after all, did accept substantive due process, he merely disagreed with Peckham and the majority about which principles were fundamental.[35]

Bork, like many others, missed the point that Holmes's objection in *Lochner* was mainly to an abuse of method, as in *Plant*. Peckham's opinion for the majority erected a general proposition in place of the inquiry of whether, as Holmes had said in *Plant*, "there is a wrong or not, and if not, why not." This is, once again, a form of the error that Ronald Dworkin condones in claiming that judges may appeal directly to rights and principles in difficult cases, and in interpreting the *Riggs* and *Henningsen* cases to represent legitimate examples of this practice. The case-specific method of the common law is evaded by appealing directly to a generalized value, caricatured in 1894 by Holmes as a "benevolent yearning."

Bork reflects the widely held view that the *Lochner* majority approved virtually all claims of contractual freedom and that Holmes consistently resisted them. Both points are wrong. *Otis v. Parker*, decided the other way in rejecting the constitutional challenge by a majority of 7–2, exemplifies that other factors often swayed the majority. In still other cases Holmes joined the court in overruling state laws even on particular

33 Id.

34 *Pennsylvania Coal Co. v. Mahon*, 260 U.S. at 413.

35 Bork, *The Tempting of America*, 45, quoted in Michael J. Phillips, "The Substantive Due Process Decisions of Mr. Justice Holmes," 36 *American Business Law Journal* at 437.

contract grounds.[36] The difference between *Otis* and *Lochner* is that Justice Peckham's opinion absolutizes free contract, voicing his view that the New York law was "passed for other motives," opening the door to regulation extending to "bankers, brokers, lawyers, real estate, and many other kinds of business, aided by many clerks, messengers, and other employees." Peckham, in effect, ignored that constitutional liability could turn on matters of degree, and applied a subjective test to find the law unreasonable. As in other dissents, Holmes would insist that the test be objective, and invoked a community standard.[37]

All this is rooted in the early common law research. Today the notion that a judge in any jurisdiction should explicitly apply principles of common law to a state or the federal constitution would be shocking. Yet the remark in *Hudson County Water Co. v. McCarter*, taking rights as matters of degree, describes Holmes's method concisely.[38] The comment illustrates line drawing at work in a constitutional context: even constitutional rights, while declaring themselves absolute, are limited

[36] The common assumption that the Supreme Court was dominated by laissez-faire conservatives wielding the Fourteenth Amendment to favor business interests overlooks the fact that the majority of state regulatory laws challenged under the Fourteenth Amendment were actually upheld by the notorious "Lochner Court"; the number of overrulings is generally inflated. Michael J. Phillips, "The Substantive Due Process Decisions of Mr. Justice Holmes," 441. As Howard Gillman noted in 1993, the court's motivation in overruling many state laws was less a bias in favor of business than antipathy to what the justices considered "class" or "partial" legislation, laws that promoted narrow interests over the general welfare, which Holmes apparently shared in joining such decisions. Howard Gillman, *The Constitution Beseiged: The Rise and Demise of Lochner Era Police Powers Jurisprudence* (Durham, N.C., and London: Duke University Press, 1993). Notwithstanding his dissent in *Lochner*, *Adkins*, *Adair*, and other now celebrated instances, Holmes did not resist every overruling of state legislation by his Court on Fourteenth Amendment grounds. Of 89 cases identified in 1999 by Michael J. Phillips in which the Court used the due process clause to strike down substantive government action while Holmes was a Justice, Holmes joined or wrote 62, principally involving utility and rate regulation. Phillips, "The Substantive Due Process Decisions of Mr. Justice Holmes," 461.

In these cases Holmes appears to have been willing to engage in "marking points on the line": of 32 cases in which the Court during his tenure overturned rate orders against such due process plaintiffs as railroads and utilities, he joined all but five. Id., 456. Of the five dissents, he wrote only one, *City of Denver v. Denver Union Water Co.*, dissenting on technical legal grounds. 246 U.S. 178, 195–98 (1918). As during his days on the SJC in rulings under the takings clause, he saw his duty as contributing to individual determinations of whether a state action against private property was confiscatory in violation of the constitutionally protected right.

[37] *Coppage v. Kansas*, 236 U.S. 1, 27 (1914) (Holmes, dissenting), and *Schlesinger v. Wisconsin*, 270 U.S. 230, 241 (1926) (Holmes, dissenting).

[38] *Hudson County Water Co. v. McCarter*, 209 U.S. 349, 355 (1908).

by contrary principles of policy, which may be found throughout the law.[39]

For a few contemporary legal scholars, there is merit to the idea of seeing a parallel between common law and interpretation of the Constitution. David A. Strauss has written:

> The common law method has not gained currency as a theoretical approach to constitutional interpretation because it is not an approach we usually associate with a written constitution, or indeed with codified law of any kind. But our written constitution has, by now, become part of an evolutionary common law system, and the common law – rather than any model based on the interpretation of codified law – provides the best way to understand the practices of American constitutional law.[40]

Comments such as this reflect a growing discomfort with treating the U.S. Constitution purely as a text, even while so much of judicial practice

39 Some clarification is required to address a criticism of Professor Patrick J. Kelley, who claims that Holmes violated "the traditional understanding of our constitutional order" because he failed to apply the principle that "legislative enactments... are deemed invalid if judged to be inconsistent with the constitution." The key word here is "judged." If, as most scholars assume, this is the exclusive prerogative of judges, then for Holmes to imply common law limits to that prerogative is a fundamental error:

> Holmes's takings jurisprudence reflects a deep-seated discrepancy between Holmes's constitutional theory and the traditional understanding of our constitutional order, which recognizes two fundamental principles as ordering norms. First, since the people are sovereign, constitutional provisions, which formally express the will of the people, have priority over legislative enactments, which are deemed invalid if judged to be inconsistent with the constitution. Second, the legislature in our system of separation of powers is a lawmaking body superior to the courts, so that statutes control over inconsistent common-law precedent." (Patrick J. Kelley, "Holmes's Early Constitutional Law Theory and Its Application in Takings Cases on the Massachusetts Supreme Judicial Court," 18 *S. Ill. U. L. J.* 357, 415 (1994))

Drawing on various comments by Holmes on policy that I have discussed, Kelley further claims that Holmes had a consequentialist theory of law in which social policy was "the object and ground of all law," including decisions under constitutional jurisdiction. In other words, Kelley attributes to Holmes the view that "[c]onstitutional law is thus just a subcategory of judge-made common law. Like all judge-made law, constitutional law can only be justified by its social consequences for the community." Id., 362–63, 364.

Kelley cites the 1872 book notice where Holmes first observes that "public policy must determine where the line is to be drawn." But as I have noted in chapter 8, this must be read in the context of Holmes's deference to community standards. Where constitutional questions are raised in litigation regarding matters yet unsettled, judges should refrain from implementing any final policy determination.

40 David A. Strauss, "Common Law Constitutional Interpretation," 63 *University of Chicago Law Review* 877–935 (1996).

and the growth of constitutional doctrine resembles the common law. But Strauss holds a judge-oriented view of common law, relying only on the text for a limiting balance, still vulnerable to the objections voiced by Justice Scalia.

As the scholarly responses to Scalia's attack on common law in *A Matter of Interpretation* demonstrate, no clear idea exists today as to precisely what "common law" means. Nor is there a general understanding as to why it should be considered a legitimate alternative to the positivist tradition. The roots of textualism are, if not grounded in analytical positivism, certainly closer to it than to common law. Professor Strauss concedes that the text, and thus aspects of strict textualism in constitutional interpretation, are important – they act as a restraining force – but he notes that "our written constitution has, *by now*, become part of an evolutionary common law system" (emphasis added).[41]

In the qualifier Strauss suggests that the common law resemblance of constitutional jurisprudence is a relatively recent development. Preoccupation with the recent past obscures that Professor Corwin, in "Due Process of Law before the Civil War" (1911), could trace this resemblance back into the eighteenth century, if not indeed to the Magna Carta.[42] Due process, the key term of the Fifth and Fourteenth Amendments, is undeniably a common law concept.[43] Something akin to common law reasoning might even be applied to the grounds on which Chief Justice John Marshall drew to defend judicial review in the first place, even while withholding its use, in *Marbury v. Madison*. At best, the framers deftly or discreetly avoided, and hence left open, whether the Supreme Court should have the final word on the constitutionality of legislation.[44]

The contemporary argument that the text governs is, we should recognize, associated with the assumption that the Court governs. That, in turn, is something that has been drawn gradually – perhaps excessively – out of the document over a long period of time. Marshall's notion of judicial

41 Id., 885.

42 Corwin, "Due Process of Law before the Civil War," in Garvey and Mason, *American Constitutional History*, 46.

43 Id.; Corwin, "The Basic Doctrine of American Constitutional Law," in Garvey and Mason, *American Constitutional History*, 25.

44 Larry D. Kramer observes that, in the national debate over adoption of the Constitution, only a "smattering" of references to judicial review was available on which to base any kind of judicial assessment of the constitutionality of legislation, and that the best assessment of its meaning at the time was something well short of judicial supremacy – that is, a final judicial say in constitutional interpretation. Kramer, *The People Themselves*, 83.

review was actually a modest one, described by Larry Kramer as falling well short of judicial determinacy or supremacy. His goal in *Marbury v. Madison* was (in Kramer's words) "to get judicial review into the record – not to establish its existence, but to deflect an incipient movement to delegitimate it."[45] In that sense Marshall had rather little to do with its subsequent emergence as the powerful trump over state and federal legislation.

"Original understanding," as the new bellwether of judicial review, is rendered more tenuous if there was no original understanding, whether by intention, compromise, or even indecision, empowering the Supreme Court to exercise such definitive review at all. It may be useful as a starting point for particular kinds of cases, as defined in Bork's *The Tempting of America*.[46] But its explanatory power seems limited to that, and by the fact that it fails to question the assumption of conclusive judicial supremacy in interpreting the Constitution as a final forum.

Original understanding is particularly hard-pressed to account for the single path that has led to the greatest expansion of the Court's most controversial work: the use of the Fourteenth Amendment to decide substantive matters involving personal rights, such as privacy. The Fourteenth Amendment was a post–Civil War enactment, moved by the immediate concerns of that tumultuous time, such that looking to its original understanding, within that of the original Constitution or Bill of Rights, requires already something of a leap.[47]

Questions regarding its scope arose later. By 1889, before the Court had yet intruded into the realm of state economic regulation, the same year that Professor Kent was ruminating fretfully that "jurisdiction exists in all this class of cases," a prize was awarded to an equally fretful graduate of Harvard Law School for a paper entitled "The True Meaning of the Term 'Liberty' in Those Clauses in the Federal and State Constitutions which Protect 'Life, Liberty, and Property' ":

> One is obliged to ask why it should include thus much and no more. If it includes the right to pursue any lawful trade, why should it not include the right to worship in any lawful manner, to print or speak in any lawful manner? Possibly, if the point

45 Id., 124.

46 Bork, *The Tempting of America*, 162–63. See also Kalman, *The Strange Career of Legal Liberalism* (New Haven: Yale University Press, 1996).

47 Originalists generally look to the original understanding of the Bill of Rights for the language of the Fourteenth Amendment, which assumes without evidence that the 1868 amenders shared or adopted precisely the earlier understanding.

should arise, it would be held to include all the above liberties, although the writer has not found any statements in the books to that effect.[48]

Thirty-five years later, in *Gitlow v. New York*, where the Court upheld a conviction of the publisher of *The Left Wing Manifesto* for advocacy of the overthrow of organized government, Holmes would write in dissent:

The general principle of free speech, it seems to me, must be taken to be included in the Fourteenth Amendment, in view of the scope that has been given to the word "liberty" as there used, although perhaps it may be accepted with a somewhat larger latitude of interpretation than is allowed to Congress by the sweeping language that governs or ought to govern the laws of the United States.[49]

Seventeen years earlier, in the majority opinion in *Patterson v. Colorado*, he had written, "We leave undecided the question whether there is to be found in the Fourteenth Amendment a prohibition similar to that in the First."[50]

I recall this to give a sense of the distance traveled by the Court during Holmes's tenure, as well as its relation to the uncertain future seen in 1889. The movement would accelerate before his retirement in 1932. The previous year, in *Near v. Minnesota*, the *Gitlow* dissent became law, with liberty of the press assimilated to the other liberties already protected. Liberty of association would follow close behind in 1937 with *De Jonge v. Oregon*. The protection of defendants in criminal cases would gather steam in the late 1930s, including right to counsel (*Powell v. Alabama*), exclusion of forced confessions (*Brown v. Mississippi*), and race discrimination in jury lists (*Norris v. Alabama*). Religious belief and exercise was included in *Cantwell v. Connecticut*, in 1940. Also in the 1930s, the separate-but-equal doctrine of *Plessy v. Ferguson* began to be gradually undermined in decisions involving state higher education.[51] All this came a full generation before Earl Warren arrived and took his controversial seat as Chief Justice.

There is little light to be shed on these developments from strict textualism or any original understanding of the Reconstruction Congress of 1866 that drafted the Fourteenth Amendment, or the states that

[48] Charles A. Shattuck, "The True Meaning of the Term 'Liberty' in Those Clauses in the Federal and State Constitutions which Protect 'Life, Liberty, and Property,'" 4 *Harv. L. Rev.* 265 (1891), cited in Freund, *On Law and Justice*, 5.

[49] *Gitlow v. New York*, 268 U.S. 652, 672 (1925).

[50] 205 U.S. 454, 462 (1907).

[51] *Missouri ex rel. Gaines v. Canada*, 305 U.S. 337 (1938). *Plessy* is 163 U.S. 537 (1896); *Near*, 283 U.S. 697 (1931); *De Jonge*, 299 U.S. 353 (1937); *Powell*, 287 U.S. 45 (1932); *Brown*, 297 U.S. 278 (1936); *Norris*, 294 U.S. 587 (1935); *Cantwell*, 310 U.S. 296 (1940).

ratified it.[52] More helpful, I submit, is Paul Freund's observation in 1963:

> All of this movement and ferment, so obscure to the vision of 1889, reflected a sensitivity to values that had emerged in the society and that were sharpened by visible and powerful threats here and abroad. It is no accident, after all, that during the tenure of [the first] Justice Roberts, which coincided with the rise of totalitarian dictatorships, the Court found occasion to set aside the action of Mayor Hague of Jersey City in handpicking the speakers permitted to use the public square, the action of a Huey Long–dominated legislature of Louisiana levying an oppressive tax on the big-city press, and the action of Governor Sterling of Texas in declaring martial law in defiance of a federal court order.[53]

For Freund, much of the expansion of due process jurisprudence was a response to world conflict and the implication of American constitutional rights in the worldwide challenge to democracy.[54] If Holmes reconstructed the common law as a theory of public inquiry – the asking of legally pertinent questions, however arising – then this attitude must color his approach to cases arising under the Constitution. The Fourteenth Amendment, adopted for reasons profound but pertinent to 1868, has since repeatedly posed the ultimate question for a free democratic society, from generation to generation: whether controversial government actions are consistent with the protection against deprivation of "life, liberty, or property without due process of law."

52 See Paul Horowitz, "The Past Tense: The History of Crisis – and the Crisis of History – in Constitutional Theory," 61 *Albany L. Rev.* 459 (1997).

53 Freund, *On Law and Justice*, 7.

54 *On Law and Justice*, 3–22. As this source reflects, Professor Freund's influence on my account of the growth of Fourteenth Amendment jurisdiction has been considerable.

10

Holmes's Theory in Retrospect

Controversies over Holmes linger, seventy-four years since his death. In retrospect we gain insight into the work of an original thinker, but one may wonder how long the settlement of Holmes's reputation must take. Not quite a half century ago, Paul Freund remarked:

> In England until recently it was a tradition that living authors were not to be cited as authority in judicial opinions. On one occasion the Lord Chief Justice, despite the tradition, could not refrain from citing Professor Holdsworth's *History of English Law*, but when he did so he was careful to refer to Professor Holdsworth as one "who is happily not an authority." The reporter of decisions, in puzzling over this passage, concluded that it must have been a slip of the pen, and so when it was published it read "Professor Holdsworth who is unhappily not an authority."[1]

While among over two thousand opinions, in fifty years of judging, there are ample matters for which Holmes is happily, as well as unhappily, not an authority, I have bypassed much relevant criticism to suggest that contemporary legal and political theory has something to gain from a comprehensive reassessment. *The Common Law* has passed its 125th year, still widely misunderstood.

Much hinges on the turn Holmes's work took in 1876, examined in chapter 6, after his early critical scholarship had developed a deep skepticism of the project of analytical classification and an alternative rooted in common law. Having debunked the prospects for a universal or fundamental legal classification offered by John Austin, and conceiving a law without determinate boundaries in which no such essentialism was

[1] Freund, *On Law and Justice*, 147.

to be found, he proposed the historical inevitability of evolution from moral toward external standards of liability. This, a less frequent objection than his pronounced skepticism and tendency to glorify struggle, has nevertheless diverted attention from the balance of his theory and continues to bedevil his reputation. Holmes would apply the precept in his Massachusetts judicial opinions, as Patrick J. Kelley has shown in some detail.[2] Kelley finds a doctrinaire character in many instances, as well as a rigidity in the results. Both he and G. Edward White have noted cases where Holmes, despite his emphasis on the jury's role in informing the court of "common experience," refused to let the jury determine and apply the relevant community standards.[3]

Holmes's overall vision of the common law might have better withstood the test of time as a more moderate statement, such as given by Sir Frederick Pollock in 1900:

> One of the most characteristic and important features of the modern Common Law is the manner in which we fix the measure of legal duties and responsibilities, where not otherwise specified, by reference to a reasonable man's caution, foresight, or expectation, ascertained in the first instance by the common sense of juries, and gradually consolidated into judicial rules of law.[4]

For Pollock (who, we may recall, published a parallel critique of Austin in 1872 that prompted Holmes to get his own developing views into print the same year[5]) the gradual specification of rules through the test of common prudence was not connected with the necessary removal of all moral (in the sense of *subjective*) standards, and it was not the *essential* principle of Anglo-American law, just "*one of* the most characteristic and important." In a looser formulation, we find Postema concluding recently that "the law is inclined only to look at behavior not on motivation."[6] For Holmes the general theory implied a uniform evolution and was sweeping and rigorous. It was the main thesis of the book that would launch his career, and the projected basis for the ongoing development of English and American law.

It required a stretch to demonstrate that subjective tests of legal liability were always reducible to an objective standard, a fact that has proved

2 Kelley, "Holmes on the Supreme Judicial Court: The Theorist as Judge," 283–99.

3 E.g., id. at 292–97 (Holmes interjecting his own view of community standards in cases involving *res ipsa loquitur* and specification). See also White, *Justice Oliver Wendell Holmes*, 381.

4 Sir Frederick Pollock, "History of the Law of Nature," in *Essays in the Law* (London: Macmillan, 1922), 69.

5 See chapter 5, n. 34, supra.

6 Postema, "Philosophy of the Common Law," 610.

inconsistent with the very local flexibility within the system that his overall conception recognizes. In effect, Holmes resisted the conclusion that locally derived standards, reflected as they are in a decentralized adjudicative framework, might insist on recognizing individual subjectivity in specific areas of law, through some approximation of an actual mental state or attitude.[7]

Although the general theory (and his judicial insistence on it) could have benefited from a larger dose of Holmes's own skepticism, part of the problem is semantic. Holmes never adequately addressed the uneasy relationship between ancient liability based on vengeance and a contemporary understanding of the term "moral." This confusion, between morality and subjectivity, would vex him in dealing with persistent examples of subjectively based liability such as libel and slander, and it has muddled his position with respect to analytical positivism. Like the ghost of Sir Henry Maine, an earlier universal evolutionist, the ghost of John Austin must share responsibility. Austin had focused attention upon a prominent feature of mature Anglo-American legal systems, which he misperceived as an innate separation of law and morals. Holmes would, in a sense, build upon both Austin and Maine by reconceiving the separation as an objectivization of liability, while turning it into an evolutionary end-state, not unlike Maine's notion of a historic shift of legal relations based on "status" to "contract."[8]

Holmes's accomplishment was more than simply following a path away from what James Herget has called the "expository" toward the "evolutionary" paradigm for law.[9] His immersion in Austin's exposition, as well as that of Chancellor Kent, obliged him to construct an alternative understanding of the ubiquitous tendency toward classification, and an explanatory mechanism for change within a putatively consistent and dispositive system. This focus on change, on the nature and weight of precedent, the role of juries and judges, the standard of prudence in original

7 Were he following the same line of inquiry today, Holmes would find a process that is messier, more divergent, and riddled with specialized legislative and administrative rules, even if still involving elements of successive approximation in the adjudicative process, not unlike what he had pictured in the early 1870s. Professor Atiyah in 1981 credited Holmes for the radical insight that juries participate in determining legal standards. It was his notion that "what commonly was called a question of 'fact' in a negligence action involved not only issues of pure fact but normative issues as well; amazingly, this was first acknowledged by English Courts only in 1955." Atiyah, "The Legacy of Holmes through English Eyes," in *Holmes and the Common Law: A Century Later*, 27–73.

8 Henry Maine, *Ancient Law: Its Connection with the Early History of Society, and Its Relation to Modern Ideas* (New York: Henry Holt, 1885).

9 Herget, *American Jurisprudence 1870–1970*, 29.

controversies, and the timing of generalization, has obscured the underlying insight that Holmes has in common with other legal theorists. One is certainly James Coolidge Carter (1827–1905), who emphasized the role of customary morality in shaping and transforming the law.[10] Another is F. A. Hayek, now the acknowledged champion of the view that law is grounded in social mores rather than state power.[11] A more unlikely bedfellow is Lon L. Fuller, notwithstanding his own severe critique of Holmes in 1940, based on a common misreading of "The Path of the Law" as separating law from morals. Though he is best known for his attack on positivism and his exegesis of the "morality that makes law possible," Fuller's vision of law privileged the "spontaneous ordering of human relations" and saw adjudication as the "collaborative articulation of shared purposes," both elements of Holmes's decidedly more skeptical approach.[12]

Contemporaneous as well as contemporary reaction to *The Common Law*, viewing Holmes as consistent with Austin, reflects the influence of Austin's strict separation of positive law from morals, while failing to discern the distinctive context.[13] If Holmes was influenced by Austin's separation thesis, it led him nevertheless in a radically different direction. Eschewing an Aristotelian separation of kinds as static and simplistic, he looked to history for a dynamic that distinguished (in practice, not in essence) the fact-specified dictates of law from the abstract dictates of morals.[14]

[10] Carter viewed the role of custom in shaping law in a manner remarkably similar to Holmes. As with Maine and Holmes, he began with a consideration of primitive society, and saw law as emerging from norms developed through the constant interactions of individuals, eventually embodied in precedent as judges discover what those norms are, but express them provisionally, subject to modification in light of new circumstances. Id., 120; James Coolidge Carter, *Law: Its Origin, Growth and Function* (New York: Legal Classics Library, 1996).

[11] As discussed in chapter 2, n. 15, Hayek drew on David Hume, who in turn was influenced by the "moral sense" theorists of the Scottish Enlightenment. Some similar influence on Holmes is suggested by his Harvard education, reading, and involvement with the Metaphysical Club. See chapter 2, n. 4, chapter 3, n. 24.

[12] Fuller, *The Law in Quest of Itself*, 110; *The Morality of Law*, 92 ("the law merely brings to explicit expression conceptions of right and wrong widely shared in the community"); Herget, *American Jurisprudence 1870–1970*, 253–61. On Fuller's criticism of Holmes's alleged positivism, see *The Law in Quest of Itself*, 62–63, 117–18.

[13] White, *Justice Oliver Wendell Holmes*, 182–91.

[14] See Touster, "Holmes a Hundred Years Ago," 684–91. Noting that *The Common Law* had sought so ambitiously to advance the projects of both Maine and Austin, Touster asks the question, "Why, then, the clear, if not always acknowledged, failure of the work?" His answer is similar to the opinion expressed in 1882, in an anonymous review, by the distinguished scholar Albert Venn Dicey, that Holmes focused too keenly on proving *where* the legal process was going and too little on the ramifications of the historical

In so doing Holmes left open a connection between law and the moral usage embedded in the community, which he distinguished from moral postulates as they appear in legal arguments or judicial opinions. This device served an important function, particularly where juries were not engaged in the judgment process, as in the labor cases *Vegelahn* and *Plant.* It restrained the encroachment of moral postulates on the gradual development of judicial consensus. In redefining judicial inquiry as coordinate with that of the jury, Holmes limited its freedom to moralize even while revitalizing the underlying legitimacy of the common law method.

While he would frequently allude to the importance of judicial deference to community standards as established through jury determinations, we find him increasingly willing (as Kelley notes) to put the judge in the place of the common law jury in defining the prudent man: to forgo sending cases back for further jury findings – if that option were available – and to look instead to himself for the relevant community standard. This form of judicial self-reliance, which Holmes had recognized before becoming a judge, is conditioned by its focus on community-derived standards and the rejection of argument from abstract "principles." As he explained in his 1880 essay "Trespass and Negligence,"

> A judge who has long sat at *nisi prius* [trying cases of first impression on their facts] ought gradually to acquire a fund of experience which enables him to represent the common sense of the community in ordinary instances far better than an average jury. He should be able to lead and instruct them in detail, even where he thinks it desirable on the whole, to take their opinion. Furthermore, the sphere in which he is able to rule without taking their opinion at all should be constantly growing.[15]

As a Massachusetts judge, Holmes routinely conceptualized close cases as invoking competing lines of precedent, involving conflicts that must be resolved through line drawing, thus applying his model of common-law rule making as it emerged in the early 1870s. Kelley has shown that

process itself. As Dicey had written in 1882, the dual influence of Maine and Austin led to the insight that "the notions and maxims which make up the common law are the slow growth of judicial decisions," but also to the chief defect of Holmes's book, "uncertainty of aim." I have argued that the full ramifications of his insight become clear only in light of Holmes's entire career and of its now evident opposition to Hobbesian positivism as it has progressed into the twentieth century and beyond. A. V. Dicey, "Holmes's 'Common Law,'" published anonymously in *The Spectator, Literary Supplement,* June 3, 1882, at 745–47, reprinted as an appendix to, Touster, "Holmes a Hundred Years Ago," 712, 714.

[15] Holmes, "Trespass and Negligence," in *Formative Essays,* 257, and in 3 *Collected Works,* 99–100.

Holmes often appears to force his conceptual framework upon resistant materials, thereby biasing the results.[16] Yet the materials of each case – claims, facts, defenses – were already packaged by counsel to suit the interests of opposing parties. Holmes's historical thesis may be flawed, but his method removes arguments from case law into a wider perspective, disrobing principles and maxims, translating conflicting precedents into the continuum of conflicting activities, and seeking a context within which he could compare previous resolutions, whether legislative or judicial. Seeing each case in this broader continuum provided considerable illumination:

> Nobody who sat on [Holmes's] court in my time had quite such a daunting personality – to a young lawyer, at least. Holmes was extremely courteous but his mind was so extraordinarily quick and incisive, he was such an alert and sharply attentive listener, his questions went so to the root of the case, that it was rather an

[16] Kelley, "Holmes on the Supreme Judicial Court: The Theorist as Judge," 283–85, 300–303, 324–40, 351–52. See also White, *Justice Oliver Wendell Holmes*, 384–85. Examples of Holmes's line-drawing analogy are rife and begin soon after his assumption of judicial responsibilities. They arose wherever competing considerations cast alternative theories of decision over a particular case, as in the examples, such as *Beadel v. Perry*, that Holmes had come across in his research for *Kent's Commentaries*. In 1879, shortly before preparing his text for the Lowell Lectures, Holmes wrote out a lengthy explanation of the relationship between judge and jury: "The court, not entertaining any clear views of public policy applicable to the matter, derives the rule to be applied from common experience. . . . But the court further feels that it is not possessed of sufficient practical experience to lay down the rule intelligently. . . . Therefore, it aids its conscience by taking the opinion of the jury." Note the context in which Holmes uses the phrase "public policy," and what he goes on to say:

> But supposing a state of facts often repeated in practice, is it to be imagined that the court is to go on leaving the standard to the jury for ever? Is it not manifest, on the contrary, that if the jury is, on the whole, as fair a tribunal as it is represented, the lesson which can be got from that source will be learned? Either the court will find that the fair teaching of experience is that the conduct complained of is or is not blameworthy, and therefore, unless explained, is or is not a ground of liability; or it will find the jury oscillating to and fro, and will see the necessity of making up its mind for itself. . . .
>
> If this be the proper conclusion in plain cases, further consequences ensue. Facts do not often exactly repeat themselves in practice; but cases with comparatively small variations from each other do. A judge who has long sat at *nisi prius* ought gradually to acquire a fund of experience which enables him to represent the common sense of the community in ordinary instances better than an average jury. He should be able to lead and to instruct them in detail, even where he thinks it desirable, on the whole, to take their opinion. Furthermore, the sphere in which he is able to rule without taking their opinion at all should be continually growing.

Hence it is clear that, however controversial it is today to speak of judges contributing to public policy, for Holmes it meant a collaborative enterprise of seeking a "common sense of the community." Holmes, "Trespass and Negligence," in *Formative Essays*, 257, and in 3 *Collected Works*, 98–99.

> ordeal to appear before him. In arguing a case you felt that when your sentence was half done he had seen the end of it, and before the argument was a third finished he had seen the whole course of reasoning and was wondering whether it was sound.[17]

The essence of this contribution is a revision of the conception of common law method inherited from sixteenth-century England as a distinctive vision of formal community inquiry into the litigated conflicts that arise in society.

I have emphasized that Holmes's model of retrospective generalization separates contemporary common law from the project of analytical positivism to come up with a fixed universal definition of law that might lead to final answers to legal questions. It proposes a theory by which legal rules are mediated by contemporary standards of prudence and policy, and offers an empirical model of rule-based conflict resolution, one that seeks to distinguish between conflicts among competing precedents and those among competing general interests. It demands that judges explain their reasoning and decisions in specific terms – comparing precedents, distinguishing interests, limiting the prospective use of generalization. In constitutional law, Holmes did not foreclose judicial inquiry into new substantive issues under the Fourteenth Amendment, but he believed that his protocols of interpretation offered a method for weighing the protections of a constitution, sweeping in their expression, in circumstances unforeseen by the framers.

Of all contemporary scholars, Gerald Postema has done the most to explore the theory of common law. For Postema, as well as for David Strauss and other writers that have lately given the matter serious thought, "common law is judge-made law."[18] This is, of course, true in a literal sense, but so describing it downplays the influence of embedded patterns of conduct and belief that form what Holmes called the external standard of prudence. That is quite close to what Postema recognizes elsewhere as "material conventionalism," or the influence on common law of "ordinary social life." As a foundation for common law, it is hard to improve on Postema's observation:

> Material conventionalism maintains that it is necessary that law be incorporated into the *ordinary social life* of the community it seeks to govern, while it will always be different and to a degree distant from it. For this, it is not necessary that legal

[17] Unpublished remarks of U.S. Circuit Judge James M. Morton, Jr., at memorial exercises for Holmes at the Supreme Judicial Court on October 9, 1937, quoted in Novick, *Honorable Justice*, at 173.

[18] Postema, "Philosophy of the Common Law," 588.

> norms be incorporated into any general theory or comprehensive doctrine about that social life or its underlying principles. Providing the soil into which law must sink its roots are "conversations" not creeds, practices not principles, ordinary affairs and activities not theories and doctrines. These resources give practical life to law's norms. Entirely without them, law's normative guidance and robust normative governance would be rootless. (emphasis in original)[19]

From this it is but a short step to the essence of Holmes's judicial method. If legal problems are seen as embedded in practices, and the practices are the concrete factors that define both the legal and the logical character of cases that come before the courts, then it follows that each case must be seen as a class of legal problem, and each problem must be seen as a continuum, a phenomenon with discrete stages in the process of inquiry and remediation.

This context illuminates such comments as in 1913 regarding a "time for law." It should not be read to suggest that judges should time their interventions, insofar as decisions may be forced by the flow of litigation; they should consider it in the nature of the response. Within the flow of disputes are varying degrees of ripeness, what Holmes referred to in 1870 as the relative opportunity to "'reconcile the cases,' as it is called, that is, by a true induction to state the principle which has until then been obscurely felt."

How this perspective applies to contemporary problems may require further insight, as Holmes's half-century of judging recedes. He has helped us to understand that judges should withhold predisposition where "opposing convictions still maintain a battle front against each other." We may yet wonder if they must put a finger to the political winds before deciding when and how to withhold. If recognition is required of a popular consensus respecting constitutional cases, how may we know when it is a consensus that is gathering, as opposed to a pendulum shift in popular feeling? If judges must confine a decision to specific circumstances, leaving open the broader dispute to further ferment in the public sphere, what if nonjudicial avenues are clogged and no resolution is likely? May it not depend on how dire the consequences of waiting? Answers do not come easily, but these are practical questions that Holmes's conception of common law uniquely recognizes, as legitimate aspects of legal and constitutional philosophy.

Another insight is the relationship of common law method and textual interpretation. In an example suggested by H. L. A. Hart, noted above in

[19] Id., 615.

chapter 3, the question was posed of whether a bicycle would constitute a "vehicle" prohibited by statute from use in a public park. Hart attributed this kind of legal question to the "open texture" of language, such that (in David Lyons's analysis) it implied the impossibility of resolution by "the law." The example demonstrated that there exist gaps in legal language that oblige the judge to "legislate."[20]

Openness of texture, even as a metaphor applied to language, carries with it the image of a fabric, a woven cloth, with intervening spaces that fail to provide the logical force of clear words in their typical function of representation. If the law is equated with authoritative legal language, the logic of the metaphor suggests that the law is without an answer to any unclear case that falls resolutely in the gaps and thus outside the operative terms – in spaces where reference seems utterly unavailing. But (as Hart himself has observed[21]) the law of precedent operates by example; and the common law is an accretion of examples, successively approximated in language.

Common law precedents may thus be drawn on to illuminate the meaning of a statutory term, such as the term "maintenance" in *Commonwealth v. Churchill.*[22] There, the question arose as to whether one defendant, as a sales employee, had participated in "keeping and maintaining" a place for the illegal sale of alcoholic beverage. The prosecution argued that sales in the presence of the employer, whose guilt was clear, assisted the latter in keeping the tenement. In an opinion remarkably similar to his common law decisions, Holmes compared competing lines of precedent in similar situations. His finding that purchases in other situations had been held outside the purview of such assistance influenced the result. Such considerations would tend to be ignored by purely textual interpretation. In *A Matter of Interpretation,* Justice Scalia draws a sharp line between common law and statutory interpretation:

> [T]hough I have no quarrel with the common law and its process, I do question whether the *attitude* of the common-law judge – the mind-set that asks, "What is the most desirable resolution of this case, and how can any impediments to the achievement of that result be evaded?" – is appropriate for most of the work that I do, and much of the work that state judges do. We live in an age of legislation, and most new law is statutory law.[23]

[20] Lyons, "Open Texture and the Possibility of Legal Interpretation," 303.

[21] Hart, *The Concept of Law,* 126.

[22] See chapter 9, n. 7.

[23] Scalia, *A Matter of Interpretation,* 13.

Here Scalia adopts a view of common law decisions as a caricature plainly rejected by Holmes: that the common law method is an open invitation to judicial license, to a subjective instrumentalism, deciding as the individual judge deems socially "desirable." Scalia excludes the possibility of a common law approach that does not invite sheer subjective result orientation. He continues:

> As one legal historian has put it, "The lion's share of the norms and rules that actually govern the country [come] out of Congress and the legislatures...." This is particularly true in the federal courts, where, with a qualification so small it does not bear mentioning, there is no such thing as common law. Every issue of law resolved by a federal judge involves interpretation of text – the text of a regulation, or of a statute, or of the Constitution.[24]

There is here an important semantic distinction between common law as a separate body of doctrine and common law as a method. When Scalia says of the federal courts, "there is no such thing as common law," he refers to the overruling of *Swift v. Tyson*, permitting federal courts to substitute their own judgment for that of the appropriate state in "diversity" cases, in *Erie Railroad v. Tomkins.*[25] Holmes had himself led the Supreme Court in this direction by his dissents in *Kuhn v. Fairmont Coal Co.* and *Black & White Taxi Co. v. Brown & Yellow Taxi Co.*[26] This only highlights that Holmes's theory of common law was focused not on content, on the common law as a discrete body of doctrine (the view he often referred to as a "brooding omnipresence in the sky"[27]), but on a method applicable to all law and legal adjudication.

When Justice Scalia in his lecture addresses what he calls the "science of statutory interpretation," he presents a compendium of "canons of construction – which have been widely criticized, indeed even mocked, by modern legal commentators." They include "*expressio unius est exclusio alterius....* [e]xpression of the one is exclusion of the other"; "*noscitur a*

[24] Id.

[25] 304 U.S. 64 (1938). Diversity cases are suits between parties of separate states, and oblige federal courts to apply state law.

[26] 215 U.S. 349, 370 (1910); 276 U.S. 518, 532 (1928). Professor White has observed: "Even though he claimed that the conception of an independent, transcendent body of federal common law was fallacious, since it ignored principles of sovereignty and resurrected the archaic image of law as 'a brooding omnipresence in the sky,' [Holmes] continued to decide federal common law cases without recourse to the law of the state in which they arose, and in negligence cases substituted the judge-made rules of federal courts for the decisions of local juries." White, *Justice Oliver Wendell Holmes*, 381.

[27] White, *Justice Oliver Wendell Holmes*, 387.

sociis, which means, literally, 'it is known by its companions'"; and "*ejusdem generis,* which means 'of the same sort.'"[28] In the case of *Commonwealth v. Churchill,* such canons would presumably have been brought to bear on the interpretation of the word "maintain," to determine whether the accused was guilty under the statute prohibiting "keeping and maintaining" the proscribed tenement. Can the canons alone satisfactorily explain the process?

It is remarkable that none of the commentaries on Scalia's essay challenged his caricature of the common law nor proffered a coherent alternative theory, demonstrating perhaps how established is either the caricature itself or the consensus that there is no coherent theory. Gordon Wood came closest to doing so, offering the following:

> I wonder whether the distinction Justice Scalia has drawn between common-law interpretation and statutory interpretation is not too sharp. In any common-law system statutory construction seems bound to take on many of the characteristics of common law interpretation. I am not a lawyer, but I do have the sense that English common-law judges, in construing parliamentary statutes, try to fit them into the body of the law; in English jurisprudence, then, knowing the text of a statute is not the same as knowing the law.[29]

Wood makes a pertinent point, but his essay was an appeal to history and tradition, tying common law practice to the development in America of an independent judiciary, and Scalia refuted it as such:

> I am not aware of any evidence that adjudicative tribunals (the Supreme Judicial Court of Massachusetts, for example, as opposed to the General Court, which is its legislature) felt free to legislate – that is, to change or depart from statutory law in the course of promulgating their adjudicative decrees. To the contrary, it was accepted (Lord Chief Justice Coke in Dr. Bonham's case notwithstanding) that courts were in principle bound by statutory enactments.
>
> This is not to say that I take issue with Professor Wood's conclusion that the problem of judicial rewriting of democratically adopted texts is "deeply rooted in our history" and that "judges have exercised that sort of presumably undemocratic authority from the very beginning." To acknowledge that is simply to acknowledge that there have always been, as there undoubtedly always will be, willful judges who bend the law to their wishes. But acknowledging evil is one thing, and embracing it is something else.[30]

28 Scalia, *A Matter of Interpretation,* 25–26.

29 Wood, "Comment," id., 59.

30 Id., 131.

This is strong language indeed, not likely to endear the common law tradition to impressionable law students.

Justice Scalia contemplates no respectable rationale for anything other than a strict, and laboratory-purified, concentration only on the statute in question, albeit part of a comprehensive body of statutes. Nonstatutory lines of precedent are plainly to be ignored. His remarks imply that statutory terms such as "maintenance" in the Massachusetts Code of 1883 could not be examined with reference to common law usage – that is, their use not only in prior decisions interpreting the statute in question, but their historical meaning as part of the common law.

Yet Scalia leaves himself an accommodation; he accepts the common law practice of *stare decisis*, while insisting that it is not an acceptance of independent judicial meaning. His canons of statutory interpretation, especially *noscitur sociis* and *ejusdem generis*, can hardly be read otherwise than as inviting, if not requiring, comparison of other cases, some of which would surely be found applicable by Holmes. In short, Scalia's strict textualism needs more room for consideration of precedent than is consistent with his own caricature of common law method.

Are we to conclude that there is little difference in the opposing schools? Not when one considers that no *nonstatutory* precedent bearing on the meaning of statutory terms is permissible for the textualist – unless perhaps it can be shown that the legislature intended to incorporate such meaning. This, however, would tread the forbidden waters of legislative history, against Scalia's conviction (with Holmes) that "the objective indication of the words, rather than the intent of the legislature, is what constitutes the law."[31] And if this were the first instance of interpreting a statutory term, the pure textualist would insist that the judge look only to the statute itself, as there would be no prior cases deciding what conduct was sufficient to fulfill the legislative standard. Scalia associates all common law with a rank form of subjective instrumentalism, leaving no room for the process of examining prior interpretations of legal concepts that Holmes describes in considerable and compelling detail.[32]

Such is the predicament of the modern judge and lawyer, absent a better conception of common law than that found in the wake of analytical positivism. Reasoning from precedent is taught at all American law

[31] Id., 23, citing Holmes, "The Theory of Legal Interpretation," in *Collected Legal Papers*, 207.

[32] David A. Strauss notes that the notion that the text of the Constitution is an effective limit on judges is plausible only if one assumes a background of highly developed precedent. Strauss, "Common Law Constitutional Interpretation," 907–25.

schools and used throughout the judicial system, but it has hardly more intellectual justification than the stability it might provide through the time-honored practice of *stare decisis.*[33] Even *stare decisis* is portrayed by Scalia as undermining the validity of majoritarian government: reasoning from precedents "would be an unqualified good, were it not for a trend in government that has developed in recent centuries, called democracy."[34] The will of the majority is embodied in a final authoritative text or not at all. With this stance the foundation for *stare decisis* is virtually incoherent, grounded in sheer tradition, but violating a putatively fundamental democratic principle.

When the discussion is brought from the abstract to the particular, in the actual world of judging, can any text qua text, any discrete form of words, handle the entire responsibility? The Churchill case affords a glimpse of the fact that there exists a diversity of problems in the application of legal language. In proscribing the "maintenance" of a tenement for illegal sale of alcohol, the legislature had expressed its intent as comprehensively and explicitly as possible. The language itself does not call for *legislative* definition of the nature of activity constituting maintenance. The legislature may not anticipate every situation to which a lawyer or prosecutor might apply its enactments.[35]

[33] A leading contemporary reference, *Corpus Juris Secundum*, says of *stare decisis*, "The rule is founded on considerations of expediency and sound principles of public policy, to preserve the harmony and stability of the law. . . . The rule represents an element of continuity in law and is rooted in the psychologic need to satisfy reasonable expectations, but it is a principle of policy and not a mechanical formula of adherence to the latest decision however recent and questionable when such adherence involves collision with prior doctrine more embracing in scope, intrinsically sounder, and verified by experience." 21 *C.J.S.*, sec. 140, 164–65 (1990) (citations omitted).

[34] Scalia, *A Matter of Interpretation*, 9.

[35] See Levi, *An Introduction to Legal Reasoning*, 27–31:

> It is customary to think of case-law reasoning as inductive and the application of statutes as deductive.
>
> The legislature may have had a particular case uppermost in mind, but it has spoken in general terms. . . . The specification of particular instances indicates that similar but unmentioned instances are not to be included. But the specification of particular instances, when in addition a word of a general category is used, may be the indication that other like instances are also intended; hence the *ejusdem generis* rule.
>
> [T]he words of advice [of Justice Reed in *United States v. American Trucking Ass'n*, 310 U.S. 534, 542 (1940)] force one to re-examine whether there is any difference between case law and statutory interpretation. It is not enough to show that the words used by the legislature have some meaning. Concepts created by case law also have some meaning, but the meaning is ambiguous. It is not clear how wide or narrow the scope is to be. Can it be said that the words used by the legislature have any more meaning than that,

The question is, then, whether a legislative or constitutional text is a comprehensive embodiment of the common will, or whether that will must be further understood to include the experience of the same community in the past and future, through relevant formal and public inquiry. Holmes's view seems to be that such words are the words of an ongoing community, and as formed over time in the legal process, they cannot be fully understood in insulation from their history of interpretation. Evaluating this insight, so central to Holmes's jurisprudence, seems foreclosed by the context of contemporary debate. Absolute textualism is more than a mere intellectual trend, a conservative ideology, or a blind commitment. It is informed by a belief concerning the nature of law, such that if democratic sourcing works only through legislative enactment, law must then remain discrete from its customary source, with a strict and identifiable boundary. By privileging the legal text, it is assumed that an identifiable entity called "law" has alone produced the outcome.

or is there the same ambiguity? One important difference can be noted immediately. Where case law is considered, there is a conscious realignment of cases; the problem is not the intention of the prior judge. But with a statute the reference is to the kind of things intended by the legislature. All concepts suggest, but case-law concepts can be re-worked.

Regarding the legislative ambiguity, Levi observes:

> This is not the result of inadequate draftsmanship, as is frequently urged. Matters are not decided until they have to be. . . . If the legislature were a court, it would not decide the precise effect until a specific fact situation arose demanding an answer. . . . Despite much gospel to the contrary, a legislature is not a fact-finding body. . . . The members of the legislative body will be talking about different things; they cannot force each other to accept even a hypothetical set of facts. The result is that even in a non controversial atmosphere just exactly what has been decided will not be clear.

11

Conclusion

I have argued that an overall consistency may be found throughout Holmes's work, in tracing his path from the earlier critical to the later constructive stage of his scholarship, and on into his judicial career. Although his place in American jurisprudence is still controversial, I have suggested that his conception of law may clearly be understood by comparison with contemporary legal positivism, as it has developed from Austin to Hart, bearing a distinct view of the nature and method of law. Having discerned a relationship between law and morals that formerly appeared to be a gloss on John Austin's strict separation, Holmes developed instead what must be described as an original common law theory. Finally, I have claimed that Holmes provides a more comprehensive and compelling approach to judicial restraint than strict textualism and original understanding, grounded as they are in the positivist tradition.[1]

[1] Given the diverse influences on Holmes, from nineteenth-century Boston, Harvard, and the Metaphysical Club to Austin, Maine, and Pollock, and the wide range of his specialized research and reading, it is not easy to characterize his "philosophy." However, Kuklick's *The Rise of American Philosophy* provides a helpful reference, shedding light on the distinctive context of philosophical speculation in the nineteenth century, especially the amateur or "club" philosophizing in which Holmes was involved, and the gradual emergence of professionalization in the twentieth, with its eventual emphasis on logic and epistemology.

By the time H. L. A. Hart came to Harvard and reinvigorated the analytical separation of law and morals in America, "noncognitivism" in philosophy had overwhelmed moral naturalism with the linguistic turn of C. L. Stevenson's *Ethics and Language* (New Haven: Yale University Press, 1933) (Kuklick, *The Rise of American Philosophy*, 496–515). This had an influence on legal theory; the analytical separation of fact and value supported Hart while obscuring the naturalistic roots of Holmes's own distinction of law and morals. The latter is rooted in the naturalist empiricist theorists of the Scottish Enlightenment,

In the following passage from *The Supreme Court and the Idea of Progress,* Alexander Bickel emphasizes that the Supreme Court does not act as a mechanical interpreter in isolation from the prevailing standards of society at large.

> The Supreme Court's judgments may be put forth as universally prescriptive; but they actually become so only when they gain widespread assent. They bind of their own force no one but the parties to a litigation. To realize the promise that all others similarly situated will be similarly bound, the Court's judgments need the assent and the cooperation first of the political institutions, and ultimately of the people.[2]

He observes that its judgments "need the assent and the cooperation first of the political institutions, and ultimately of the people." We should expect such an obvious and significant fact to be incorporated in our theory of legal interpretation.

Contemporary legal philosophy, dominated by the debate of whether law and morals are separate, recognizes no dynamic relation between popular assent and the interpretation, as opposed to the enactment, of law. With Holmes, legal interpretation is understood as continually informed by the standards of conduct of the community at large. His conception replaces the question of *whether* law is separate from morals by the inquiry of *how* the two may be understood to interact. He may not have left us with an entirely complete and satisfactory account of the dependent relation between interpretation and popular assent, but this should not detract from the fact that the relation is, uniquely among contemporary theories, fully recognized. It is informed by the account Holmes provided of the origin and specification of rules and the resolution of conflicts between them, and his attempt to define and distinguish constitutional review as an aspect of the same relation.

Holmes abandoned the positivist effort to gain a comprehensive analytical understanding of law in favor of a naturalized historical one. He did not simply reject Aristotelian logic, a logic rooted in classification and deduction based on natural kinds, leaving nothing in its place but empty skepticism. He replaced it with an account drawn from historical materials

especially the anti-Hobbes "moral sense" theories of Shaftesbury, Hutcheson, Kames, and Adam Smith, and their influence on the intellectual attitudes of other major theorists and on eighteenth- and nineteenth-century American attitudes, as well as in the influence of Alexander Bain and others on the early "pragmatism" of the Metaphysical Club. See chapter 3, n. 33, and chapter 5, n. 5 supra.

[2] Alexander Bickel, *The Supreme Court and the Idea of Progress* (New York, Evanston, and London: Harper & Row, 1970).

showing how common law concepts have emerged, with the growth and reconciliation of diverse legal classes, assisted in part by logic, but in fact deeply driven by practice and judgment, the repeated outcomes of cases informed by the standards of the ordinary person. This naturalized understanding is remarkably explicit in the 1899 article "Law in Science and Science in Law," where Holmes stressed that law is inescapably the study of the history of legal precepts in order to understand their true scope and limits.

> It is perfectly proper to regard and study the law simply as a great anthropological document. It is proper to resort to it to discover what ideals of society have been strong enough to reach that final form of expression, or what have been the changes in dominant ideals from century to century. It is proper to study it as an exercise in the morphology and transformation of human ideas.[3]

Holmes's account of deciding difficult cases addresses an issue in contemporary political theory, in particular the nature of social and political reasoning. It might be said that he has taken a naturalist detour around Hegelian logic.[4] Rather than the idealist vision of thesis engendering antithesis and leading to synthesis, his is a concrete and antirationalist model of conceptual development through a succession of litigants encountering each other in the courts. In the case-by-case negotiation of clashing purposes and interests, and the judicial abstraction of responses to them, conflicting principles (which lack "commensurability" not from logical incompatibility but because they are rooted in independent courses of conduct) may eventually be reconciled.

The insight came from the historical common law, discovered in the 1870s within the dry, citation-filled pages of *Kent's Commentaries on American Law*. Resolutions come not from the mind of a single heroic judge, the Hercules of Ronald Dworkin or the philosopher-king caricatured by Justice Scalia, or even, strictly speaking, from the minds of many judges. They eventuate over time, even across succeeding generations,

[3] Holmes, *Collected Legal Papers*, 212.

[4] As Professor Friedrich summarizes Hegel's view, "Law is the embodiment of the ethical idea emanating from the state; as such it is embedded in history which consists in the unfolding of the world spirit's idea of freedom by way of the states which progressively realize it" (Friedrich, *Philosophy of Law*, 237). The notion that law embodies an innate ethical idea undervalues the real struggles that produced recognition of areas of constitutionally protected conduct, by presuming that a "world spirit" was inexorably pushing human history toward them, and ignores the need for continued vigilance and the possibility of retrogression. Holmes often mocked the Hegelian concept of *Geist*; his diary records reading secondary sources on Hegel in 1865–66; Little, "The Early Reading of Justice Oliver Wendell Holmes," 172.

through a combination of judicial and popular thought and action. When points marked over time eventually suggest a reconciliation of conflicting views, it is one reflecting increasing experience and adjustment, among all the actors in the ongoing field of conflict, within and without the courtroom.

We might compare this with the detached rationalist model of the philosopher John Rawls, who constructs the notion of a "reflective equilibrium" under given hypothetical conditions (and behind a "veil of ignorance") to explain the derivation of general principles of justice from specific conditions.[5] Holmes's model also aims at reconciling diversity through the application of rules reached reflectively. But it is vastly dissimilar in its dependence on historical detail rather than ivory-tower reflection on presumptive competing ideas and interests. Insofar as it embodies principles of liberalism, they are rooted in the historical experience of a civic republican community and its legal tradition, including the conditions of adoption and implementation of the United States Constitution.[6]

Liberal and communitarian political theorists have battled in recent years over the competing demands of individual rights and social solidarity. The emergence of communitarianism in the late twentieth century came in reaction to liberalism's foundationalist or a priori picture of individual rights. Michael J. Sandel, in *Liberalism and the Limits of Justice*, identified this "deontological" view of rights as rooted in the utilitarian and Kantian traditions and reflected in the depiction by Rawls in his *A Theory of Justice*.[7] Holmes rejects such a view in his critique of John Austin, applying a naturalized view of emerging consensus to the rights enshrined in the United States Constitution. Rights are defined through experience, not as innately "higher" principles that trump competing considerations. They maintain a communitarian vitality in Holmes's theory of law as public inquiry. Rather than fundamental propositions, they are fundamental questions. In place of "deontological" foundations, Holmes gave constitutional rights a naturalized, popular foundation, a meaning hard-earned over time, hammered out in the real trials of an ongoing national community.

5 John Rawls, *A Theory of Justice* (Cambridge, Mass.: Belknap Press, 1971).

6 Rawls addressed the objection that his original position was overly foundationalist in *Political Liberalism* (New York: Columbia University Press, 1993); see Richard Rorty, *Objectivism, Relativism, and Truth* (Cambridge: Cambridge University Press, 1991), 175–96.

7 Michael J. Sandel, *Liberalism and the Limits of Justice* (Cambridge: Cambridge University Press, 1982), 1–10.

So described, this entails a vision of law with a unique notion of judicial timing and restraint. Beneath each final ruling lies a tacit, multifaceted, multiparty, slow-moving negotiation approaching at last some semblance of a civic consensus. As such, a truly desirable outcome, indeed the notion of "social desirability" itself, embodies something more complex than a choice between the policy views on either side of a given controversy. Judges must avoid proposing a formula too early, before all aspects of the matter have been explored. As he explained in an opinion for the Massachusetts court in 1900:

> We do not forget the continuous process of developing the law that goes on through the courts, in the form of deduction, or deny that in a clear case it might be possible even to break away from a line of decisions in favor of some rule generally admitted to be based upon a deeper insight into the present wants of society. But the improvements made by the courts are made, almost invariably, by very slow degrees and by very short steps. Their general duty is not to change but to work out the principles already sanctioned by the practice of the past. No one supposes that a judge is at liberty to decide with sole reference even to his strongest convictions of policy and right. His duty in general is to develop the principles which he finds, with such consistency as he may be able to attain.[8]

In constitutional law, Holmes's common law vision is illuminating, even if tenuous and difficult in practical application. Unlike contemporary conservatives, many of whom still decry with Professor Corwin the abandonment of strict procedural due process, Holmes yielded to what Corwin conceded to be the powerful exigency to find room in the text to weigh urgent new disputes against constitutional values. Conservatives and liberals alike would agree that such values must be carefully weighed somewhere in the governing process, or remain meaningless as they did in the Soviet constitution.[9] Holmes suggests a model through which constitutional evaluation may take place concretely, without conceding final judicial authority to determine their meaning for all time.

The Justices, while unable to enlist direct input from the public, are largely bound by prevailing public standards and restrained where standards are yet undeveloped or cannot be known. This is not to say that they must remain silent when they believe that a widely accepted practice – such as forced confessions in the twentieth century – is plainly

[8] *Stack v. New York, NH & HRR*, 177 Mass 155, 158, 58 NE 686, 687 (1900), quoted in Tushnet, "The Logic of Experience: Oliver Wendell Holmes on the Supreme Judicial Court," 1005.

[9] See Harold J. Berman, *Justice in the U.S.S.R.: An Interpretation of Soviet Law* (New York: Vantage Books, 1963), 376–80.

inconsistent with the Bill of Rights. Yet the language of the Constitution, and its Fourteenth Amendment, speaks to everyone, not just to the Supreme Court. A way must be found, even in original controversies, for the "absolute compulsion of the words" to have some force, without conceding a license to make new law ahead of the popular conscience.

What, we might ask, is constitutional law, and how does it protect values so fundamental as liberty, equality, and freedom of expression? What it does is not different from what the common law has done in multiple contexts throughout centuries of experiment with free institutions in England: it has focused the inquiry, it has forced the question, repeatedly. This is what is meant by First, or Fifth, or Fourteenth Amendment jurisdiction: it asks whether a given public purpose is consistent with free expression, equal protection, or denial of liberty without due process of law. It does so in a continuing succession of urgent but particular controversies, in which the stakes are high and all are held to account; and it has asked relentlessly. Answers gradually have come out, but they were and are not final. "Clear and present danger," a test for free speech first suggested by Holmes in 1919, now plays a subordinate role in First Amendment law.[10] The answers have not come only from inherent content in the document, the understanding of its framers, or patent logical inconsistencies between statutory and constitutional language. They emerge within a tradition, and have arisen from the specific exigencies of maintaining popular government through civil strife and world war, on into a risky and uncertain future.

[10] See Kellogg, "Learned Hand and the Great Train Ride," 56 *American Scholar* 471 (1987).

Appendix

A. Duties of all the World.

1. To the Sovereign

a. Law of prize (applying to persons not subject as well as subjects).
b. Military service — some taxes (*e. g.* poll tax.).
c. Criminal law.

2. To all the World.

a. Law of libel and slander (civil actions).
b. Injuries to the person — false imprisonment, &c.
c. Some nuisances?
d. Fraud independent of contract or special relations.

3. To persons in particular situations or relations (some of these are only special applications of the class A. 2).

a. Law of offices — corporations.
b. Monopolies, such as patent-rights.
c. Possession.
d. Ownership. Easement. Rent? &c.
e. Contract?
f. Domestic relations.

B. Duties of Persons in Particular Situations or Relations.

1. To the Sovereign (perhaps for reasons of convenience to follow duties of all the world to the Sovereign).

a. Duties of officers — impeachment, &c.
b. Eminent domain.
c. Taxes on property.

2. To all the World (perhaps to be put with duties of all the world to persons in the same situations. Some of these are special applications of A. 2).

a. Corporations?
b. Duties of land-owners not to make nuisances on their land, &c., &c.

3. To persons in particular situations or relations (including some more special applications of A. 2, and A. 3).

a. Members of corporation to each other.
b. Landlord and tenant, &c.
c. Trustee and *cestui que trust*.
d. Contractor and contractee.
e. Master and servant.
f. Guardian and ward.
&c., &c.

1. Holmes's classification of law as a system of duties (from 7 *American Law Review* 48 (1872)).

SUCCESSIONS.

A. UNIVERSAL, *or successions to the entire* PERSONA *of another, subject to greater or less exceptions.*

1. By will or death (executors and administrators).

2. By act *inter vivos:*

a. By assignments in bankruptcy (assignees)?

b. By marriage (husband to wife)?

B. PARTIAL, *or successions to a special* PERSONA, *or group of rights and duties, severable from the other rights and duties of the party first sustaining it.*

1. By descent (lands).

2. By will (lands, chattels).

3. By act *inter vivos:*

a. By voluntary change of possession (feoffment, delivery of chattels out of market overt, either with or without consideration).

b. By deed (land or chattels).

c. By other formalities, irrespective of consideration, such as transfer of shares on the books of a corporation.

d. By conveyance, either oral or in writing not under seal, for a consideration but without change of possession (chattels).

e. By simple agreement or mutual assent without consideration or change of possession (certain gifts in equity).

To which may be added SUBDIVISIONS of a *persona.*

Joint administration. Joint tenancy, coparcenary, tenancy in common. Particular estates and remainders, &c.

REPRESENTATIONS.

Or introduction of one individual under a *persona* sustained by another.

1. For purposes indefinite in number and kind — slaves, servants, wives, some general agents.

2. For definite purposes — agents.

2. Holmes's classification of succession (from 7 *American Law Review* 67 (1872)).

	In which the Consciousness of the Party liable is an Element.	Determined by Acts or Events exactly Defined.	Determined by Acts or Events not exactly Defined.
Duties of all to all.	Fraud. Wilful or malicious injuries. Negligence *stricto sensu*.	Assault and battery formerly. Extreme cases, shading into negligence *latiori sensu*, which are not left to the jury.	Negligence *latiori sensu*.
Duties of Persons in Particular Situations to All.		Liability of master for servant. Ferocious animals. Cattle. Other things having an active tendency to do damage; *e.g.* Reservoirs.	
Duties of All to Persons in Particular Situations.	Maliciously causing breach of contract. Domestic relations?	Franchise or monopoly. Possession. Property. Easements exactly defined by deed, or by an arbitrary rule of law.	Prescriptive easements not exactly defined.

3. Holmes's classification of duties in his 1873 essay "The Theory of Torts" (from 7 *American Law Review* 663 (1873)).

Bibliography

Books

Ackerman, Bruce. *We the People.* Cambridge, Mass.: Belknap Press, 1991.

Alschuler, Albert W. *Law without Values: The Life, Work, and Legacy of Justice Holmes.* Chicago and London: University of Chicago Press, 2000.

Aichele, Gary J. *Oliver Wendell Holmes Jr.: Soldier, Scholar, Judge.* Boston: Twayne Publishers, 1989.

Austin, John. *Lectures on Jurisprudence or the Philosophy of Positive Law.* London: John Murray, 1869.

———. *The Province of Jurisprudence Determined and the Uses of the Study of Jurisprudence.* London: Weidenfeld and Nicolson, 1955.

Baker, Liva. *The Justice from Beacon Hill: The Life and Times of Oliver Wendell Holmes.* New York: HarperCollins, 1991.

Bentham, Jeremy. *Works of Jeremy Bentham,* ed. J. Bowring. 11 vols. Edinburgh, 1838–43.

Berger, Raoul. *Government by Judiciary: The Transformation of the Fourteenth Amendment.* Cambridge, Mass.: Harvard University Press, 1977.

Berman, Harold J. *Justice in the USSR: An Interpretation of Soviet Law.* New York: Vantage Books, 1963.

Bickel, Alexander M. *The Least Dangerous Branch: The Supreme Court at the Bar of Politics.* Indianapolis: Bobbs-Merrill, 1962.

———. *The Morality of Consent.* New Haven: Yale University Press, 1975.

———. *The Supreme Court and the Idea of Progress.* New York, Evanston, and London: Harper & Row, 1970.

Bickel, Alexander M., and Benno C. Schmidt, Jr. *The Oliver Wendell Holmes Devise History of the Supreme Court of the United States,* vol. 9: *The Judiciary and Responsible Government, 1910–1921.* New York: Macmillan, 1984.

Biddle, Francis. *Justice Holmes, Natural Law, and the Supreme Court.* New York: Macmillan, 1961.

———. *Mr. Justice Holmes.* New York: Charles Scribner's Sons, 1942.

Blackstone, William. *Commentaries on the Laws of England.* 4 vols. New York and London: Garland Publishing, 1978.

Bobbitt, Philip. *Constitutional Fate.* Oxford and New York: Oxford University Press, 1982.

———. *Constitutional Interpretation.* Oxford and Cambridge, Mass,: Blackwell, 1991.

Boorstin, Daniel J. *The Mysterious Science of the Law: An Essay on Blackstone's Commentaries.* Cambridge, Mass.: Harvard University Press, 1941.

Bork, Robert H. *The Tempting of America.* New York: Free Press, 1990.

Brint, Michael, and William Weaver. *Pragmatism in Law and Society.* Boulder, San Francisco, and Oxford: Westview Press, 1991.

Broadie, Alexander, ed. *The Cambridge Companion to the Scottish Enlightenment.* Cambridge: Cambridge University Press, 2003.

Burke, Edmund. *Reflections on the Revolution in France,* ed. L. G. Mitchell. New York and Oxford: Oxford University Press, 1993.

Burrow, J. W. *Evolution and Society: A Study in Victorian Social Theory.* Cambridge: Cambridge University Press, 1966.

Burton, Stephen J., ed. *The Path of the Law and Its Influence.* Cambridge: Cambridge University Press, 2000.

Calabresi, G. *A Common Law for the Age of Statutes.* Cambridge, Mass.: Harvard University Press, 1982.

Carter, James Coolidge. *Law: Its Origin, Growth and Function.* New York: Legal Classics Library, 1996.

Coke, Sir Edward. *Reports.* Dublin: J. Moore, 1793.

———. *The Second Part of the Institutes of the Laws of England.* Buffalo, N.Y.: William S. Hein, 1986.

Coleman, Jules. *The Practice of Principle: In Defense of a Pragmatist Approach to Legal Theory.* New York and Oxford: Oxford University Press, 2001.

Corwin, Edward S. *American Constitutional History.* New York: Harper & Row, 1964.

Cross, Rupert. *Precedent in English Law,* 3rd ed. Oxford: Clarendon Press, 1977.

de Witte, Bruno, and Caroline Forder. *The Common Law of Europe and the Future of Legal Education.* Deventer, The Netherlands, and Cambridge, Mass.: Deventer, 1992.

Dicey, Albert Venn. *Introduction to the Study of the Law of the Constitution.* London: Macmillan, 1897.

———. *Lectures on the Relation between Law and Public Opinion in England During the Nineteenth Century.* London: Macmillan, 1905.

Dworkin, Ronald. *Freedom's Law: The Moral Reading of the American Constitution.* Cambridge, Mass.: Harvard University Press, 1996.

———. *Justice in Robes.* Cambridge, Mass.: Belknap Press, 2006.

———. *Law's Empire.* Cambridge, Mass.: Belknap Press, 1986.

———. *Taking Rights Seriously.* Cambridge, Mass.: Harvard University Press, 1977.

Ely, John Hart. *Democracy and Distrust.* Cambridge, Mass.: Harvard University Press, 1980.

Fifoot, C. H. S. *Lord Mansfield.* Oxford: Clarendon Press, 1936.

Finnis, John. *Natural Law and Natural Rights.* Oxford: Clarendon Press, 1979.

Fiss, Owen M. *Oliver Wendell Holmes Devise History of the Supreme Court of the United States*, vol. 8: *Troubled Beginnings of the Modern State, 1888–1910*. New York: Macmillan, 1993.

Flower, Elizabeth, and Murray G. Murphey. *A History of Philosophy in America*. New York: G. P. Putnam's Sons, 1977.

Frank, Jerome. *Law and the Modern Mind*. Garden City, N.Y.: Anchor Books, 1963.

Frankfurter, Felix. *From the Diaries of Felix Frankfurter*, ed. Joseph P. Lash. New York: Norton, 1975.

———. *Mr. Justice Holmes and the Supreme Court*, 2nd ed. Cambridge, Mass.: Harvard University Press, 1961.

Frankfurter, Felix, ed. *Mr. Justice Brandeis: Essays with an Introduction by Oliver Wendell Holmes*. New Haven: Yale University Press, 1932.

Freund, Paul A. *On Law and Justice*. Cambridge, Mass.: Belknap Press, 1968.

———. *The Supreme Court of the United States*. Cleveland and New York: Meridian Books, 1949.

Friedrich, Carl J. *The Philosophy of Law in Historical Perspective*. Chicago: University of Chicago Press, 1967.

Fuller, Lon L. *Anatomy of the Law*. New York and Toronto: New American Library, 1968.

———. *The Law in Quest of Itself*. Chicago: Foundation Press, 1940.

———. *Legal Fictions*. Stanford: Stanford University Press, 1967.

———. *The Morality of Law*, rev. ed. New Haven: Yale University Press, 1969.

Gillman, Howard. *The Constitution Beseiged: The Rise and Demise of Lochner Era Police Powers Jurisprudence*. Durham, N.C., and London: Duke University Press, 1993.

Gilmore, Grant. *The Ages of American Law*. New Haven: Yale University Press, 1977.

———. *The Death of Contract*. Columbus: Ohio State University Press, 1974.

Gordon, Robert W., ed. *The Legacy of Justice Oliver Wendell Holmes, Jr.* Stanford: Stanford University Press, 1992.

Gottlieb, Stephen E., ed. *Public Values in Constitutional Law*. Ann Arbor: University of Michigan Press, 1993.

Gray, John. *Post-Liberalism: Studies in Political Thought*. New York and London: Routledge, 1993.

Gray, John Chipman. *The Nature and Sources of the Law*, 2nd ed. New York: Macmillan, 1921.

Gunther, Gerald. *Learned Hand: The Man and the Judge*. New York: Knopf, 1994.

Hale, Matthew. *A History of the Common Law of England*, ed. C. M. Gray. Chicago: University of Chicago Press, 1971.

Hand, Learned. *The Bill of Rights*. Cambridge, Mass.: Harvard University Press, 1958.

Hart, Henry M. Jr., and Albert M. Sacks. *The Legal Process: Basic Problems in the Making and Application of Law*. Westbury, N.Y.: Foundation Press, 1994.

Hart, H. L. A. *The Concept of Law*, 2nd ed. Oxford: Oxford University Press, 1994.

———. *Essays on Bentham: Jurisprudence and Political Theory*. Oxford: Oxford University Press, 1982.

———. *Essays in Jurisprudence and Philosophy*. Oxford: Oxford University Press, 1983.

Hayek, F. A. *The Constitution of Liberty*. Chicago: University of Chicago Press, 1960.

———. *Law, Legislation and Liberty: A New Statement of the Liberal Principles of Justice and Political Economy*. Chicago and London: Chicago University Press. Vol. 1, *Rules and Order*, 1973; vol. 2, *The Mirage of Social Justice*, 1978; vol. 3, *The Political Order of a Free People*, 1979.

Herget, James. *American Jurisprudence 1870–1970*. Houston: Rice University Press, 1990.

Hill, Christopher. *Intellectual Origins of the English Revolution*. Oxford: Clarendon Press, 1997.

Hobbes, Thomas. *A Dialogue between a Philosopher and a Student of the Common Laws*, ed. J. Cropsey. Chicago and London: Chicago University Press, 1971.

———. *Behemoth*, ed. W. Molesworth. New York, n.d.

———. *Elements of Law*. Cambridge: Cambridge University Press, 1928.

———. *Leviathan*. Hamilton, Ont.: McMaster University, 1999.

Holmes, Oliver Wendell. *Collected Legal Papers*. New York: Harcourt, Brace and Howe, 1920.

———. *The Collected Works of Justice Holmes: Complete Public Writings and Selected Opinions of Oliver Wendell Holmes*, ed. Sheldon M. Novick. 3 vols. Chicago and London: University of Chicago Press, 1995.

———. *The Common Law*, edited and with introduction by Mark DeWolfe Howe. Cambridge, Mass.: Harvard University Press, 1963.

———. *The Occasional Speeches of Justice Oliver Wendell Holmes*, ed. Mark DeWolfe Howe. Cambridge, Mass.: Harvard University Press, 1962.

———. *Justice Oliver Wendell Holmes: His Book Notices and Uncollected Letters and Papers*, ed. Harry C. Shriver. New York: Central Book, 1936.

Holmes and the Common Law: A Century Later. The Holmes Lectures 1981, occasional pamphlet no. 10. Cambridge, Mass.: Harvard Law School, 1983.

Hooker, Richard. *Of the Laws of Ecclesiastical Polity*. Books 1–4. New York: Legal Classics Library, 1998.

Horwitz, Morton J. *The Transformation of American Law 1780–1860*. Cambridge, Mass., and London: Harvard University Press, 1977.

———. *The Transformation of American Law 1870–1960*. New York and Oxford: Oxford University Press, 1992.

Howe, Mark DeWolfe. *Justice Oliver Wendell Holmes: The Shaping Years, 1841–1870*. Cambridge, Mass.: Harvard University Press, 1957.

———. *Justice Oliver Wendell Holmes: The Proving Years, 1870–1882*. Cambridge, Mass.: Harvard University Press, 1963.

Howe, Mark DeWolfe, ed. *Holmes-Pollock Letters: The Correspondence of Mr. Justice Holmes and Sir Frederick Pollock*. Cambridge, Mass.: Belknap Press, 1961.

———. *The Occasional Speeches of Justice Oliver Wendell Holmes*. Cambridge, Mass.: Belknap Press, 1962.

Hudson, John. *The Formation of the English Common Law*. London and New York: Longman, 1996.

Hurst, James Willard. *Justice Holmes on Legal History*. New York: Macmillan, 1964.

Introduction to Law: Selected Essays Reprinted from the Harvard Law Review. Cambridge, Mass.: Harvard Law Review Association, 1968.

Jones, William. *An Essay on the Law of Bailments.* London: J. Nichols, 1781.
Kalman, Laura. *The Strange Career of Legal Liberalism.* New Haven: Yale University Press, 1996.
Kaplow, Louis, and Steven Shavell. *Fairness versus Welfare.* Cambridge, Mass.: Harvard University Press, 2002.
Kellogg, Frederic Rogers. *The Formative Essays of Justice Holmes: The Making of an American Legal Philosophy.* Westport, Conn.: Greenwood Press, 1984.
Kelsen, Hans. *General Theory of Law and State,* trans. Anders Wedberg. Cambridge, Mass.: Harvard University Press, 1949.
———. *Pure Theory of Law,* trans. Max Knight. Berkeley and Los Angeles: University of California Press, 1967.
———. Kent, James. *Commentaries on American Law,* ed. Oliver Wendell Holmes, Jr. 12th ed. Boston: Little, Brown, 1873.
Kramer, Larry D. *The People Themselves: Popular Constitutionalism and Judicial Review.* Oxford: Oxford University Press, 2004.
Lerner, Max, ed. *The Mind and Faith of Justice Holmes; His Speeches, Essays, Letters and Judicial Opinions.* Boston: Little, Brown, 1943.
Levi, Edward H. *An Introduction to Legal Reasoning.* Chicago and London: University of Chicago Press, 1949.
Lewis, Frederick P. *The Context of Judicial Activism: The Endurance of the Warren Court Legacy in a Conservative Age.* Oxford and New York: Rowman & Littlefield, 1999.
Llewellyn, K. N. *The Bramble Bush: Some Lectures on Law and Its Study.* New York: Columbia University School of Law, 1930.
———. *The Common Law Tradition: Deciding Appeals.* Boston: Little, Brown, 1960.
———. *On Legal Realism.* Birmingham, Ala.: Legal Classics, 1986.
Lodge, Henry Cabot, ed. *Selections from the Correspondence of Theodore Roosevelt.* 2 vols. New York: Scribner & Sons, 1925.
Lyons, David. *Moral Aspects of Legal Theory: Essays on Law, Justice, and Political Responsibility.* New York and Cambridge: Cambridge University Press, 1993.
Madden, Edward H. *Chauncey Wright and the Foundations of Pragmatism.* Seattle: University of Washington Press, 1963.
Maine, Henry S. *Ancient Law: Its Connection with the Early History of Society, and Its Relation to Modern Ideas.* New York: Henry Holt, 1885.
———. *Early Law and Custom.* London: John Murray, 1891.
Maitland, Frederick William. *The Letters of Frederick William Maitland.* Cambridge, Mass.: Harvard University Press, 1965.
———. *The Life and Letters of Leslie Stephen.* London: Duckworth, 1906.
Margolis, Joseph. *Reinventing Pragmatism: American Philosophy at the End of the Twentieth Century.* Ithaca, N.Y.: Cornell University Press, 2002.
Marmor, Andrei. *Interpretation and Legal Theory.* Oxford: Clarendon Press, 1992.
Menand, Louis. *The Metaphysical Club.* New York: Farrar Straus and Giroux, 2001.
Mill, John Stewart. *A System of Logic.* London: Longmans Green, 1930.
———. *The Collected Works of John Stuart Mill,* ed. J. M. Robson et al. 21 vols. Toronto: University of Toronto Press, 1963.
Milsom, S. F. C. *Historical Foundations of the Common Law.* London: Butterworths, 1969.

Misak, Cheryl, ed. *The Cambridge Companion to Peirce.* Cambridge: Cambridge University Press, 2004.

Monagan, John S. *The Grand Panjandrum: Mellow Years of Justice Holmes.* Lanham, Md.: University Press of America, 1988.

Montesquieu, Baron de. *The Spirit of the Laws (L'esprit des lois),* trans. Thomas Nugent. New York: Hafner Publishing, 1949.

Morison, W. L. *John Austin.* Stanford: Stanford University Press, 1982.

Novick, Sheldon M., ed. *The Collected Works of Justice Holmes: Complete Public Writings and Selected Opinions of Oliver Wendell Holmes.* 3 vols. Chicago and London: University of Chicago Press, 1995.

———. *Honorable Justice: The Life of Oliver Wendell Holmes.* Boston, Toronto, and London: Little, Brown, 1989.

Oakeshott, Michael. *On Human Conduct.* Oxford: Clarendon Press, 1975.

———. *The Politics of Faith and the Politics of Skepticism.* New Haven and London: Yale University Press, 1996.

———. *Rationalism in Politics.* London, 1962.

Patterson, Dennis, ed. *A Companion to Philosophy of Law and Legal Theory.* Oxford and Malden, Mass.: Blackwell, 1996.

Peirce, Charles Sanders. *Collected Papers.* 8 vols. Vols. 1–6, ed. Charles Hartshorne and Paul Weiss. Vols. 7 and 8, ed. A. W. Burks. Cambridge, Mass.: Belknap Press of Harvard University Press, 1931–35.

———. *Philosophical Writings of Peirce,* ed. Justus Buchler. New York: Dover, 1955.

Perry, Ralph Barton. *The Thought and Character of William James.* Boston: Little, Brown, 1936.

Plucknett, T. F. T. *A Concise History of the Common Law,* 2nd ed. Boston: Little, Brown, 1956.

Pocock, J. G. A. *The Ancient Constitution and the Feudal Law.* Cambridge: Cambridge University Press, 1957.

Pohlman, Harold L. *Justice Oliver Wendell Holmes and Utilitarian Jurisprudence.* Cambridge, Mass.: Harvard University Press, 1984.

Pollock, Frederick. *Essays in the Law.* London: Macmillan, 1922.

———, and Frederic Maitland. *The History of English Law.* 2 vols. Cambridge: Cambridge University Press, 1968.

Posner, Richard A. *The Economics of Justice.* Cambridge, Mass.: Harvard University Press, 1981.

———. *The Problems of Jurisprudence.* Cambridge, Mass., and London: Harvard University Press, 1990.

Posner, Richard A., ed. *The Essential Holmes: Selections from the Letters, Speeches, Judicial Opinions, and Other Formative Writings of Oliver Wendell Holmes, Jr.* Chicago and London: University of Chicago Press, 1992.

Postema, Gerald J. *Bentham and the Common Law Tradition.* Oxford: Clarendon Press, 1986.

Postema, Gerald J., ed. *Philosophy of the Law of Torts.* New York and Cambridge: Cambridge University Press, 2001.

Pound, Roscoe. *Interpretations of Legal History.* New York: Macmillan, 1923.

———. *The Spirit of the Common Law.* Boston: Beacon Press, 1921.

Rawls, John. *A Theory of Justice.* Cambridge, Mass.: Belknap Press, 1971.

———. *Political Liberalism.* New York: Columbia University Press, 1993.
Raz, J. *The Authority of Law: Essays on Law and Morality.* Oxford: Clarendon Press, 1979.
———. *The Concept of a Legal System*, 2nd ed. Oxford: Clarendon Press, 1980.
———. *Practical Reason and Norms.* London: Hutchinson, 1975.
Riley, Woodbridge. *American Philosophy: The Early Schools.* New York: Russell & Russell, 1958.
Rorty, Richard. *Objectivism, Relativism, and Truth.* Cambridge: Cambridge University Press, 1991.
Rosenberg, David. *The Hidden Holmes: His Theory of Torts in History.* Cambridge, Mass.: Harvard University Press, 1995.
Rumble, Wilfred E. *The Thought of John Austin.* London and Dover, N.H.: Athlone Press 1985.
Sandel, Michael J. *Liberalism and the Limits of Justice.* Cambridge: Cambridge University Press, 1982.
Scalia, Antonin. *A Matter of Interpretation: Federal Courts and the Law.* Princeton: Princeton University Press, 1997.
Schauer, Frederick. *Playing by the Rules: A Philosophical Examination of Rule-Based Decision-making in Law and in Life.* Oxford: Clarendon Press, 1991.
Schmidt, Paul F. *Perception and Cosmology in Whitehead's Philosophy.* New Brunswick: Rutgers University Press, 1967.
Schneider, Herbert W. *A History of American Philosophy.* New York: Liberal Arts Press, 1946.
Shiner, Roger A. *Norm and Nature: The Movements of Legal Thought.* Oxford: Clarendon Press, 1992.
Shriver, Harry C. *What Gusto: Stories and Anecdotes about Justice Oliver Wendell Holmes.* Potomac, Md.: Fox Hills, 1970.
———. *What Justice Holmes Wrote, and What Has Been Written about Him: A Bibliography.* 1866–1976. Potomac, Md.: Fox Hills, 1978.
Smith, Adam. *The Theory of Moral Sentiments*, ed. Knud Haakonssen. Cambridge: Cambridge University Press, 2002.
Stephen, Leslie. *History of English Thought in the Eighteenth Century.* London: Smith, Elder, 1902.
Stevenson, C. L. *Ethics and Language.* New Haven: Yale University Press, 1933.
Stoner, James R. *Common Law and Liberal Theory: Coke, Hobbes, and the Origins of American Constitutionalism.* Lawrence: University of Kansas Press, 1992.
Sunstein, Cass R. *One Case at a Time: Judicial Minimalism on the Supreme Court.* Cambridge, Mass., and London: Harvard University Press, 1999.
Thayer, H. S. *Meaning and Action: A Critical History of Pragmatism.* Indianapolis and New York: Bobbs-Merrill, 1977.
Thayer, James B. *John Marshall.* Boston: Houghton Mifflin, 1901.
Tushnet, Mark. *The New Constitutional Order.* Princeton and Oxford: Princeton University Press, 2003.
———. *Taking the Constitution away from the Courts.* Princeton: Princeton University Press, 1999.
Warren, Charles. *Congress, the Constitution and the Supreme Court.* 1925. Rpt. Boston: Little, Brown, 1935.

Warren, Charles. *The Supreme Court in United States History.* 1921. Rpt. Boston: Little, Brown, 1935.
Westbrook, Robert B. *John Dewey and American Democracy.* Ithaca, N.Y.: Cornell University Press, 1991.
White, G. Edward. *The American Judicial Tradition: Profiles of Leading American Judges.* New York: Oxford University Press, 1976.
———. *Justice Oliver Wendell Holmes: Law and the Inner Self.* Oxford: Oxford University Press, 1993.
———. *Tort Law in America: An Intellectual History.* New York: Oxford University Press, 1980.
White, Morton. *A Philosopher's Story.* University Park: Pennsylvania State University Press, 1999.
———. *A Philosophy of Culture.* Princeton and Oxford: Princeton University Press, 2002.
———. *Social Thought in America: The Revolt against Formalism.* 1947. Rpt. New York: Oxford University Press, 1976.
Wiener, Philip P. *Evolution and the Founders of Pragmatism.* Cambridge, Mass.: Harvard University Press, 1949.
Will, Frederick L. *Induction and Justification.* Ithaca and London: Cornell University Press, 1974.
Willey, Basil. *The Eighteenth Century Background.* New York: Doubleday, 1953.
Wilson, Edmund. *Patriotic Gore: Studies on the Literature of the American Civil War.* New York: Oxford University Press, 1962.

Articles

Aleinikoff, T. Alexander. "Constitutional Law in the Age of Balancing." 96 *Yale L.J.* 943 (1987).
Atiyah, P. S. "The Legacy of Holmes through English Eyes." In *Holmes and the Common Law: A Century Later,* occasional pamphlet. Cambridge, Mass.: Harvard Law School, 1983:76.
Bix, Brian. "Legal Positivism." In *The Blackwell Guide to the Philosophy of Law and Legal Theory,* ed. William A. Edmundson and Martin P. Golding. Oxford and Malden, Mass.: Blackwell, 2004:29.
Boorstin, Daniel. "The Elusiveness of Mr. Justice Holmes." 14 *New England Q.* 478 (1941).
Bork, Robert P. "Neutral Principles and Some First Amendment Problems." *Indiana L.J.* 47, 1 (1971).
Cohen, Felix S., ed. "The Holmes-Cohen Correspondence." 10 *Journal of the History of Ideas* 14–15 (1948).
Cohen, Morris R. "The Place of Logic in the Law." 29 *Harv. L. Rev.* 622 (1916).
Coleman, Jules, and Brian Leiter. "Legal Positivism." In *A Companion to Philosophy of Law and Legal Theory,* ed. Dennis Patterson. Oxford and Malden, Mass.: Blackwell, 1996.
Corwin, Edward S. "The Impact of the Idea of Evolution on the American Political and Constitutional Tradition." In *Evolutionary Thought in America,* ed. Stow Persons. New Haven: Yale University Press, 1950:182.

Dewey, John. "Justice Holmes and the Liberal Mind." 53 *New Republic* 210 (1928).
———. "My Philosophy of Law." In *Credos of Sixteen American Scholars.* Boston: Boston Law Book, 1941:77.
Dicey, Albert Venn. "Holmes's Common Law." *The Spectator*, library supplement, June 3, 1882, pp. 745–47, published anonymously. Reprinted as an appendix to Touster, "Holmes a Hundred Years Ago: The Common Law and Legal Theory," 10 *Hofstra L. Rev.* 673, 712 (1982).
Dolinko, David. "Alschuler's Path." 49 *Fla. L. Rev.* 421 (1997)
Dworkin, Ronald. "Law as Interpretation." 60 *Texas L. Rev.* 527–50 (1982).
———. "Thirty Years On." Review of Jules Coleman, *The Practice of Principle: In Defense of a Pragmatist Approach to Legal Theory.* 115 *Harv. L. Rev.* 1655 (2002).
Elliott, E. Donald. "Holmes and Evolution: Legal Process as Artificial Intelligence." 13 *J. Legal Studies* 113 (1984).
Epstein, Richard A. "Pennsylvania Coal v. Mahon: The Erratic Takings Jurisprudence of Justice Holmes." 86 *Geo. L. J.* 875 (1998).
———. "The Static Conception of the Common Law." 9 *J. of Legal Studies* 253–75 (1980).
Fisch, Max. "Justice Holmes, the Prediction Theory of Law, and Pragmatism." 39 *Journal of Philosophy* 85, 94 (1942).
———. "Was There a Metaphysical Club in Cambridge?" In *Studies in the Philosophy of Charles Sanders Peirce,* ed. Edward C. Moore and Richard S. Robin. Amherst: University of Massachusetts Press, 1964:15.
Frankfurter, Felix. "The Constitutional Opinions of Justice Holmes." 29 *Harv. L. Rev.* 683 (1916).
———. "The Early Writings of Oliver Wendell Holmes, Jr." 44 *Harv. L. Rev.* 717 (1931).
Freund, Paul A. "Oliver Wendell Holmes." In *The Justices of the United States Supreme Court*, ed. Leon Friedman and Fred. L. Israel. New York: Chelsea House, 1980:1755.
Fuller, Lon L. "Positivism and Fidelity to Law – A Reply to Professor Hart." 71 *Harv. L. Rev.* 630 (1958).
Gergen, Mark P. "The Jury's Role in Deciding Normative Issues in American Common Law." *Fordham L. Rev.* 68, 407 (1999).
Goldsmith, M. M. "Hobbes on Law." In *The Cambridge Companion to Hobbes,* ed. Tom Sorell. Cambridge: Cambridge University Press, 1996:274.
Gordley, James. "When Paths Diverge: A Response to Albert Alschuler on Oliver Wendell Holmes." 49 *Fla. L. Rev.* 441 (1997).
Gordon, Robert W. "Holmes' Common Law as Legal and Social Science." 10 *Hofstra L. Rev.* 719 (1982).
Gottlieb, Stephen E. "The Paradox of Balancing Significant Interests." 45 *Hastings L. J.* 825 (1994).
Grey, Thomas C. "Holmes and Legal Pragmatism." 41 *Stan. L. Rev.* 787 (1989).
———. "Molecular Motions: The Holmesian Judge in Theory and Practice." 37 *Wm & Mary L. Rev.* 19 (1995).
Hale, Sir Matthew. "Reflections by the Lrd. Chiefe Justice Hale on Mr. Hobbes His Dialogue of the Lawe." In W. Holdsworth, *A History of English Law*, 7th ed. London, 1956: vol. 1, pp. 499–513.

Hantzis, Catherine Wells. "Legal Innovation within the Wider Intellectual Tradition: The Pragmatism of Oliver Wendell Holmes, Jr." 82 *Nw. U. L. Rev.* 541 (1988).

Hart, Henry M. "Holmes' Positivism – An Addendum." 64 *Harv. L. Rev.* 929 (1951).

Hart, H. L. A. "Positivism and the Separation of Law and Morals." 71 *Harv. L. Rev.* 593 (1958).

Henkin, Louis. "Infallibility under Law: Constitutional Balancing." 78 *Colum. L. Rev.* 1022 (1978).

"Holmes, Peirce and Legal Pragmatism." 84 *Yale L.J.* 1123 (1975).

Horowitz, Paul. "The Past Tense: The History of Crisis – and the Crisis of History – in Constitutional Theory." 61 *Albany L. Rev.* 459 (1997).

Hough, Charles M. "Due Process of Law – To-day." 32 *Harv. L. Rev.* 218 (1919).

Howe, Mark DeWolfe. "Holmes' Positivism – A Brief Rejoinder." 64 *Harv. L. Rev.* 937 (1951).

———. "The Positivism of Mr. Justice Holmes." 64 *Harv. L. Rev.* 529 (1951).

Kaplan, Benjamin. "Encounter with Oliver Wendell Holmes, Jr." In *Holmes and the Common Law: A Century Later*, occasional pamphlet. Cambridge, Mass.: Harvard Law School, 1983.

Kelley, Patrick J. "A Critical Analysis of Holmes's Theory of Torts." 61 *Wash. U. L. Q.* 681 (1983).

———. "Holmes on the Supreme Judicial Court: The Theorist as Judge." In *The History of the Law in Massachusetts: The Supreme Judicial Court 1692–1992*, ed. Russell K. Osgoode. Boston: Supreme Judicial Court Historical Society, 1992: 275.

———. "Oliver Wendell Holmes, Utilitarian Jurisprudence and the Positivism of John Stuart Mill." 30 *Am. J. Jurisprudence* 189 (1985).

———. "Was Holmes a Pragmatist? Reflections on a New Twist to an Old Argument." 14 *S. Ill. L. J.* 427 (1990).

Kellogg, Frederic R. "Common Law and Constitutional Theory: The Common Law Origins of Holmes's Constitutional Restraint." 7 *George Mason L. Rev.* 177 (1984).

———. "Justice Holmes, Common Law Theory, and Judicial Restraint." *John Marshall L. Rev.* (2003).

———. "Law, Morals and Justice Holmes." 69 *Judicature* 214 (1986).

———. "Legal Philosophy in the Temple of Doom: Pragmatism's Response to Critical Legal Studies." 65 *Tulane L. Rev.* 15 (1990).

———. "Who Owns Pragmatism?" 6 *Journal of Speculative Philosophy* 67 (1992).

Kennedy, Gail. "The Pragmatic Naturalism of Chauncey Wright." In *Studies in the History of Ideas*, vol. 3. New York: Columbia University Press, 1935:477.

Komesar, Neil. "A Job for Judges: The Judiciary and the Constitution in a Massive and Complex Society." *Michigan L. Rev.* 86, 657 (1988).

LaPiana, William. "Victorian from Beacon Hill: Oliver Wendell Holmes's Early Legal Scholarship." 90 *Colum. L. Rev.* 809 (1990).

Leiter, Brian. "Legal Indeterminacy." 1 *Legal Theory* 481 (1995).

Little, Eleanor N. "The Early Reading of Justice Oliver Wendell Holmes." 8 *Harv. Library Bull.* 163 (1954).

Luban, David. "Justice Holmes and the Metaphysics of Judicial Restraint." 44 *Duke L. J.* 449 (1994).

Lyons, David. "Founders and Foundations of Legal Positivism." 82 *Mich. L. Rev.* 722 (1984).

———. "Human Rights and General Welfare." 6 *Philosophy and Public Affairs* 113–29 (1977).

———. "Open Texture and the Possibility of Legal Interpretation." 18 *Law and Philosophy* 297–309 (1999).

Novick, Sheldon M. Editor's Introduction. In 1 *Collected Works of Justice Holmes*, vol. 1 (1995), at 1.

———. "Justice Holmes and the Art of Biography." 33 *Wm. & Mary L. Rev.* 1219 (1992).

———. "Justice Holmes's Philosophy." 70 *Wash. U. L. Q.* 703 (1992).

Oakeshott, Michael. "The Concept of a Philosophical Jurisprudence." *Politica* 3 (1938):203–222, 345–360.

Oldham, James. "The Survival of Sir William Jones in American Jurisprudence." In *Objects of Inquiry: the Life, Contributions, and Influences of Sir William Jones (1746–1794), ed.* Garland Cannon and Kevin R. Brine. New York: New York University Press, 1995.

Olivecrona, K. "The Will of the Sovereign: Some Reflections on Bentham's Concept of 'a Law.'" 20 *American J. of Jurisprudence* 95–110 (1975).

"The Origin of the Modern Standard of Due Care in Negligence." 1976 *Wash. U. L. Q.* 447 (1977).

Perry, Stephen R. "Judicial Obligation, Precedent, and the Common Law." 7 *Oxford J. of Legal Studies* 215 (1987), 234.

———. "The Varieties of Legal Positivism." 9 *Canadian Journal of Law and Jurisprudence* 361–81 (July 1996).

Phillips, Michael J. "The Substantive Due Process Decisions of Mr. Justice Holmes." 36 *American Business Law Journal* 437–77: (Spring 1999).

Pierce, Richard J. "Public Utility Regulatory Takings: Should the Judiciary Attempt to Police the Political Institutions?" 77 *Geo. L. J.* 2031 (1989).

Pollock, Sir Frederick. "Law and Command." *Law Magazine and Review*, New Series, no. 3 (1872):191.

———. "The Merger Case and Restraint of Trade." 17 *Harv. L. Rev.* 151 (1904).

Postema, G. J. "Bentham and Dworkin on Positivism and Adjudication." *Social Theory and Practice*, 5 (1980):347–76.

———. "Co-ordination and Convention at the Foundations of Law." *Journal of Legal Studies* 11 (1982):165–203.

———. "The Expositor, the Censor, and the Common Law." *Canadian Journal of Philosophy* 9 (1979):643–70.

———. "Law's Autonomy and Public Practical Reason." In *The Autonomy of Law: Essays on Legal Positivism*, ed. Robert P. George. Oxford: Oxford Clarendon Press, 1996.

———. "The Philosophy of the Common Law." In *The Oxford Handbook of Jurisprudence and Philosophy of Law*, ed. Jules Coleman and Scott Shapiro, Oxford: Oxford University Press, 2002:593–95.

Pound, Roscoe. "Judge Holmes' Contributions to the Science of Law." 35 *Harv. L. Rev.* 449 (1921).

Rasmussen, David M. "Jurisprudence and Validity." *Cardozo L. Rev.* 17, 1059 (1996).

Raz, J. "Authority and Justification." 14 *Philosophy and Public Affairs* 3–29 (1985).

———. "Authority, Law, and Morality." 68 *Monist* 295–324 (1985).

———. "Legal Principles and the Limits of Law." *Yale L. Rev.* 81 (1972), 823–54.

———. "On the Functions of Law." In *Oxford Essays in Jurisprudence: Second Series,* ed. A. W. B. Simpson. Oxford: Oxford University Press, 1973:278–304.

Rogat, Yosal. "Mr. Justice Holmes: A Dissenting Opinion." 15 *Stan. L. Rev.* 3, 254 (1962–963).

Schauer, Frederick. "Easy Cases." 58 *So. Cal. L. Rev.* 399 (1985).

———. "Precedent and the Necessary Externality of Constitutional Norms." 17 *Harv. J. L. & Pub. Pol.* 45 (1994).

Scheiber, Harry N. "Comment: Public Rights and the Rule of Law." 71 *Cal. L. Rev.* 217 (1984).

Schwarz, Joan I. "Oliver Wendell Holmes's 'The Path of the Law': Conflicting Views of the Legal World." 29 *American J. L. History* 235 (1985).

Seipp, David J. "Holmes's Path." 77 *B. U. L. Rev.* 515 (1997).

Shattuck, Charles A. "The True Meaning of the Term 'Liberty' in Those Clauses in Federal and State Constitutions which Protect 'Life, Liberty, and Property.'" 4 *Harv. L. Rev.* 265 (1891).

Simpson, A. W. B. "The Common Law and Legal Theory." In *Oxford Essays in Jurisprudence: Second Series.* Oxford: Clarendon Press, 1973: 77–99.

Spann, Girardeau A. "Simple Justice." 73 *Georgetown L. J.* 1041 (1985).

Strauss, David A. "Common Law Constitutional Interpretation." 63 *U. Chi. L. Rev.* 877–935 (1996).

Strauss, Leo. "On the Spirit of Hobbes's Political Philosophy." In *Hobbes Studies,* ed. K. C. Brown. Cambridge, Mass.: Harvard University Press, 1965.

Sullivan, Kathleen M. "Categorization, Balancing, and Government Interests." In *Public Values in Constitutional Law,* ed. Stephen E. Gottlieb, Ann Arbor: University of Michigan Press, 1993.

"Symposium: The Path of the Law after One Hundred Years." 110 *Harv. L. Rev.* 989 (1997), containing essays by William W. Fisher III, Robert W. Gordon, Tracey E. Higgins, Martha Minow, Sheldon M. Novick, Richard D. Parker, Richard A. Posner, David Rosenberg, and G. Edward White.

"Symposium: The Path of the Law 100 Years Later: Holmes' Influence on Modern Jurisprudence." 63 *Brook L. Rev.* 1 (1998), (containing essays by Neil Duxbury, David Dyzenhaus, John C. P. Goldberg, Thomas C. Grey, Gary Minda, Richard A. Posner, Anthony J. Sebok, William Twining, Catharine Pierce Wells, and G. Edward White.

"Symposium: The Path of the Law Today." 78 *B. U. L. Rev.* 78 (1998), containing essays by Jack Balkin, Jack Beerman, Robert Cooter, Ruth Gavison, Clayton

P. Gillette, Lewis Kornhauser, Gerald Leonard, Sanford Levinson, Richard McAdams, Frederick Schauer, and Robin L. West.

Thayer, James B. "The Origin and Scope of the American Doctrine of Constitutional Law." 7 *Harv. L. Rev.* 129 (1893).

Touster, Saul. "Holmes a Hundred Years Ago: The Common Law and Legal Theory." 10 *Hofstra L. Rev.* 673 (1982).

———. "In Search of Holmes from Within." 18 *Vanderbilt L. Rev.* 437 (1965).

Tushnet, Mark. "Anti-Formalism in Recent Constitutional Theory." 83 *Mich. L. Rev.* 1502 (1985).

———. "The Logic of Experience: Oliver Wendell Holmes on the Supreme Judicial Court." 63 *Va. L. Rev.* 975 (1977).

Utz, Stephen G. "Maine's Ancient Law and Legal Theory." 16 *Conn. L. Rev.* 821 (1984).

Vetter, Jan, "The Evolution of Holmes: Holmes and Evolution." In *Holmes and the Common Law: A Century Later*, occasional pamphlet no. 10. Harvard Law School, 1983:75.

Wechsler, Herbert. "Toward Neutral Principles of Constitutional Law." 73 *Harv. L. Rev.* 1 (1959).

White, G. Edward. "From Realism to Critical Legal Studies: A Truncated Intellectual History." 40 *S. W. L. J.* 819 (1986).

———. "From Sociological Jurisprudence to Realism: Jurisprudence and Social Change in Early Twentieth-Century America." 58 *Va. L. Rev.* 999 (1972).

———. "The Integrity of Holmes' Jurisprudence." 10 *Hofstra L. Rev.* 633 (1982).

———. "Looking at Holmes in the Mirror." 4 *Law and History Rev.* 440 1986).

———. "The Rise and Fall of Justice Holmes." 39 *U. Chi. L. Rev.* 51 (1971).

Wigmore, John. "Justice Holmes and the Law of Torts." 29 *Harv. L. Rev.* 601 (1916).

Wright, Chauncey. "The Evolution of Self-consciousness." In *Philosophical Discussions.* New York: Henry Holt, 1877:205–29.

———. "The Philosophy of Herbert Spencer." 100 *N. American Rev.* 427 (1865).

Yale, D. E. C. "Hale and Hobbes on Law, Legislation, and the Sovereign." 31 *Cambridge L. J.* 121–56 (1972).

Collections

Oliver Wendell Holmes, Jr., Papers, Harvard Law School Library, Cambridge, Massachusetts.

Index

For EU product safety concerns, contact us at Calle de José Abascal, 56–1°,
28003 Madrid, Spain or eugpsr@cambridge.org.

www.ingramcontent.com/pod-product-compliance
Ingram Content Group UK Ltd.
Pitfield, Milton Keynes, MK11 3LW, UK
UKHW010900060825
461487UK00012B/1270

* 9 7 8 0 5 2 1 3 2 1 9 2 1 *